Blood in the
Moonlight

Blood in the Moonlight

Michael Mann and Information Age Cinema

Mark E. Wildermuth

McFarland & Company, Inc., Publishers
Jefferson, North Carolina, and London

LIBRARY OF CONGRESS CATALOGUING-IN-PUBLICATION DATA

Wildermuth, Mark E., 1956–
  Blood in the moonlight : Michael Mann and information age cinema / Mark E. Wildermuth.
      p.   cm.
  Includes bibliographical references and index.

  ISBN 0-7864-2059-6 (softcover : 50# alkaline paper) ∞

  1. Mann, Michael (Michael Kenneth)—Criticism and interpretation. I. Title.
  PN1998.3.M3645W56   2005
  791.4302'33'092—dc22   2005000096

British Library cataloguing data are available

©2005 Mark E. Wildermuth. All rights reserved

No part of this book may be reproduced or transmitted in any form or by any means, electronic or mechanical, including photocopying or recording, or by any information storage and retrieval system, without permission in writing from the publisher.

Cover photograph: Robert Prosky as Leo in the 1981 film *Thief*
Background image ©2005 PhotoSpin

Manufactured in the United States of America

McFarland & Company, Inc., Publishers
  Box 611, Jefferson, North Carolina 28640
  www.mcfarlandpub.com

To my mother, my father, my sister,
and the singer outside the window

Acknowledgments

I sincerely wish to acknowledge the people who helped make this book possible. This project could not have been completed without funding from the Kathlyn Cosper Dunagan Grant at the University of Texas. I must express gratitude to the library staff of the Dunagan Library at the University of Texas, especially Anita Voorhies, whose efforts as the interlibrary loan librarian have always been outstanding. My heartfelt thanks to Dr. Shawn Watson for encouraging research in English as the Chair of Humanities and as the English Area Coordinator at the University. I am also much in debt to the research assistants who contributed so much energy and enthusiasm to this and other projects, Jeanetta Calhoun and Robert Walker. I must also express my thanks to Tom Stracener, whose wizardry with the computer and the digital camera added greatly to the professional quality of the final manuscript. Special thanks also go to Victoria Wildermuth, whose support and critical insight were essential to the completion of this work. And finally, heartfelt thanks to my mentor at the University of Wisconsin at Madison, Howard D. Weinbrot, who showed me the way.

Table of Contents

Acknowledgments	vii
Preface	1
1. Introduction: Symbolic Exchange, Informatics, and Michael Mann's Cinema	15
2. Sympathy and the Devil: Doing Time in *The Jericho Mile* (1979)	35
3. It's a Criminal World: Artifice, Nature, and Humanity in *Thief* (1981)	55
4. History, the Unconscious, and Hyperreality: Gothic Doubles in *The Keep* (1983)	77
5. Renewed Dialogue: Indirect Light, Complexity, and Exchange in *Manhunter* (1986)	93
6. Translating Ritual Time and Symbolic Exchange: Colonialism and Nationalism in *The Last of the Mohicans* (1992)	115
7. The Decay of Dialogue: Disguise and Duplicity in *Heat* (1995)	135
8. Reviewing the Dialogue: Information as Commodity in *The Insider* (1999)	151

9. A Blast from the Past: Being the People's
   Champion in *Ali* (2001)   173

10. Summation and Conclusion   195

Bibliography   205

Index   209

Lecktor: If this pilgrim imagines he has a relationship with the moon, he might go outside to look at it. Have you ever seen blood in the moonlight, Will? *It appears quite black. If one were nude, it would be better to have privacy for this sort of thing.*
Graham: That's interesting.
Lecktor: No, it's not. You thought of it before.
Graham: I'd considered it.
Lecktor: You came here to look at me—to get the old scent back, didn't you? ... Do you know how you caught me, Will? ... The reason you caught me is we're just alike. You want the scent? Smell yourself.

A conversation on the uses
and abuses of information
from Manhunter (1986)*

---

*The screenplay and film adapted by Mann from the novel changes the spelling of the killer's name from Lecter to Lecktor. All other films based on Thomas Harris's novels maintained the "Lecter" spelling (as it appeared in the novels).

Preface

> *In the real world, there are ramifications.... How do you stay secure? How do you afford security? How do you protect your telephonic communications from being invaded? ... [T]hat's where the pressure hits.*
>
> Michael Mann speaking with
> Michael Sragow about issues
> raised by *The Insider*

Even in the wake of the theoretical and methodological revolutions in film and literary criticism since the 1960s, the desire of any critic undertaking a critical study of a major filmmaker is to bring as many biographical and historical facts to bear on a director's work as possible. One of the strengths of Donald Richie's seminal *The Films of Akira Kurosawa* (1965) was its capacity to integrate details about the director's culture, as well as his private and professional life, with the close analyses of plot, character, and theme in each of the films discussed. Some forty years later, nothing has changed; witness David Weddle's recent fascinating study of Sam Peckinpah's life and films in *If They Move, Kill 'Em* (1994). Information on production history, and interviews with the director regarding his or her personal philosophy on film and stylistics are useful for grounding analysis, even for critics and filmmakers who, living in this postmodern and postquantum age of ours, most probably will regard the idea of factual objectivity with considerably more skepticism than earlier generations of directors and critics.

That being the case, anyone undertaking a study of the works of Michael Mann typically would follow suit, integrating extensive bodies of information about the artist's personal and professional life with discussion of the films—but thus far that has not happened, and, in all likelihood, it is not about to happen any time soon. The only book-length study of all of Mann's films, Mark Steensland's *Michael Mann* (2002), cites some interesting details on the individual films' production history, and reports the basic facts regarding Mann's birth and education, but otherwise includes little biographical information on the director. Apparently there is a reason for this: Mann likes it that way. When asked by interviewer Michael Sragow to discuss his personal life and politics in relation to the movie *The Insider*, Mann replied, "Do you remember De Niro in *Heat*? ... Gray! ... That's what I aspire to—Gray!" As Sragow said, "This is Mann-talk for keeping the personal out of interviews. Mann doesn't want to speak about his non-working life. He feels abashed every time he does"(1).

This, however, does not mean that we know nothing about Mann— there are interesting facts that do emerge from a handful of interviews, which may explain why he is such an elusive individual, and also help provide an interesting context for his films. I will use these facts and other relevant aspects of Mann's cultural milieu to explain why an extraordinary methodology must be devised for explicating the works of an artist who seems to insist on our seeing them as public works that stand on their own without any invasion of the artist's private life.

As Steensland said, in 1943 Mann was born in a tough neighborhood in Chicago known as the "Patch" (13), a place that some of the tough-guy characters of his crime dramas would also claim as a place of origin. After graduating from high school, he obtained a B.A. in English at the University of Wisconsin at Madison, where he was introduced to two elements destined to become powerful attractors in his life: film studies and political radicalism. As Mann indicated in his interview with the American Film Institute (AFI) in their documentary *The Directors*, Madison was in what he considered its "Golden Age," when it was "one of three or four radical campuses" in America, along with Berkeley and Columbia. This mixture of art and politics led Mann, as the documentary also indicates, to leave America in 1965 for two reasons: to study film in the London International Film School and to thereby avoid being drafted to fight in Vietnam.

Both the American and the European experience would set the foundation for a film career in which he would focus on the impact of information in our culture by examining the lives of human beings—some real, some the creations of fiction—who would represent radical alternatives to the status quo. Both before and after Madison, there had been a certain fascination with radicals from all parts of the political spectrum. Mann met Malcolm X in 1963 where he "felt his assault on society, a much needed assault" (Dzenis 1). Later, in 1969, he would meet former

Nazi SS commando Otto Skorzeny, the architect of Mussolini's rescue from Italian partisans and of the failed attempt on Eisenhower's life during the Battle of the Bulge in World War II. After that latter conversation, which apparently was the motive for his attack on Nazism in Mann's Gothic film *The Keep*, the shaken Mann, a "self-described 'nice Jewish kid from Chicago,'" felt "haunted by that meeting" (Steensland 31–32). Then, after the London experience, came the opportunity to observe leftist radicalism in action: Mann found himself in Paris in May of 1968, somehow getting close to the group of young French radicals that took over the television station there (when few if any network television crews could establish contact with the radicals) and making his first professional film about it, the documentary *Insurrection* from which NBC would later show clips on their First Tuesday news show (Steensland 13).

These experiences, and the interests that they sparked and nurtured in the young filmmaker, appear to have led Mann to examine the potentially coercive capability and possibly negative impact of the media and information on society within the context of the various types of radicalism and resistance that they have helped to spawn. His concern with these issues surfaces not only in his films but also in the few interviews he has conducted with the press over the years. For example, in her interview with Mann, Cynthia Rose (2003) indicated that "Mann ... thinks TV sitcoms cause crime" because, as Mann said, on television, people see "'Janitors with two-story houses, expensive cars, and Cuisinarts. If you can't get that stuff yourself, it's bound to make you feel substandard.'" Rose indicates that Mann's experience with the television medium, as he was preparing for a career as a director, taught him about "the heady nature of wielding media power." Hence arose, as Mann said in that interview, his close attention to style and detail after he became a director: "'A sound here will change your sense of a shape that appears seconds later'" (3). Not one detail can be overlooked if one is to achieve the right effect in a scene; and thus it was that, for example, not a single right angle appeared in the final and deliberately disorienting climactic sequence in *Manhunter* (4).

While working with network television, Mann also sometimes experienced the power of the corporate world over the creative control of the artist. According to Graham Fuller, Mann, while he was the producer of *Miami Vice* during the 1980s, sometimes endured criticism from NBC's executives who felt the show was becoming "unacceptably dark" (1). Mann would face a more serious confrontation with NBC in the late 1980s when producing and directing the made for television crime film

L.A. Takedown, the precursor of his mid–1990s theatrical release *Heat*. NBC forced the perfectionist director to cut some seventeen minutes from *Takedown*. As Mann said of the movie in his AFI *Directors* interview, "It was not the film I made," and "anybody who was seeing that film was being cheated by this mutilated product." In protest, Mann insisted that his name be taken off the film as its director. In 1995, Mann said in his *Directors* interview, he went "back to the full form of the screenplay" he had written in the 1970s when he decided to reshoot the full-length version as *Heat*. It was as if he could not let go of the project until he had full control over its final execution without any influence from the media bureaucracy that, in his eyes, had wrongfully tampered with it.

But while Mann is clearly concerned with the control the media asserts over us—something reiterated in his interview with Sragow on *The Insider* cited in the epigraph—he does not give associates the impression of being a lone radical himself. Quite the contrary, interviews with Mann and his colleagues that do briefly touch on his personal beliefs emphasize his attachment to what seem to be basic human values. In the Cynthia Rose interview, Daniel Day-Lewis, star of *The Last of the Mohicans*, indicated that Mann is "an optimist ... committed to a constructive viewpoint" (3). In that same interview, Mann, while critical of the values the British characters stood for in *Mohicans*, nevertheless expressed great respect for the tribal societies of the Native Americans, praising, "The native American warrior [who] used his strength to serve his family, his tribe and the life of his nation" (5). In his interview with Fuller he also praised the Native Americans' "generosity in sharing agricultural techniques and food" with the Europeans (4). In his interview with Sragow on *The Insider*, he simultaneously seemed to question the larger political and economic system while still emphasizing the need for people to connect with other human beings socially. Mann quit smoking after making *The Insider* because, as a father, "You have to think of the impact on your children of cigarette smoking, and of the impact on them of your own potential for early disease and earlier death." He depicted the tobacco industry as a business creating "a market addicted to their product." Nevertheless, kicking the habit was a very difficult thing for him to do because that addiction was itself something that had worked its way into his life as a social being. Ever since his student years in Europe, he had shared cigarettes with friends and thus there was "an association, for me, with a certain kind of conviviality" (4).

This is an interesting moment of revelation: Mann's struggle with nicotine brings to mind the basic conflicts of many of his protagonists.

They want to share in the exchange of human society but live in a culture and an economic system that somehow always charges a terrific price for that exchange, something that requires a compromise of values to exist in the system if one is to be established as a social being capable of making exchanges. Whether it is Frank in *Thief* or Cuza in *The Keep* or Wigand in *The Insider*, the larger socioeconomic system (and its implicit epistemologies) can make demands that compromise one's humanity, that seem to prey upon it. And, as we will see in the analyses below, the key means to oppressing the protagonists is information—specifically disembodied types of information such as television and cyberspace (and sometimes film) that can invade the privacy of the home and the mind as if no physical barriers between the inside and the outside existed. Mann's protagonists face the same dilemma that their author (and all of us) sometimes must face: how to stabilize boundaries and value systems in a world where a new kind of information, unlike the physically embodied spoken word (the medium his protagonists tend to trust) seems to consume our social reality, perhaps consume meaning itself, and make it impossible to stabilize an identity as a social being. Mann's protagonists yearn for a world where they can be like the good father or the true warrior, giving their spoken word as a sign of honor and living by it. But the socioeconomic systems they live in make designs on human beings that prevent them from evading the kind of isolation, alienation, and falsification that become the norm in their postmodern world.

Hence, the task of writing a critical analysis of Mann's films is daunting. Here is an artist who insists on maintaining his privacy and integrity as an individual. He has indicated that this should apply to his fellow artists as well. Asked by Sragow how Russell Crowe prepared for his role in *The Insider*, Mann replied on p. 4 that the Freedom of Information Act did not apply to that kind of work.[4] Moreover, Mann and his protagonists represent something of a paradox. They reject the isolation of contemporary life in their values for human society and contact, yet they apparently reject some of the larger political and economic mechanisms that human society is dependent upon for its existence. There is a kind of radicalism here and one that does not seem to promote a complete rejection of humans as social beings but nevertheless seems to question some of the more conservative elements of our culture. Hence the primary challenge in developing a systematic approach to Mann's films is in finding a means to make sense of what seems to be an inherent paradox in the director's vision of contemporary life and the problems it creates for all of us. How, in short, does one apply or develop a theory or methodology adequate to the task of interpreting such a director's works?

The first key, I argue, is to accept Mann's films as public expressions of a philosophy mainly concerned with the impact of information on human culture, one that must stand on its own with little or no extraneous commentary from the author. The second key is to focus on what precisely those films say about information, because this may provide a means of drawing on appropriate critical theories in the realm of informatics that will enable the implementation of a method for fully explicating the films' content.

As I make clear in the following chapters, the two most useful theoretical approaches for studying Mann are those of N. Katherine Hayles and Jean Baudrillard. They are appropriate because they examine the two areas of main interest to Mann's films: *informatics* and *the posthuman*. The term informatics refers to the various ways in which human beings interact with information systems. As Hayles's studies argued, these systems exhibit such complexity in the global information sphere that they suggest that a greater degree of control over human beings can be exerted than ever before (and hence could threaten our freedom). At the same time, they perhaps point to a human potential for liberation if individuals can somehow escape this network of information. What emerges is the culture of the postmodern, or more precisely the post human, where, as Hayles indicated in the criticism quoted in the next chapter, the most significant aspects of human experience—space, time, context, language, and identity—are denatured, characterized as nothing more than disembodied cultural and linguistic constructs that deconstruct themselves in the conflicted informatics and ideologies of the cultural matrix.

Blood in the Moonlight (this title derives from a phrase used by Hannibal Lecktor whose oppressive approach to informatics is discussed in the chapter on *Manhunter*) situates Mann's films in this cultural matrix because Mann has addressed the uses and abuses of information in each of his motion pictures. So far only two book length studies of Mann's films have been published—Steensland's *Michael Mann* and Nick James's *Heat* (2002)—neither of which has considered Mann's films in this context. Indeed, neither work is a systematic theoretical study of Mann's films. They are instead appreciations of his work that offer some insight into his themes and characters but are more useful as summaries of production methods and backgrounds to Mann's films than as critical studies. Only one writer has made a solid connection between Mann and posthuman, Jean Baptiste Thoret (2000), who drew parallels between

Mann and posthumanist thinker Jean Baudrillard. I will discuss both Thoret's and Steensland's approach to Mann in more detail below, but briefly I will explain here how my application of Hayles's and Baudrillard's work has led me away from Steensland and Thoret and toward a somewhat different methodology and set of conclusions about Mann's films.

The main problem with Steensland's and Thoret's approaches is their focus. Both writers overemphasize the isolation of Mann's protagonists and overlook their need for and their occasional successes in establishing meaningful human social contact. Steensland, for example, drawing parallels between Mann and some forms of existential thought, argued that Mann ultimately wants his protagonists to cut off all "entanglements" with people and things (17). Similarly, Thoret argued that, above all else, the Mann protagonist wants to vanish (9). There is no denying that Mann's protagonists have moments like that, but there are occasions when they connect with those whom they love and establish meaningful relationships. The rising action and ending of *The Last of the Mohicans* (a film that Thoret largely ignored and which Steensland argued in his chapter on the film was one of Mann's weaker efforts, partly because of its hero's success in love) clearly showed a successful and meaningful romantic relationship between Nathaniel (Daniel Day-Lewis) and Cora Munro (Madeleine Stowe). How is one to explain the difference between a relationship like this versus the disastrous one between Vincent Hanna (Al Pacino) and his wife in *Heat*? For that matter, why could Jeffrey Wigand find happiness exchanging information with high school students in *The Insider* when his attempts to do so with corporate America made him paranoid and miserable? Either Mann was being utterly inconsistent or another approach to his films is needed to explain Mann's thinking on how human beings communicate.

I argue that the best approach is to situate Mann with such theoreticians as Baudrillard, Hayles, and, later in Mann's career, Paul Virilio, to better appreciate and describe how Mann distinguishes between good and bad uses of information. Moreover, as I show in the Introduction, the most important of these theorists to bring to bear on Mann's texts is Baudrillard because he shared with Mann the capacity to differentiate between the abstract disembodied informatics associated with acquisitiveness and power, that Mann has decried, and the fully embodied dialogical discourse of *symbolic exchange* that both Mann and Baudrillard have praised as an alternative to the informatics of oppression. Baudrillard saw such symbolic exchange as the antithesis of a digitalized capitalist culture that separated subjects from objects, that engaged in the kind of dualism between form and substance that both Hayles and Mann decry. Hence, what will emerge in my study is a description of Mann's approach to informatics that shows parallels between Mann and Baudrillard that Thoret's focus leads him to overlook.

Specifically, I draw attention to how Mann's philosophy and even his narrative and visual styles speak to his interest in the phenomenon of symbolic exchange that influenced the early, more optimistic stage of Baudrillard's thinking when he focused on this exchange as a means of resisting the oppressive aspects of informatics. Baudrillard initially saw an oppression taking place as a result of the reigning informatic system's monological denial of a response from the masses who are coerced by the information presented by media that they are not allowed to respond to dialogically. In late capitalist culture, where selfish acquisition and the selling of images in the society of spectacle is the norm, orality degenerates and with it the original dynamic of symbolic exchange that was the norm in primitive oral cultures. There the focus was not on selfish amassing of wealth and power but rather on the concepts of loss, indebtedness, and sacrifice. Things are exchanged to meet the immediate needs of individuals who, in the ritual of gift giving, show that they are not attached to themselves but rather to the social unit, the tribe, or clan, wherein no surplus of goods or capitalistic exchange value ever appears. Instead, value is exhausted with the exchange, just as signification is in oral exchanges where meaning is likewise exhausted with the exchange of the gift of the word. Information in a ritual of symbolic exchange is not coercive but rather represents the very essence of the reciprocal social bonding that creates the society. Words and individuals in symbolic exchange have real presence and do not exist in the disembodied *simulacrum* of the culture, the *hyperreality* that is Baudrillard's trope for the oppressive posthuman informatics that inevitably kills meaning and society. Mann's protagonists have their most successful and meaningful moments as social human beings when they engage in symbolic exchange. They suffer most when the larger oppressive system of disembodied informatics prevents them from making such exchanges.

In order to do justice to such a philosophical outlook in the films, I have developed a methodology appropriate to explicating the works of an artist who has decried abstract disembodied discourses and applauded the kind of embodied symbolic exchange that Baudrillard has described as best exemplified by street language, graffiti, and those types of poetic discourse that immediately exhaust meaning as a gift of symbolic exchange. This methodology may try some readers' patience since it does not present the analysis of the films in a purely abstract way. Instead, I implement a literary descriptive essay style that presents the analytical synthesis of the film's themes as emergent patterns embedded in the cinematic narrative via a discourse representative of the cognitive distancing that evolves from interpretation of stylistic detail in individual scenes discussed in roughly chronological order. The result works much the same as traditional analysis—stylistic detail supports analysis, form is connected to content—but this takes place in a much subtler fashion than what one typically sees in analytical essays. The analysis does not divorce style and content and thereby reiterate the inherent posthuman dualism implicit in the more traditional method's epistemic. Rather it seeks to embody the abstract in the concrete materiality of the film's narrative and dialogue, just as Mann's films do in moments of symbolic exchange with the audience.

The inspiration for this method is N. Katherine Hayles's book *How We Became Post Human*. Therein Hayles demonstrated how her methodology worked to combat the potential harm that disembodiment does to human subjects:

> To contest it [the metanarrative of human disembodiment], I want to use the resources of narrative itself, particularly its resistance to various forms of abstraction and disembodiment. With its chronological thrust, polymorphous digressions, located actions, and personified agents, narrative is a more embodied form of discourse than is analytically driven systems theory. I hope to replace a teleology of disembodiment with historically contingent stories about contests between competing factions, contests whose outcomes were far from obvious.... Though overdetermined, the disembodiment of information was not inevitable, any more than it is inevitable we continue to accept the idea that we are essentially informational patterns [22].

Hayles here faced the hard task of reporting the rise of disembodied cybernetics without capitulating to its assumption that its outcome as disembodied discourse, supporting the idea of human beings as disembodied information patterns, was set by some kind of deterministic law. Hence, she turned to narrative, with its emphasis on chronology, shared human space, context and time, the very antithesis of the posthuman condition of disembodied informatics. At times in her study she sounded quite literally, more like a novelist than a theoretician, as when she used descriptive detail to bring to life as a human presence Janet Freed, the secretary for the Macy conferences on cybernetics, a living woman embedded in her context (83).

It is appropriate to bring similar sensibilities and methods to Mann's films because, as we will see later, he too has discerned much harm in the disembodiment of information and has adopted a style appropriate to his occasion. Unlike many other postmodern artists such as Godard and Quentin Tarentino, he has shown no interest in deserting normal plot chronology but instead has tended to use fairly conventional narrative structures driven by suspense and character development located in specific actions. This is absolutely necessary to bringing to life the embodied discourse of symbolic exchange, and it is equally needed for allowing the audience to experience a fundamental symbolic exchange with the film, much like what Baudrillard said happened with poetics (described in greater detail in the introduction). I argue that Mann has made film a type of symbolic exchange with his audiences when they come to understand the full discharge of meaning between protagonists who resist the coercive aspects of the informatic system as best they can. My own discursive style preserves the integrity of that exchange by following (for the most part) the chronology of the film and its development of character in narrative chronological time. This is the best way to explore the themes that Thoret and Steensland undervalue in Mann's films, love and friendship, themes that are essential to understanding Mann's conception of humans as social beings engaging in symbolic exchange.

This method, my analyses will show, is the best way to do justice to these films. Time, as we will see below, is a significant topic for Mann. It is the ultimate gift shared by his protagonists, it is the only means, as a gesture in symbolic exchange, to counteract (if only temporarily) the effects of the coercive and oppressive form of informatics. Mann's arguments are developed through narrative time in such a fashion that allows a reader like myself to engage the films dialogically. Hence my own readers will sense a type of pattern emerging in my essays. I will begin with a brief overview of the topics addressed in the film. I will then present a description and analysis of the opening scene of the films to show how each sets up the thematic conflicts that reflect the conflicted nature of the protagonists who in turn reflect the conflict between dialogical and coercive (disembodied) types of informatics in their culture. I will then show how the unfolding of the plot in time engages us in questions about how these conflicts can be resolved. I will present what appears to be the film's mode of resolving those conflicts and what this implies about Mann's commentary on information. More often than not, however, Mann's commentary will lack closure—as befits an artist who does not wish to be coercive and who implicitly wishes to keep open possibilities for new exchanges with audiences in the future.

In addition to the theoretical advantages to this approach, there are

Preface

also pragmatic benefits. First, there is no need to supply separate plot summaries for each film for readers who have not seen them. Enough detail is preserved from each film to ensure that anyone who has not seen any of the given films will be able to understand the essay. Second, the detail presented is, I hope, sufficiently rich to whet the appetite for readers to seek out films by Mann that they have not seen. At least two of his films—*The Jericho Mile* and *The Keep*—have become quite rare and are available only on VHS. Unfortunately, no digitized VHS prints, letterbox prints, or DVD versions of these films exist. Where there is increased demand for a product, there is always hope.

After the analyses of these individual texts, I will present an overview of what Mann's collected works imply about the uses and abuses of information. Briefly, the chapters of this book will cover only those films that Mann directed and wrote (usually with help from a screenwriter).

Chapter 1, the introduction, provides backgrounds on posthuman culture and its significance for Mann's films. It also describes the parallels between Mann and Baudrillard as it provides background on the concepts of symbolic exchange originally formulated by Marcel Mauss and Georges Bataille in the twentieth century.

Chapter 2 discusses Mann's most optimistic appraisal of the significance of symbolic exchange in his first full-length made for TV movie, *The Jericho Mile* (1979). Here Mann presents a protagonist (Rain Murphy) whose isolation from the larger system as an inmate in Folsom Prison makes it possible for him to create a stable identity as a tribal leader who beats the system at its own game by using shared time (depicted as a form of symbolic exchange) as a means to resist the system. From this point on, time becomes a major theme in Mann's films because its role in symbolic exchange is one of the main means for measuring the protagonists' capacity to fight against the system and establish an identity.

Chapter 3 on *Thief* (1981) discusses the impact of urban life (city as complex information system) on the protagonist's search for freedom, and shows how the city complicates the search for freedom and identity because its economics and technologies make the hero more vulnerable to the system's coerciveness.

Chapter 4 discusses the Gothic film *The Keep* (1983) that takes us back to World War II to comprehend how things got the way they have in postmodern society, by examining how the Nazis first exploited the subconscious as a means to assert control over human subjects.

Chapter 5 investigates *Manhunter* (1986), focussing on what Paul Virilio has called the videoscopic revolution (indirect light) in TV and video in order to demonstrate how they make possible even greater invasion of the human subject's territoriality and consciousness by further eroding humanity's capacity to stabilize boundaries in space and time that make possible meaningful communication and symbolic exchange.

Chapter 6, which analyzes *The Last of the Mohicans* (1992), shows how Mann once again takes an historical approach to demonstrate how the rise of disembodied imagined nationalist (and colonialist) communities destroyed tribal cultures based on symbolic exchange and replaced them with the hyperreal politics of greed.

Chapter 7 investigates how Mann's next film, *Heat* (1995), describes the decay of dialogue in late postmodern society that further diminishes the efficacy of symbolic exchange in a culture where deception becomes the norm, and violence expresses the anxiety created by the destruction of context, territorial space, and stable identity boundaries.

Chapter 8 describes Mann's *The Insider* (1999) as a depiction of how the modern news media have become a form of terrorism that further erodes the capacity of the protagonists to empower themselves in a society that has become an implosive vortex where information is a commodity and truth, like meaning, ceases to exist.

Chapter 9 on *Ali* (2001), shows how Mann still evinces fascination for the concept of symbolic exchange when Ali's encounter with African culture in Zaire empowers him at the end of the film in unexpected ways (albeit in a context where Mann suggests that oppressive informatics could perhaps be more successfully resisted in the 1960s than they can be today).

Finally, Chapter 10 summarizes Mann's approach to informatics and further clarifies the significance of symbolic exchange for his films. The act of sacrifice and symbolic sharing of time represents something that individuals can still engage in regardless of gender, ethnicity, or economic class. In the early twenty-first century the global system of information that manifests itself through coercive strategies cannot be changed, but the experience of the exchange at the local level for the individual is still significant as the defining characteristic of our humanity. Mann has argued this consistently throughout his career for reasons that will become evident as we begin our investigation of his place in the posthuman milieu of informatics.

Two final notes before I turn to discussing Mann's milieu and analyzing his films. Stills from the films accompanying my analyses of individual scenes and shots are what are known as "frame grabs" taken from DVD and VHS with the use of a computer. They may not represent the best possible quality in terms of clarity but they will serve to illustrate my discussions. And finally, readers will note that in my documentation at the end of each chapter I generally cite the VHS versions of the films, but nevertheless describe any significant differences between DVD and VHS versions in my endnotes when necessary. Because not all of Mann's films are available on DVD and because the versions on VHS are generally better known to the public, I typically cite the VHS versions of the films for the sake of consistency.

1

Introduction: Symbolic Exchange, Informatics, and Michael Mann's Cinema

Power consists in the monopoly of the spoken word; the spoken word ... is no longer exchanged.
Jean Baudrillard, 1997

By August 2003 it had all become apparent. A do not call registry was established in the United States to prevent telemarketers from violating the sanctity of the home, thus triggering a war between legislators and federal judges concerning the rights of citizens to defend themselves against such invasions of their privacy. In the same month, a cell phone was used by terrorists in Jakarta to trigger a car bomb as part of a global Jihad that had accelerated after September 2001 when the World Trade Center and the Pentagon were attacked as viewers watched the events live on television in their homes and at the workplace. In August 2003, identity theft had become the number one complaint dealt with by the Federal Trade Commission, which was processing as many as seven million such cases a year. Information technology had become a kind of agency with seemingly unlimited potential for wreaking havoc in people's lives. Information could be a weapon, one that could be used to bypass any kind of physical boundary. It was an instrumentality that promised seemingly unlimited potential for empowering those who could wield it, to have a stunning impact by controlling human beings via the manipulation of the flow of information and energy that had made possible the technological system that sustained the very existence of our information based society. Our dependency on and our complete integration into such systems would be made apparent again as the entire power grid from New York City to Michigan, and including an area north of Toronto, shut down in August 2003, and workers in New York City instantly evacuated office buildings en masse as if they were facing a terrorist attack.

But for Michael Mann this must have seemed less like breaking news than the fulfillment of carefully considered prognostication. Since the late 1970s he had been making films that described the significance and potential dangers of an emerging informatics whose impact on our culture has been profound. N. Katherine Hayles, in her study *How We Became Post Human* (1999), offered a description of informatics that helps illuminate its significance for Mann and others who have studied with keen interest (and concern) human beings' interaction with information systems in modern times. In note 4, page 313, Hayles indicated that the term *informatics* refers to all of "the material, technological, economic and social structures that make the information age possible." Informatics therefore included "the patterns of living that emerge from and depend on access to large data banks and instantaneous transmission of messages," plus the "reconfiguring of the human body in conjunction with information technology." It also "includes the following: the late capitalist mode of flexible accumulation; the hardware and software that have merged telecommunications with computer technology." It refers not only to Donna Haraway's (2000) concept of information as a potential mode of domination but also to the study of the "cultural impact and significance of information technol-ogies."

In this study, Hayles warned society of the rise of a new cybernetics and an information culture in which a model of a "computational universe" implied that human beings would someday be seen as inferior to machines: "If the name of the game is processing information, ... the days of the human race are numbered" (243). This is taking place today because in the wake of postmodernism and posthuman informatics, everything in our world including the human subject, can be reduced to disembodied abstract information. In both the realm of cybernetics and in postmodern cultural theory, the human subject is losing any kind of physical presence, and thus both the sciences and the humanities have "collaborated in creating the postmodern ideology that the body's materiality is secondary to the logical or semiotic structures that it encodes." In such a context, a human being is "primarily, if not entirely, a linguistic and discursive construction." Hence, both the sciences and the humanities make "pronouncements supporting an ideology of disembodiment" (192).

1. Introduction

This is an especially disturbing idea because it implies that boundaries between human beings and information systems may be highly permeable—and this raises concerns, as Hayles said in her (1990) study *Chaos Bound*, regarding the use of information to control human subjects individually and en masse. As information and technological "systems became more complex and encompassing, they could also become more oppressive." This has been made especially clear since World War II: "In more than one sense, the Cold War brought totalitarianism home to Americans. As information networks expanded and data banks interlocked with one another, the new technology promised a level of control never before possible"(5).

That Michael Mann should share with Hayles an interest in the impact of information systems on culture may surprise some readers who would normally associate such themes with science fiction rather than with the genres that Mann has mastered—action films, crime sagas, psychological thrillers, historical dramas, docudramas, and at least one venture into the Gothic (*The Keep*, 1983). Certainly most of his critics do not focus on his interest in communication and informatics. As noted in the Preface, both Steensland's (2002) and James's books on Mann (2002) are primarily appreciations of his films rather than systematic scholarly or theoretical analyses. Only one critic, Thoret, has made the connection between Mann and the posthuman interaction between humans and information technologies.

Thoret's analysis requires discussion as it does shed light on some of Mann's interests in posthuman informatics. Thoret has connected Mann's unusual conception and exploration of space in cinema to culture critic Jean Baudrillard's (1975, 1997) descriptions of the implosive quality of social space in postmodern life, where the exterior and the interior no longer can be distinguished. This is reflective of posthuman informatics, as defined by Hayles in *Chaos Bound* (1990). For her, this new informatics leads to the denaturing of human experience, the very essence of what for her and others the term posthuman means—the deconstruction of the human subject on the grounds that every element of human experience, language, context, space, and time, can be deconstructed by virtue of the fact that they are artificial cultural constructs rather than natural creations (265). Baudrillard's theory that human beings now live in a simulacrum, a culture of simulation rather than a real physical world, his theories on the hyperreal quality of life, said Hayles, parallel similar posthuman conceptualizations of space where "context is seen as a construction to be manipulated rather than a preexisting condition" (274). "Like cyberspace, the hyperreal presupposes a radical erosion of context" leading to a denatured reconfiguration of spaces (275–276).

Thoret detected such a conception of space in Mann's films paralleling the aquarium syndrome in Baudrillard's theories where exterior and interior spaces can no longer be distinguished. Thoret said, "In Mann's America ... the interface exterior/interior has disappeared" (7). This presented Mann and his protagonists with a profound question: "If a distinction between the exterior and the interior is no longer allowed, how do you withstand the cataclysm of spaces, so that they can be public, professional and intimate?" (7). The answer, very simply, is that you can't: "From then on, the expulsion of the Mann hero to the outside of the enclosure ... only emphasizes his profound desire to simply disappear" (9).

This represents a dark reading of Mann, one that argues that there can be no hope or optimism for human beings as they struggle with the oppressive nature of posthuman informatics that seem to evince the potential to invade and control every aspect of human life. Thoret implied that the human subject simply disappears (or yearns to disappear) in Mann's world, that there is no hope for resistance, no alternative to a culture in which all the stabilizing elements in human existence—boundaries that create contexts within which human beings can define their relations to space, time, self, society, technology—cease to exist as they succumb to the implosive posthuman vortex created by the conflicted, deconstructed nature of human society. This contrasts with the more optimistic, humanistic impression that Steensland (2002) offered in his appreciation and praise of Michael Mann's protagonists:

> Their zeal is nothing short of religious. And although they may be alone at the end of their stories, their victories are never Pyrrhic but very real. They succeed as martyrs do. Their sainthood is guaranteed. They are not destroyed because these men know they are alone and because of that, the worst crime in a Michael Mann film is not thievery or killing, but betrayal of self [8].

Steensland is not an academic critic and he has not approached Mann from a theoretical perspective, but he has seen all of Mann's films and offers consistent, relatively optimistic readings of these texts. The question now becomes: if we do read Mann in the context of informatics, does the analogy with Baudrillard's thinking hold, and does it necessarily exclude any reading of Mann as an optimist with regards to resisting the oppressive nature of the world his protagonists live in? The

1. Introduction

argument of the present study *Blood in the Moonlight* can be put very plainly: The parallels between Mann and Baudrillard (not to mention other theoreticians investigating the posthuman and informatics that we will explore in later chapters) are even stronger and more complex than Thoret could describe in his necessarily shorter study. A careful examination of Mann's films—those that we know he both directed and scripted or cowrote—will reveal that much of his thinking about the human condition is dark, implying that in the age of informatics human freedom is compromised by a system that, as Baudrillard implied in the chapter epigraph, exercises such absolute control over human communication, that the human subject seems to deconstruct and lose any capacity for empowerment in the invasive dehumanizing postmodern world of informatics.

Nevertheless, both Mann and Baudrillard, like other posthuman thinkers, have explored other possibilities, other alternatives to the present system, and various means of resisting it. Both show an interest in what French thinkers such as Georges Bataille and Marcel Mauss called *symbolic exchange*. Both show an interest in the capacity of the spoken word to resist the effects of the seemingly pervasive influence of what Hayles calls a *disembodied informatics*, technologies of communication that at times seem to deny human freedom. Mann and Baudrillard show both optimism and pessimism at different times, depending on the focus of their investigations of the human quest for freedom in the context of posthuman informatics.

There is no easy means for explaining the surprising degree of parallelism between Mann and Baudrillard. Nevertheless, as Hayles says in *Chaos Bound*, parallels between different types of discourses, different modes of thought, different disciplines, can be explained by the complex networks of information that are created by the information feedback loops resulting from innovations in informatics since World War II:

> The recurrent image I use to explain the complex interconnections of theory, technology, and culture is a feedback loop. ... [T]he feedback cycle connected theory with culture and culture with theory through the medium of technology. Literary texts and theories were also involved in this cycle, for they too were affected by technology at the same time that they were affecting it. It should be no surprise, then, that many of the presuppositions that underlie the literary texts are also embedded within the scientific models and theories of the period [xiv].

This would clearly apply to film as well as literature because film as a medium and as a mode of communication is even more directly connected to the various technologies of informatics than other forms of literature are. Hence, Mann could easily evince concerns about information in his films similar to those voiced by such theoreticians as Hayles and Baudrillard if he is likewise focusing on the importance of information in our culture. However, the parallelism between Mann and Baudrillard may have begun in part also because of an unusual incidence of synchronicity, a fortunate coincidence that perhaps prompted each man to consider the relationship between power, control, and information in the late twentieth century.

Mann's first film, a documentary, *Insurrection*, chronicled "the student uprisings in Paris, France, in May 1968" (Steensland, 13). The 25-year-old filmmaker had managed to get close to the radical student leaders when no one else could. More than likely this was made possible in part because of the radical politics that Mann shared with them, politics that, as the American Film Institute's (AFI) *The Directors* indicated, he had absorbed in Madison and which had prompted him to go to London and avoid service in Vietnam. Decades later, in an interview with Cynthia Rose, he referred to "the spring of 1968" as "thrilling history," a radical time leading to radical change (3). Mann's career began just as Baudrillard's critical consciousness of post-modern culture was also emerging with the events of 1968.

The insurrection these men observed was a remarkable moment for a filmmaker or a philosopher to experience and chronicle because, as Baudrillard indicated, one thrust of this radical action was to take control of the television medium and thereby resist its influence over the masses. As Steven Connor said in his analysis of Baudrillard, this event took on special significance for the French thinker who ironically saw it as an illustration of the most oppressive effects of the media that helped create a code of conformity:

> Baudrillard argues that it is not possible simply to take over the form of the mass media and change their content to any good purpose, since what is oppressive about the media is precisely the "code" which in their very form they embody. ... A mass medium talks to its audience, says Baudrillard, while never allowing its audiences to respond to it and, indeed, confirms its audience's muteness by simulating audience response via phone-ins, studio audiences ... and other forms of bogus 'interaction.' The mass media ... "fabricate non-communication...." The experience of the events of May 1968 in France, in which radio and TV stations were taken over by revolutionary groups, was that every form of subversive message can be made harmless by this means, since every "transgression and subversion never gets 'on the

1. Introduction

air' without being subtly negated as they are: transformed into models, neutralized into signs, they are eviscerated of meaning" [53].

Connor referred here to Baudrillard's discussion of the May 1968 event in his early 1972 essay "Requiem for the Media." This event continued to be significant to Baudrillard even in later works like the 1981 *Simulacra and Simulation* (which was not published in English until the 1990s). At the stage of Baudrillard's thinking that Connor described, the early to mid-1970s, Baudrillard believed that the main problem with postmodern culture and society was that the media do not allow the masses to respond—it is the tyranny of the monological over the dialogical, abstract informatic technology over the individuated voice. As Connor said, at this point Baudrillard wanted to believe that such things as street talk and visual art like graffiti showed subversive potential as forms of what he called *symbolic exchange*, which can resist the codes of an oppressive system that, in turn, deny the masses a response (55). Nevertheless, later in his career, Baudrillard, in *Simulacra*, eventually said that the problem was more complex than that, because the masses and the media, to some degree, help sustain each other in a system that is oppressive to all. This represents an irreconcilable paradox for him. Is it the case where "the media neutralize meaning and produce the ... masses," or is it the masses who resist the media by not "responding?" Thus there is a paradox in this strange relationship between the masses and the media (84). Therefore, the prevailing strategy of the masses today is silence, a hyperconformism that resists the system while perpetuating it (85–86).

Hence, the student revolution of May 1968 takes on new significance for him by the time he writes the *Simulacra*. As Connor said, by this point in his career, he had given up on the idea that human beings can take back the power of the spoken word from the system and respond meaningfully, so for him the idea of society cannot exist, for in a system like this we are burying it beneath its "simulation" even as the system desperately attempts to give the masses "an identity," which they themselves resist through their thoughtless simulation (59). The result is the collapse of society itself into a "'black hole'" (59). This, Baudrillard realized in *Simulacra*, was what he was seeing in May 1968, the first instance of implosion, not revolution: "May 1968 was ... the first implosive episode" precipitating the "involution" of society (73).

Tracing the development of Baudrillard's theories on control and resistance brings to mind perhaps a first time viewing of *Easy Rider*: what starts seemingly as a manifesto on revolutionary reform, ends in a sad recognition of a pervasive, nihilistic, incomprehensible implosion of violence. It is violence that seems to confirm the power of the social even as it seeks to deny its reality, its existence. Reclaiming the spoken word, seeking new ways to rebel against and reform a technocracy of informatics, gives way to a type of criticism that, in some ways, as Connor indicated, helplessly recapitulates the very ills of the culture it criticizes (60–62). There is no escaping the explosive vortex of society and its sign systems, not even for the critic.

In any event, the implosion of a society in an information cultural matrix where traditional conceptions of space and context and subjecthood seem to implode or deconstruct, as described by Baudrillard, reflect concerns shared by others like Hayles who comment on this milieu of informatics and how it impacts human culture. Each commentator has a special take on all of this, and Michael Mann, who witnessed the events of May 1968 even more intimately than Baudrillard, is no exception. Perhaps because of this shared experience with Baudrillard, he began with similar questions but he nevertheless reached somewhat different conclusions. He has never completely lost his faith in the significance of oral exchanges in this age in which, as Walter Ong once said, the word has become technologized. Mann still sees some value in orality and in street art like graffiti in various situations (at the local level), even though he evinces concern for the global situation similar to Baudrillard's. He also evinces similarities with other posthuman thinkers, as we shall see. But the key for understanding his films and to what extent they voice concerns similar to and yet divergent from Baudrillard's thinking, is the concept of *symbolic exchange*. This phenomenon has remained significant to both men throughout their careers for it is a form of human discourse and action without which their special critiques of modern informatics and posthuman culture cannot be made. It is the foundation of both men's philosophies, a phenomenon all human beings have experienced but one which few have come to comprehend and value as deeply as Baudrillard, Michael Mann, and their immediate predecessors who described symbolic exchange from an anthropological and an economic perspective, namely Marcel Mauss and Georges Bataille. A brief survey of these thinkers' theories on exchange will make possible a description of what is distinctive about Mann in the context of Baudrillard's conceptions of informatics and the postmodern.

Symbolic Exchange versus the Acquisitive Monopoly of the Capitalist Enterprise

Two of the first systematic studies of symbolic exchange in primitive societies were prompted by critiques of capitalism made by the French

1. Introduction

anthropologist Marcel Mauss (and his colleague Henri Hubert) who in turn influenced the economic theories of Georges Bataille. Mauss, looking at the financial crises of the 1920s and 1930s contrasted the so-called primitive preindustrial societies of the past (and their remaining counterparts in the present such as Native American tribes of Northwestern America) and concluded that present-day industrial societies suffered from an excess of acquisitiveness and selfishness that was destroying the moral fiber of the society. Key to maintaining the social fabric of primitive cultures is the idea of reciprocity, as exemplified through gift giving, a type of symbolic exchange. Mauss said, "Many ideas and principles are to be noted in systems of this type. The most important of these spiritual mechanisms is clearly the one which obliges us to make a return for a gift received" (5). Primitive cultures emphasize and exemplify this principle, according to Mauss, because they do not engage in an economic system of barter in which one seeks selfishly to acquire more than one's competitor can. Primitives "replace our system of sale and purchase with one of gifts and return gifts" (30). Gain is less important than loss and reciprocity. Thus, "Material and moral life, as exemplified in the gift-exchange, functions there in a manner at once interested and obligatory" (31).

Without this process in the archaic society, there is no honor or integrity—having "face" means not pursuing purely selfish interests but pursuing interests that meet mutual needs of more than one party. In Melanesia, for example, commerce is honorable but "when it is carried out ... for immediate gain, it is viewed with the greatest disdain" (36). Failure to establish the proper form of contract means loss of "face" and "rank" (38), and it can also result in death and destruction (39). "If things are given and returned it is precisely because one gives and returns such 'respects' and 'courtesies.'" A man "gives himself, and he does so because he owes himself—himself and his possessions—to others" (45). This applies to both patriarchal and matriarchal societies, where, in the latter case, the gift exchange may result in polyandry or the existence of a governing property woman (54). Either way, people in archaic societies "have not reached the stage of pure individual contract, the money market, sale proper, fixed price and weighed down coin money" (45).

Without the precedent of such archaic societies, our own society would be without moral guidance or rule: "Much of our everyday morality is concerned with the question of obligation and spontaneity in the gift." Moreover:

> It is our good fortune that all is not couched in terms of purchase and sale. Things have value which is emotional as well as material ...

Our morality is not solely commercial.... The gift not returned debases the man who accepted it, particularly if he did so without thought of return.... We must always return more than we receive; the return is always bigger and more costly [63].

And, by implication, it is also more rewarding if it represents, therefore, a genuine sacrifice. Hence, Mauss argued, we "should return to the old and elemental" way of behaving for it is the "very heart of social life" (67). Otherwise, by implication, we risk destroying the very fabric of our social existence.

Social economist Georges Bataille agreed and used Mauss's studies of these symbolic exchanges to formulate an even more radical critique of capitalism. Like Mauss, whom he quoted in *The Accursed Share* (originally published in the late 1960s), he contrasted modern materialist economics with a superior archaic system wherein the (symbolic) gift exchange was the basis for dealing with abundance, with the excess of "useful wealth" (59). All natural processes promote excess, and all living systems must find ways to deal with luxurious excess. Modern economies do not deal well with excess; many of our society's "problems ... follow from the existence of surpluses" that lead to uneven distribution of wealth (poverty) warfare, "the first explosive character of the world." Thus a "curse obviously weighs on the human life insofar as it does not have the strength to control a vertiginous movement" (40). As a result, "Under current conditions, everything conspires to obscure the basic movement that restores wealth to its function, gift giving, to squandering without reciprocation" (38).

For Bataille, it is less a matter of the primitives having superior ethics, as Mauss argued, than it is a matter of successful management of energy, economy, and surplus—but the principle needed is the same: an exchange of gifts that symbolizes for the participants respect for and renewal of the community through reciprocity. Archaic cultures made sure that things were used. Yes, the Aztecs were as warlike as we are, but their violence signified something different to them. For them "Consumption loomed just as large in their thinking as production does in ours." There was an essential difference between the Aztecs and we moderns: "They were as concerned about sacrificing as we are about working" (46), working to create more excess, accumulated for our own profit. War for them in their time was a religious form of sacrifice (54–55), something done as a gift to the sun god (49) who was fed just as the sun fed the world with its energy and radiance. Such "Sacrifice restores to the servile world that which servile use has degraded, rendered profane" (55). Victims of vio-

1. Introduction

lence are the "surplus taken from the mass of useful wealth" to save the community from "a mortal danger of contagion" (59). "This was the price men paid to escape the downfall and remove the weight introduced in them by the avarice and cold calculation of the real order" (61).

By the same token, the Aztec merchant "did not sell; he practiced the *gift exchange*; he received riches from the 'chief of men' (from the sovereign, whom the Spanish called the *King*); he *made a present* of these values to the lords of the lands he visited" (65). "The gift that one made ... was a sign of glory, and the object had the radiance of glory" (65). As in the Northwestern Native American ritual of "Potlatch," the ritual is based not on "the need to acquire but rather the contrary need to lose or squander" (67). It is about "the dissipation of useful wealth" (68). The giver "enriches himself with a contempt for riches, and what he proves himself to be miserly of is in fact his generosity." The exchange thus takes place in another's presence because the giver "has actually acquired, in the other's eyes, the power of giving or destroying"(69). The "exemplary virtue" of such activity "is given in this possibility for man to grasp what eludes him, to combine the limitless movements of the universe with the limit that belongs to him" (70). By contrast, our "present forms of wealth make a shambles and a mockery of those who think they own it" (76). Hence, today's society is a "counterfeit" of a real community and its "lie destines life's exuberance to revolt" (77).

Thus for both Mauss and Bataille, a culture based on acquisitiveness and selfish profit cannot be said to constitute a real society. Genuine social ties can only be established via economies based on destruction of surplus through mutual sacrifice and selfless gestures symbolizing the deeper social ethos of reciprocal and mutual exchange. For Baudrillard, these conceptions of symbolic exchange initially presented an opportunity to criticize the incapacity of Marxism to effectively disengage itself epistemologically and ideologically from the materialistic capitalism it sought to critique and subvert through its revolutionary rhetoric. In the long run, however, his thinking about the exchange led him directly to a model of postmodern culture as a simulacrum of reality that cannot be reformed even through the dialogical power of the spoken word as a type of symbolic exchange.

As Connor said (1989), initially in his career Baudrillard contrasted the "synthesized communication" represented by the television stations the students commandeered in 1968 with the "ideal of free, immediate exchange, in which the hierarchical split between the transmitter and the receiver is transmuted into a mutual responsiveness and discursive responsibility in spontaneous dialogue" (53–54). This primitivism derived from Mauss and Bataille is part of his "attack on the tendency of Marxist economics to subsume everything in the primitive societies to the principle of economic production; on the contrary, he argues, everything in primitive society is based upon the principle of continuous symbolic exchange, which maintains social stability and reciprocal relations between man and nature by never allowing the process of exchange to be blocked, cornered or constrained to produce profit." This is "opposed to conditions under capitalism" (i.e., the monopolistic stage of it) "in which every giving away of value is really only a detour on the way to greater accumulation or profit" (54).

One can add that the concept of symbolic exchange becomes for him an essential means for understanding the power of the spoken word as well as the consciousness of the human subject—essential because his quest for linguistic liberation in the context of informatics led him to question and subvert the idea of subjecthood itself in the context of symbolic exchange.

For Baudrillard, the excesses of capitalism had killed exchanges between human beings and nature. In *The Mirror of Production* (1975) he argued that postindustrial man prohibited all types of symbolic exchange between humanity and the natural world (58). By contrast, primitive peoples conceived even everyday acts like eating as acts of exchange; otherwise they do not come into being (79). The things exchanged do not exist as isolated material objects but instead represent a means to an exchange meant to supply mutual needs. Production appears nowhere for it is "negated ... by reciprocal exchange" that consumes itself endlessly (8).

Such exchanges work the way language naturally works when it is an unbounded oral milieu evoking spontaneous responses: "Language is produced by certain people and consumed by others; everyone is at the same time a producer and a consumer" (97). In such an exchange, identity cannot be described as a kind of subject differentiated from an object. Rather, "just as there is no separation between the sphere of producers and the sphere of consumers, there is no true separation between ... the ... subject and ... object" (98). Subject and object do not really have places in symbolic exchange. The exchange exists only to meet the needs of the community, its members—there is no objectification of the real, of the things or the people involved in the symbolic exchange. The term *symbolic*, as Baudrillard said later in *Mirror*, means "non-universalized" and "non-rationalized " (164). It is a reply to a need that is discharged with the reply (101). There is no surplus, no remainder: the function exists only in the dynamic exchange, the shared instance, that time in

1. Introduction

which it exists and defines the social fabric in that moment. Subject and object do not exist; the exchange is symbolic in the sense that it stands for something else (here, a process designed to answer mutual needs of participants), and in that moment does not signify an objective meaning or inert thing but a dynamic function. Meaning is exhausted as the word is spoken or as the act of reciprocity or sacrifice is performed. Society is a function resulting from these dynamic processes of shared exchanges dramatized and realized by the society's cultural rituals.

The effect of industrialization, or, more specifically, the effect of the technologization of language, in what we now would call the *postmodern milieu*, is to negate our capacity for this type of reciprocity in language that produces a real society of thinking and action. With this new stage that constitutes a monopolization of the code to ensure conformity, comes a radical alteration of how signs function for "The signifier becomes its own referent" and all reality becomes the place "of a structural simulation" (127-128). Thus, even at this early stage of his career, Baudrillard confronted the fact that we live in a simulacrum of reality because language has lost its value as a mode of symbolic exchange. As Connor said, this "simulation takes the form, not of unreality, as many of Baudrillard's followers wish to believe, but of manufactured objects and experiences which attempt to be more real than reality itself—or, in Baudrillard's term, 'hyperreal'" (57).

At this stage Baudrillard still believed that there might be means of opposing all of this through an aesthetic mode, poetry, but with time he seemed to despair of a solution, though the symbolic exchange gesture remained important to his theories even later in his career. In *Symbolic Exchange and Death* (published in France in 1976), he argued that poetry still preserved symbolic exchange, despite the despotism of the system's code. The "poetic creates the situation of primitive societies in linguistic material: a restricted corpus of objects whose uninterrupted circulation in the gift-exchange creates an inexhaustible wealth, a feast of exchange" (203). A good poet engages in ritual and magic; he or she is like a shaman or prophet who exhausts the meaning of words through ritual, and hence in poetry reciprocity enables user value and exchange value to cancel each other out, resulting in the "nothingness of value" which is the source of the pleasure of the text (204).

Thus, the poem as gesture of symbolic exchange fully actualizes the potential of the symbol to avoid the divisive, alienated quality of human experience in the postmodern world, the posthuman nonreality in which the subject yearns to connect with an exterior world, with some object or Other, in a world where time and space (context), as Hayles had said, lose meaning as reference points. This is because "The symbolic ... puts ... an end to the opposition between the real and the imaginary." It extinguishes the disjunctive code and its binary terms that were the symptom of the postmodern linguistic and cultural collapse occurring in the kind of monopolistic economies he described in *The Mirror of Production*. Here in *Symbolic Exchange* he described how the symbolic undoes the "topologies of soul and body, man and nature, the real and the non-real." In binaries like man/nature, male/female, each disjunctive term excludes its other, which is transformed into its "imaginary" (133). This cannot happen in the symbolic act, which does not deconstruct these opposites but rather creates a field of operation where the binary epistemic of subject/object does not exist in the exchange, which puts the word's meaning to death like a god or self-sacrificing hero (199).

The ultimate consequence of this is that we realize that there has never been either a *"subject of the consciousness" or "a subject of the unconscious"* (222) for symbolic modes cannot be *"the labor of the unconscious"* (223). The dichotomy of conscious and unconscious are fictions created by the oppressive code of the system and its binaries. Poetry can perhaps remind us of this different field of activity, in this other space where symbolic action precludes materialist reference (236). Instead, there is *jouissance*: the destruction of the oppressive logos of the dominant Code (230).

In his later work, Baudrillard still held onto this conception of symbolic exchange but he had come to better comprehend the pervasiveness of the Code and its irresistible nature. When he spoke of resistance, he usually came to recognize the futility of it as he did here in *Simulacra*. He wanted to be a nihilistic terrorist in theory, but Baudrillard came back to the lesson of May 1968—the system absorbs everything of a subversive nature that you can throw at it because it nullifies the only real exchanges that exist for society, whether it reacts with anger or indifference (163). What is left is the simulacrum where simulations or models precede reality in a hyperreal world, and power is a mere "hallucination" recapitulating the implosive forces of a society consuming itself (23). If one defies at all, one should do it without the feeble value of hope (152).

This is perhaps the most pessimistic assessment of the posthuman scene one can find. Michael Mann shares some of that pessimism, but he has also kept alive some optimism regarding the value of symbolic exchange in his consideration of many aspects of posthuman culture.

1. Introduction

The Value of Film and Symbolic Exchange in Mann's Cinema

What follows here is a summation of the attitudes Mann evinced in his films regarding the cultural scene Baudrillard described. This is not an attempt to persuade the reader to embrace this reading of his films; that is the role of ensuing chapters, each of which presents a critical study of a particular film's commentary on the potentially oppressive nature of informatics. The proof of this study is in the individual analyses, just as the proof of what Mann has had to say about this cultural scene is in his films.

If Baudrillard saw all of the media, including film, as being irresistible sources of corruption and coercion by the end of his career, Mann, throughout his career, has kept alive some limited optimism for the efficacy of symbolic exchange and the capability of film to use it as an aesthetic means for challenging and interrogating the system. For Baudrillard, in *Simulacra*, cinema had lost much of its power in the context of hyperreality, especially under the influence of television, because it is a main means of instituting the simulacra:

> The cold collage ... of two cold media that evolve in an asymptotic line toward each other: the cinema attempting to abolish itself in the cinematographic (or televised) hyperreal [47].

In all of his films, Mann has shown his concern for the way in which informatics, especially when associated with visual media, can become a damaging influence in human lives. Like Baudrillard, he has been especially suspicious of the culture's master code because of its association with a socioeconomic system based on acquisitiveness and profit. As Steensland noted, one of the recurring motifs in Mann's films is that of the Faustian contract or deal that goes wrong:

> Every protagonist in a Michael Mann film has three common characteristics. First, they are alone in their dedication to what they do. Second, they enter a deal they believe will give them something they lack. Third, they ultimately realize the deal is dangerous because it is beyond their control, and the only thing within their control is their inner self [17].

Most of these observations are valid—certainly these patterns emerge but their significance is greater and more complex than Steensland asserted. The deal always goes wrong, yes, but it goes wrong for specific reasons that have to do with the most salient differences between the protagonists and the antagonists that they deal with. Moreover, while the protagonists do realize that they are losing control of the deal, they also realize that controlling and comprehending the "inner self" is far more difficult than they initially realize. These characters, in short, are as deeply divided as the culture of signs that they inhabit, a culture that makes attempts at asserting some kind of identity or subjecthood problematic, as Baudrillard's assessment of this culture and its economic system would lead us to anticipate.

The most significant difference between protagonists and antagonists in Mann's films is their relationship to the system. The protagonist rejects it while the antagonist accepts it and is a willing proponent of its politics of greed and domination, its use of the social code as an informatics of domination. But these differences do not result mainly from differences in politics or personality or philosophy. They stem from different attitudes toward the value of language and, more specifically, the value of the sacrifice that can be made through symbolic exchange. Mann's protagonists believe in the value of the exchange and are capable, at least at times, of utterly selfless exchange with other individuals who engage with them in the exchange. They believe in the power of the spoken word as a sign of integrity—they seek to prove their value by maintaining *face*, by living up to their word, by keeping promises. The antagonists are just the opposite. They seek only self-satisfaction. They pursue power in disregard of its hallucinogenic and pathogenic properties. They use information for purely coercive purposes—they are monologists. The protagonists, male and female, at least in their best moments, speak dialogically—they persuade rather than coerce, when they can, and they believe in freedom of choice. They want to restore the ritual of exchange via the power of that choice.

This, however, proves to be a difficult undertaking. Some protagonists are more capable of disentangling themselves from the coercive system of informatics than others. Sometimes this is because of their social or economic situation, but mainly it is because of how their character interacts with the cultural milieu that they find themselves in. Either way, the pervasiveness of the culture of greed and coercion makes the quest difficult, as does the epistemology and values that the sign system promotes. Protagonists wanting to achieve freedom from the oppressive system sometimes seek economic empowerment or empowerment over technology and communication systems to fight the system with its own fire. They usually do not succeed—these systems, with rare exception, typically burn everyone who touches them. Other protagonists look to conventional ideas of empowerment through society's notions of sub-

1. Introduction

jecthood. This fails for the reason Baudrillard gave—you can become a subject only by making someone or something else an object, and this puts you into the simulacrum with its binary semiotics that contrast reality and unreality, body and soul, male and female. This only leads to implosion, loss of identity. There is only one way to find identity and real power, and that is through the dynamic of symbolic exchange and sacrifice wherein subject and object disappear in a dialogical space that defines self and society through nonobjectifying acts of reciprocity. Quests for more conventional forms of subjecthood and power end disastrously.

The films and their respective protagonists and antagonists discussed in ensuing chapters illustrate these principles. These films, by the way, were chosen because they represent work that we know Mann both directed and scripted. His television series work is not discussed here because it represents a more complicated field of study—he did not write or direct most of the episodes of *Miami Vice*, *Crime Story*, and *Robbery Homicide Division*, so a different kind of critical approach will be required for these series that are sufficiently complex to merit a separate book length study. Also omitted are his documentaries and TV docudramas that likewise represent a different corpus of work. The youth film *Band of the Hand* (1986) is omitted because it was produced but not directed or written by Mann. And the made for television *L.A. Takedown* (1989) is omitted because this film is best seen as a draft for the more expansively developed *Heat* (1995) featuring the same characters and a similar plot.

Each film discussed has presented Mann with the opportunity to consider to what degree symbolic exchange can exist in modern society and to what degree it can have a positive effect on people's lives in the context of a culture under the gun of a coercive informatics that seeks to deny the power of the spoken word, that seeks to rob human beings of identity and the capability of shaping their lives as they choose. Mann's most successful protagonists were his first and one of his most recent, Rain Murphy of *The Jericho Mile* (1979) and Muhammad Ali in *Ali* (2001). Murphy, an inmate in Folsom Prison, established himself as a tribal leader who engaged in an exchange of total self-sacrifice that enabled him to secure an identity that was as liberating for his fellow inmates as it was for himself in his brief rebellion against the system. Ali's experience in Africa at the end of the film allowed him to understand the value of symbolic exchange when his encounter with the local people in Zaire taught him the value of art and symbol in ways he could not have anticipated in the postmodern American culture of his origin.

All of the other protagonists struggle with doppelganger antagonists who show that the protagonists are tainted in various ways by the society they live in. From this examination emerges what seems to be Mann's hypothesis concerning domination and information that he presents as a kind of cultural history. By looking back on history in movies like *The Keep* (set in World War II) and *The Last of the Mohicans* (set in eighteenth-century America), as well as *Ali* (set in the 1960s), he has shown that, as information technology has grown more sophisticated, it has become more dangerous, more effectively coercive, more capable of undermining our human sense of reality (as defined and instantiated by the discourse of the symbolic exchange) via the influence of the hyperreal simulacrum. Hence emerged his main thesis: as time goes by, the dialogics and oral rhetoric of symbolic exchange and sacrifice have less chance of changing the global situation of the coercive system of informatics. Indeed, attempts to globalize the locally effective exchange will inevitably be poisoned by the information technology and its associated values and epistemologies (this was most poignantly illustrated by one of Mann's most brilliant films, *The Insider*). With the passage of time, the spoken word is losing its power. But Mann still has not given up on its potential at the local level to make a difference. It is still alive. Hence, like Baudrillard, he is pessimistic, but he nevertheless does emphasize the importance of maintaining some optimism. To do otherwise, he seems to imply in his films, would be to surrender to the oppressive system, to violate the deeper significance of symbolic exchange.

Also emerging here is a preoccupation with time, a major theme in all of his films. Molly Graham in *Manhunter* (1986) said it best: "Time is luck," which is just another way of saying that time is what you make of it. For Mann, the only way to make anything of it, the only way to substantiate time in these postmodern times, is through the symbolic exchange, one of the reasons that love is such an important theme in his movies. It is the measure of how human beings use time to help themselves and each other simultaneously. Mann, as we will see, is extremely sensitive not only to the denaturing of space/context but the denaturing of time as well. As Hayles says in *Chaos Bound*, in posthuman culture, "time sinks into the media experience of constructive, repetitious packages and becomes a series of disconnected intervals." As a result, "Time still exists in cultural postmodernism, but it no longer functions as a continuum along which human action can be meaningfully plotted" (279). Mann has insisted that the symbolic exchange between individuals can still impact time and space, no matter what may be happening elsewhere in our cultural continuum. Time and space can and should be shared,

1. Introduction

in the territory defined by symbolic exchange, by the serving of mutual needs in the immediacy of the moment. The difference between doing that and failing to do so is the difference between the high romance shared by Cora Munro (Madeleine Stowe) and Nathaniel (Daniel Day-Lewis) in *The Last of the Mohicans*, and the sad, bitter destruction of domestic bliss exemplified by Justine (Diane Venora) and Vincent Hanna's relationship (Al Pacino) in *Heat*.

One other thing has emerged here: Mann's faith in the film medium itself. He has seemed to recognize, as the analyses below will show, that film is both an aural and a visual medium. As such, it can instantiate the coercive and hyperreal nature of the visual medium as described below in discussions of Virilio and Kittler in relation to Mann's films. But it can also produce the clean analog of sound, a medium that, as Kittler attests (1999), can represent a physical realm in ways that the disembodied visual media cannot (119). (Kittler's ideas will be presented in more detail in the chapter on *Manhunter*). Thus Mann has used film to recreate dialogue and exchange with stunning effect. The street art Baudrillard once admired also is extolled as an alternative to the system in *The Jericho Mile* and in *Ali* as discussed in later chapters. Indeed, some of the most memorable moments of Mann's films have involved dialogue that seems to command the attention of the viewer more powerfully than the images do. And it is the key to explaining the kind of powerful reaction that Steensland has to the martyrlike characters. They seem physically present at times. They make us cheer for them even when, sometimes, they make mistakes. They represent the real deal.

So too, by implication, does their creator. Mann's films have seldom made much money at the box office; only *The Last of the Mohicans* was highly profitable (perhaps because it was released shortly after Kevin Costner's successful frontier adventure *Dances with Wolves*). Probably fewer than a third of Mann's films received a majority of positive critical reviews when they were new. (Critical and financial success has eluded much of Mann's TV work as well; *Miami Vice* was an exception; *Crime Story* was cancelled by NBC in its second season, while CBS eliminated *Robbery Homicide Division* after fewer than a dozen episodes were aired). What then is the motive for making these movies, and how does one maintain status in profit-driven Hollywood under such conditions? Steensland indicated that to initiate production on *Ali*, Mann had to offer his own money to secure the project (86). Making *The Insider* shortly after the scandals with Big Tobacco and CBS clearly involved some risk for Mann because either of them could have considered suing him for his blunt indictment of both institutions. Each of these projects involved risks and therefore sacrifices. In both cases, the reward seems mainly to have been in the sacrifice; or, to put it another way, the gesture was its own reward. Perhaps, then, these films are attempts at exchange that in a way support the director's implicit thesis. The message may not be something one can make global in such a profit-driven and conformist system as Hollywood and the world at large. Nevertheless, its greater significance as a form of exchange is still there for those who, perhaps only at the local level of the individual's life, appreciate it for what it is.

2

Sympathy and the Devil: Doing Time in *The Jericho Mile* (1979)

> *You are running a game down on us.*
> [Rain Murphy confronts an Olympic official
> near the conclusion of *The Jericho Mile*.]

There are at least two kinds of games being played among the inmates and corrections officials within, and the people from outside, the walls of Folsom Prison in *The Jericho Mile*. The first is the game of egocentric dominance, selfish acquisition, and the oppressive global informatics used to create a hyperreal cultural text that blinds its captive audience to the insubstantial, meaningless, and divisive quality of life in postmodern society. The second is the game that resists the inherent narcissism of this culture with an oral, dialogical culture of symbolic exchange. The latter game, for Mann in this film, is preferable to the former and could briefly use some of the information technologies and their deconstructive epistemologies as effective weapons for fighting the global system. However, *The Jericho Mile* demonstrates that such resistance can succeed only on the local level. The subversive tribal society that can exist briefly on the local level cannot hope to compete with an oppressive informatics on the global level. The very means for realizing globalization on this scale defeat such attempts as they do not and cannot promote true intimate symbolic exchange. Nevertheless, Mann uses both the aural and visual aspects of his medium to dramatize how dialogics and symbolic exchange can offer effective resistance on the local level even if they cannot completely overcome the oppressive machinery of postmodern civilization.

The conflict between these two gaming activities/cultures is brilliantly dramatized in the opening montage sequence of the film, which can also serve as a proem to all of Michael Mann's works. The initial image, a full shot of an African-American inmate listening to a boom box (playing the film's theme, *Sympathy for the Devil*) on headphones, moving to the beat of a song only he and the audience can hear, suggests immediately the kind of isolation and alienation instantiated by the prison experience. The technology promotes a narcissistic movement away (escape) from the social reality he inhabits—an electronic hallucinogenic narcotic that becomes identified in this film with the simulacrum culture that Mann examines and decries in this and his other films. There are rapid succession of cuts, which we are consciously aware of because they are not used in a classical style here to relate narrative, but rather are implemented reflexively and formalistically to interrupt the usual chronological linear flow of space and time (important topics for the film). The cuts thus underscore, through style and content, the alienation of other men we view in the yard even as they seem to interact socially. We see men playing chess, stickball, and basketball; men lifting weights, men styling each other's hair—but we gradually realize that they have all segregated themselves ethnically. Blacks, Chicanos, and whites do not appear together in the same social spaces. Here, as if in anticipation of Baudrillard's theories on the implosion and disappearance of true social structures in the simulacrum, even social units reflect separation and division.

And yet, simultaneously, the cuts reveal alternatives to this divisive social aesthetic; contrasts and significant synchronicities emerge here that indicate possibilities for meaningful human contact that will be realized later in the film through symbolic exchange. Two protagonists who will initiate that exchange, Rain Murphy (Peter Strauss) and R. C. Stiles (Richard Lawson), a white man and a black man, run together in the yard, in contrast to the other prisoners who accept the boundaries laid down between ethnic groups in the yard. Moreover, not all of the games and activities going on around them are identical. The game of the main antagonist, Dr. D. (Brian Dennehy), the selling of liquor, is the only one that involves an exchange of money, profit. Other games seem to be purely for sport and competition; some gestures such as the styling of the hair seem to involve a nonprofiting, fairly selfless type of exchange. The latter type is the more common. Nevertheless, the series of cuts shows a greater number of hands taking part in the economic exchange for the liquor that promises, once again, escape from an oppressive social reality. Dennehy's network seems larger and very empowering—at least for him. And subsequent dialogue reveals that despite the segregation,

2. Sympathy and the Devil

he has ties to the blacks and Chicanos because he offers them the opiate they believe they need. Eventually we will realize that he is in control, every bit as much as the faceless guards who suddenly announce over the electronic communication system—the loudspeakers—that the prisoners must "*Clear the yard!*"

The opening montage, in short, points to the dominance of acquisitive economics and the power of electronic media to control the masses, despite their psychological isolation and social divisiveness in an economically and socially oppressive environment. As a representation from post–Vietnam, late 1970s America, it can be taken for a microcosm of the conflicted American cultural scene. Simultaneously, it suggests alternatives that will be dramatized by the relationship between Murphy and Stiles that allows Mann to illustrate how genuine symbolic exchange works, an exchange that represents an alternative to the hallucinogenic simulacrum invoked by the politics of selfishness and greed.

A key metaphor developed to illustrate this concept is represented throughout the film by how the prisoners, especially Murphy, manage time. Keeping and giving time are the symbolic gestures of exchange that allow localized subversion of the system because they show how a temporally liberating space can be achieved dialogically via reconfiguration of space/time relations in such a way as to resist the posthuman deconstruction of space and time associated with the prison as a microcosmic representation of the oppressive simulacrum. These dialogical relations allow Rain Murphy to find means of resisting the objectifying epistemologies that inform the hyperreal realm and its oppressive antisocial economics by allowing him to connect the previously deconstructed interior and exterior spaces in meaningful and productive ways. This is the means, realized through dialogue and street art (graffiti), by which walls of many kinds come tumbling down and promote a deeper kind of human social sympathy among these men who have been demonized by an equally oppressive outside world. As we study the unfolding of the film's narrative, the development of plot and characterization make clear how Mann's guarded yet very real optimism regarding resistance of the simulacrum expresses itself as a faith in the value of symbolic exchange as an alternative to an oppressive informatics identified with the simulacrum politics of selfishness and avarice. Let us turn now to an analysis of these themes as they develop in the film's narratology.

Initially, Murphy might seem to be an unlikely hero for Mann's project. Although he runs with Stiles, he evinces no connectedness to the other man, especially when Stiles becomes winded and stops. Murphy keeps moving, oblivious to the other man's presence. He appears to be doing his own time, living in even greater isolation than the other men.

He seems the last man one would expect to be able to engage in a selfless symbolic exchange of sacrifice. He runs in circles—he participates in the nonlinear cyclical quality of the inmates' lives later decried by Warden Gulliver who laments that the "comic book" mentality of the men renders them incapable of dealing with the real world and keeps them cycling back into the prison after they are released. It calls to mind the turnstile gate guarded by the Black Brotherhood who thus prevent any nonblacks from entering the weight lifting facility. Murphy thus initially seems to be an icon for this strangely deconstructed space where human time is not plotted in a linear fashion that allows any meaningful progress. In short, he appears to typify the problems of the posthuman that Hayles and Baudrillard discuss (see Chapter 1). Disconnected from context, time, and space, Murphy, in the opening scenes, would seem to show no capability for pursuing the forms of symbolic discourse that might be used to resist or represent an alternative to the disembodied information systems used by the guards and by Dr. D. to ensure that the inmates cannot define themselves as human subjects with control over their environments or their own destinies. By disconnecting from the system, Murphy seems to capitulate to it in a form of hyperconformity (as Baudrillard would call it) to the oppressive situation he finds himself in.

But as he interacts with Stiles, and as Stiles sadly becomes susceptible to the politics of Dr. D., a very different aspect of Murphy's character gradually emerges—one that points to his capacity to embrace and thereby exemplify for Mann an alternative to this conformity to the system. After a mesmerizing session watching *Let's Make a Deal* on television (and what better icon for the politics and informatics of greed in the simulacrum of an American culture that can still take possession of these inmates?), the men are back in their individual cells where their mail is delivered to them in—of all things—supermarket baskets. Stiles receives a photo of his wife and newborn daughter whom he has never seen because, like all of his children, she was sired during a conjugal visit. This triggers Stiles's obsession with linear time—he does not want to wait the three months required before his next conjugal visit; he wants to break out of the cyclical dehumanizing simulacrum of time instituted by the prison environment. He thus places a new demand on Murphy as he forcibly shares the pictures with him in Murphy's cell, his own private space, despite Murphy's initial reluctance to become involved in the man's private life. This is the first step toward a meaningful sharing of time on Murphy's part, the first step toward representing in the film the idea of time as a form of selfless and meaningful symbolic exchange. Murphy's increasing attachment to Stiles will illustrate this, even as Stiles becomes

2. Sympathy and the Devil

Before *The Jericho Mile*'s Rain Murphy (Peter Strauss) initiates them into the tribal culture of symbolic exchange, most of the prison inmates live isolated existences in the simulacrum of a society created by an oppressive technology of informatics.

victim to the politics of greed, an example of how the system inevitably destroys those who accept its dehumanizing methods and ideologies.

As time passes other people also place demands on Murphy, demands that will eventually reveal his capacity to share time selflessly. The prison counselor Janowski has had Murphy's running timed with a stopwatch, and he discovers that Murphy is doing a four-minute mile. Janowski uses this to approach Murphy, to see if the hard exterior of the man can be made more permeable and admit access to Rain's interior life. He asks him why he never contacts his family, why does he run, and just where is he when he runs. Murphy replies predictably: "I am *here* ... Doing *my own time*." Nevertheless, Janowski discovers that Murphy can share time if no immediate sacrifice is demanded of him. Asked if he will run with some athletes from the outside world when they come to the prison, Murphy replies that he will if they show up "on time"; that is, when he is ready to run. Janowski is pleased, the first step toward an exchange of some kind has been taken, the first step toward sharing interior and exterior spaces with Rain Murphy. This process in turn informs Murphy's evolving relationship with Stiles who will draw out from Murphy his unexpected and extraordinary capacity for sacrifice and symbolic exchange.

Stiles's descent into the simulacrum and its greed accelerates the process. Stiles strikes up a deal with Dr. D. in what Steensland would call a kind of Faustian gesture (23) that will undo him and his capacity to make time. Desperate to see his family, he makes a contract with Dr. D., the "Captain of Industry" who will "trick out" Stiles's "jacket" (his personal information file) to enable him to see his wife and child immediately. Dr. D. controls money and information: he can manipulate time and space through deception because in his world information is reality and reality is something less than an illusion. Mann's point is clear: Dr. D. *is* the system; he *is* the simulacrum. Even the naïve Stiles realizes that this favor from such a man must come with a price and asks: "What's it cost?" He thinks this contract can be sanctioned honorably and equitably because he can offer D. sugar for his inoperative still, but D.'s cryptic reply, "If we can't help each other do easy time, who's gonna do it?" implies this prince of deception has something more in mind. He is a purely selfish individual and will do nothing that directly benefits another. Information and industry always cycle directly back to him in the oppressive paradigm that he institutes for his own self-interest. Mann has thus created the perfect villain for symbolizing the evil of the simulacrum that only Murphy can effectively resist through symbolic exchange. Mann's point again is clear: D. is the opposite of people who can make sacrifices for he serves only one master—himself.

Mann shows how dialogue is a significant part of the strategy that can be developed through the symbolic exchange to combat the oppressive materialism of D. When Stiles tells Murphy what has happened between himself and Dr. D., the typically immovable Murphy is outraged and says, "You are a *slave*." Stiles dialogically counterattacks, and says, "I ain't waitin' no damn three months," and suggests that he has social needs unlike Murphy. Murphy enters the rhetorical space, the dimension of orality that will become part of his (and by implication, Mann's) strategy against the simulacrum. Initially Murphy resists being drawn into this dialogical space, defending himself with a Zen-like trope that prefigures Franks' prison-born philosophy in Mann's next film *Thief*: "I am into *nothing*. That is how I do my time." Stiles replies with even greater rhetorical fury implying that Rain is not what he seems, that he is dissembling; he compares Murphy to a "glue sniffer," someone who simply runs away from reality and social obligations like all of the rest.

2. Sympathy and the Devil

Murphy appears to be hurt by this—and regardless of whether it is because he believes Stiles or not, the dialogical space has brought him out of himself and has put him into a space where he is vulnerable but now interacts more intimately, sharing space and interior life through a purely verbal exchange. (The two men are speaking on two sides of the prison wall that separates them—they cannot see each other.) Mann's point is becoming clearer here: the power of voice and dialogue should not be underestimated. Rain Murphy's humanity is emerging here, even as he still attempts to run away, to disconnect from himself and others. Dialogue can be a transforming force in human lives if given a chance.

As time passes in the film, we begin to realize that Rain is in truth a deeply sympathetic individual who is capable of tremendous self-sacrifice. Ironically, it is this very sensitivity that has caused him to develop defensive strategies to protect himself, to conceal himself (even from himself) in his own private space. He is actually a much less narcissistic individual than Stiles who, just before the conjugal visitation session looks in a mirror and says to himself, "You all right. You outrageous." The less self-centered Murphy is indeed capable of deeply empathic connections with others. But at this point in the film he seems unaware that someone in this selfish, acquisitive economy could connect with others in such a manner, and this temporarily arrests his development as an individual. For example, when he is observed by his future trainer, who describes the sensation of "floating" that a runner experiences when he is in the groove, and who also tells Rain he has a pulled hamstring, Murphy replies, "How'd you know that?" Murphy here, as in Janowski's office, cannot believe that such imaginative sympathy and relative disinterestedness could exist in anyone, certainly not an authority figure. Thus when the trainer suggests they "get down to business," he turns away, assuming wrongly that this places the benevolent authority figures in the same category as Dr. D. For Murphy, any kind of authority figure is identified with the acquisitive power driven system of the simulacrum. But Mann's narrative proceeds to disprove this assumption—perhaps as much for the audience as for Murphy.

The ensuing disaster with Stiles eventually helps Mann illustrate how even an individual as isolated as Murphy can become part of a symbolic exchange that could help him resist the system while enabling him to establish and stabilize an identity through the exchange process. The deal with D., of course, goes down badly: D. has sent not Stiles's wife but a prostitute with two balloons of drugs for purchase by D.'s men. Stiles, like other Mann characters, is learning a sad lesson—deal with the devil (the system) and you will always lose because the game is rated to prevent you from obtaining what you want. Outraged to discover that he has been exploited, Stiles walks out and as a result the prostitute is arrested and D.'s operation is compromised. Murphy, however, does not desert Stiles at this moment, and his loyalty here again helps Mann begin to show the value of the exchange and how it can be instantiated through gesture and dialogue. When the Black Brotherhood confronts Stiles for fraternizing with whites, Murphy resists as the leader of the Brotherhood strikes Stiles. Later Murphy advises Stiles to "Get off the main line. Get out" because D.'s men are like an army. Stiles, in turn, shows his desperation, saying that he can't do "isolation time"—and Murphy, likewise desperate for his friend says, "Mr. Stiles—they invented the hard time you can't handle? Or is it just me you can't live without?" He dialogically shares the interior space of his hopes with Stiles, says he will do the Olympic trials that Janowski has urged him to do—anything to save Stiles from his descent into depression and isolation. Murphy is growing more intensely connected to Stiles, hoping through the dialogue and a promised gift exchange to help Stiles. But Stiles insists it's all "Dreams ... Nothin' happens." There is no pretense here; Murphy is naked and vulnerable as he pleads with Stiles, "Oh. Man. Come on. Come on," and offers to cover his back when he makes his break tomorrow. It is Murphy's first selfless pledge, his first use of language to make a genuine attempt at symbolic exchange in the film.

But it is doomed to fail. A padlock is placed on his door and he cannot help Stiles who appears oblivious to Murphy's cries not to go without him. Stiles is murdered by the white power fascists who serve Dr. D., and Murphy is devastated. Holding the blood covered body of Stiles, he shares physical space and human contact for the first time in the film, before releasing the body, and sinking to the floor, submerged in his impotent rage and his private grief.

Despite this newly imposed and more intense form of isolation, Murphy decides to pursue a new symbolic exchange in order to avenge the death of his friend, a pivotal moment in the film for it allows Mann to illustrate just how powerful a symbolic exchange can be as a mode of resistance, as a meaningful alternative to the system. Murphy makes a new deal with Janowski, one which represents what Mauss and Hubert (1966) have indicated is typical of such exchanges. Both parties will receive something, both will simultaneously be in debt and discharge their debt through their indebtedness in an exchange that involves nonmaterial, nonquantifiable value—immediate value that is expended without surplus value. Murphy agrees to run but says, "You gotta give me what I want." And what he wants is free time, not the "license to kill some-

2. Sympathy and the Devil

body" that Janowski wrongly anticipates. He wants a gift of time—thirty minutes in D's metal industries, "alone," with no one sharing the space. He then sums up the grounds of the contract that involves for him a type of selfless involvement with Stiles's life: "You owe me. I wanna do something for Stiles." And Janowski agrees because the deal makes sense. Stiles in death still cries out for justice. He has awakened in Murphy a sensibility that, as we learn later, has lain dormant since he murdered his father to protect his stepsister. Murphy is about to become part of a society of exchange.

His plan of attack is brilliant and helps Mann show how genuine sacrifice is so antithetical to the informatics of greed and coercion that it can effectively work as a counter measure to the culture and power structures associated with that informatics. Murphy does not descend to D.'s level but instead commits an act of exchange that is the precise opposite of its violently oppressive politics of selfish profit. Murphy enters the metal works as D.'s men exit, men wearing metal masks that represent them for what they are—inert, metallic robots bending and twisting metal in the service of their dehumanizing master—cold, hard cash. Alone, Murphy finds the money made off of the drug deal, then takes it out into the public space of the yard for all to see. Pulling it from the paper bag, he places it on the ground as everyone, including D. and his crew, watches while he sets it on fire. D. experiences the impotence of rage in this public space that Rain had felt in his private grief with Stiles lying dead in his arms. As D. screams, "I'll kill you, you're a dead man," Murphy walks away, unconcerned, despite the fact that he knows this man can destroy him. But that is the point. The money is worthless, as is the violence and command structure of D.'s army. Killing Murphy would be a meaningless gesture, even by D.'s standards. It will not return what is of value to D. But symbolically, it returns the value of Stiles's life to Murphy, for that value is precisely what has been instantiated by contrast with the sacrifice of the worthless money. As in the Hindu sacrifices Mauss and Hubert describe, priest and victim are one (88). Stiles's symbolic significance as a victim is embodied in Murphy whose commitment to the value of human life as something utterly opposed to the politics of greed is so powerful that he does not fear for himself. That is the only way to combat D.'s materialism and violence—via a genuinely nonviolent resistance that cannot be undone once consummated. The act is not cyclical but linear, purposeful, and final—as irreversible and as irresistible in this public humanized social space as chronological time itself. In short, Murphy resists successfully the system's tendency to deconstruct human subjects, their language, their time, and their space.

In the shared space and time of the symbolic exchange, the time, space, and language that Murphy and Stiles shared dialogically is made meaningful by his complete and selfless devotion to his friend, and his contempt for the empty, meaningless economics and politics of Dr. D. Mann *at this moment in time* in the film thus uses Murphy to show how D. and all he stands for can be defeated.

Predictably, D. later stages a counterattack—one that is doomed to fail for reasons that Mann explains in narrative time through the unfolding symbolic actions of his characters. D. convinces the members of the Brotherhood that it was Murphy who seduced Stiles into betraying himself. The leader of the Brotherhood, a power lifter who is much larger and stronger than Murphy, confronts him and attempts to beat him into submission—only to discover that it cannot be done. Rain keeps coming back for more because the Brotherhood leader has insulted Stiles. "You badmouthed my friend," says Murphy, "The man was my brother." The leader is astonished as Murphy pledges to "nail" him for lying about Stiles. The leader undergoes a complete reversal in the face of this selfless devotion and returns the gesture, saying, "C'mon man, I'll give you a hand." It is the second time Murphy shares space with another human being, and it is the moment when the entire society of the prison will be transformed in defiance of what D. represents. Mann is scoring a coup here; he will show us how not only the individual but a genuine social group, bonding through a sacrificial symbolic exchange, can work to defeat the coercive economics and informatics of Dr. D.'s simulacrum of a society. The scene's point is clear—exchange can move through a group of people and quickly begin to unite them in a social unit when they begin to perceive common needs, goals, and shared capacities for exchange. That is why D.'s counterattack cannot work—one act of exchange and defiance will lead quickly to others.

This is clearly illustrated by the ensuing action of the film. D. has used his white power thugs to commandeer the yard so that an official Olympic style track cannot be built in time to enable Murphy to compete in the trials and be given an official qualifying Olympic Athletes' Union (OAU) running time. Unexpectedly, however, the leader of the Brotherhood, extending Murphy's sacrificial symbolic exchange to an even wider public space, joins forces with Rubio and his Chicano handball team and forms an alliance against D. via the exchange process. A dialogue between these men takes place under the immense graffiti on the yard, one portraying a huge grim reaper figure seen earlier in the opening montage. There it was a terrifying figure, holding a viper and thorns in its hands, almost never seen in its totality but fragmented by the editing, as if to symbolize the fragmentation of the social groups of men in the yard. Here, by contrast, in long shot, we see it in its totality towering above the black and Chicano leaders, the rays of force and light radiating from it connecting the men in a triangular mise-en-scène that suggests a kind of dynamic social unity, thus foreshadowing the result of the dialogical interaction. These men are sharing time beneath this icon that points to the finiteness of human action while also evincing symbols that suggest means of defying the potentially oppressive nature of time through sacrifice and renewal. As a unit, the inmates will make sacrifices allowing Murphy to have his time so that everyone in the yard can share in that liberating energy. Mann will use this symbolic gesture to illustrate a point he shares in common with the early (1970s) philosophy of Baudrillard—namely that street language, working as a form of collective dialogical exchange with individuals, like the street art or graffiti that is likewise produced as a collective answer to the system, can at least temporarily challenge the coercive informatics of materialism, as localized in the organizational unit of D. and his fascist thugs. Indeed, at this moment, Mann incorporates street art into his own symbolic gesturing in the scene, involving us visually, sympathetically, and cognitively with the rebellion these inmates organize against the system.

Representing themselves as the "United Front Labor Brigade and Militia," the inmates confront D., saying, "This is not a political situation, this is a pocket situation. *Your* pocket." Thus they collectively reject the coercive informatics and materialism that D. and the white power faction represent. Rubio says, "If we can't work out on the yard, we gonna work out on your head." Outraged that a former business associate would say this, D. and his people hurl racist epithets at Rubio. The leader of the black Brotherhood takes offense and in yet another gesture of collective exchange says, "Now I'm Mexican too." Hence, the divisions of race and ethnicity that D. once counted on to prevent the men from becoming truly an integrated social force, instead of the mere simulacrum of one, have gone. A riot ensues, and D. and his men lose the yard. Mann's point is simply this: genuine social action is still feasible through symbolic exchange; it can indeed disempower the architects of greed.

In the next shot we see further evidence of the effectiveness of the symbolic exchange as we see men of all ethnicities working in the yard to finish the track before Murphy's time runs out. In the mean time, Murphy has become even more deeply involved in symbolic change, to the point where he now begins to trust those authority figures who also share time and in the same manner as the men in the yard. These men in Folsom are not faceless bureaucrats; they genuinely want to help Murphy. Warden Gulliver muses to the trainer and the counselor, "One Murphy that can play into street values instead of jailhouse values is worth so much" because he can stop "the games they play" and keep them from returning to the prison. All three men understand what Murphy represents to the inmates because they relate to him in the same way. Murphy can help these dehumanized men adopt a more human, more meaningful, and purposeful linear sense of time through the shared exchange. He is not a shallow icon, a disembodied image of success that can be created by the media and used to manipulate a mass audience. He is more like the tribal chieftains that Mauss and Bataille describe—a man like the Aztec chieftain who stands for the entire tribe, whose worth is created and reflected through the exchange. He is, in short, the real deal, as the inmates demonstrate when they selflessly give him their food in the cafeteria—much to his embarrassment. He has become a living symbol of exchange to the inmates and the authorities—showing that the exchange can unite human beings regardless of ethnicity or status, in defiance of the artificial boundaries created by the economics of the simulacrum.

He is also deeply human, not at all a paragon, as we learn in his verbal exchanges with his trainer, and especially with Janowski. This is important to Mann's thesis—the paragons and images of success are products of the world associated with D. and his followers, the realm of the disembodied informatics created by the coercive politics of greed and selfishness. By contrast, Murphy, like all of Mann's protagonists, is a deeply conflicted and imperfect individual, as he shows in his final and most revealing interview with Janowski. He is someone who has been torn apart by the conflicting demands of culture and family history—but as such he perfectly exemplifies the human dimensions that make feasible the symbolic exchange. When Murphy speaks to Janowski, we learn of how he committed patricide to save his stepsister from the father's alcohol induced violence—but we also see his utter devotion to his father. It was from his father, after all, that he first learned the value of symbolic exchange. He speaks of how his father would take him to the carnival, win him a goldfish, show him how to shoot in the arcades and carry him on his shoulders "all day." The father sacrificed time selflessly, and yet brought to the family's shared private space the same violence and hallucinogens associated with D.'s oppressive acquisitive culture. In short, the father simultaneously represented the simulacrum and the potential for resisting it via symbolic exchange. Hence Murphy says to Janowski, "I loved the man," but worries that "Maybe I'm telling myself a jack story." In an astonishing gesture where he both sympathetically (or sym-

2. Sympathy and the Devil

bolically) identifies with Rain and analyzes him, Janowski says, "Maybe both feelings are true." They are, but Murphy still struggles with his own double nature, his simultaneous identification with and rejection of this authority figure who created him. He says, "This [i.e., prison] is where I belong." Janowski, hoping that he can find some sign that Murphy can forgive himself, can stop being frozen in time, can move forward in service of himself as he does in service to others asks, "You still believe that?" Murphy's answer is painfully honest: "I don't know. Everything's mixed up." And how can it be otherwise, Mann seems to suggest, since Murphy's father introduced him to everything he would hate about the system and everything he would use to fight it? Amazingly, Murphy's confidence in himself is undaunted. He seems to sense the strange power implicit in this tension between self and other that makes him the perfect protagonist in this symbolic struggle against the system, the very things that allow him in the final acts of the film to fully realize his potential as a symbolic leader for himself and the others who live at Folsom. He thus assures the deeply concerned Janowski and possibly Murphy himself that, "I am going to make it."

And indeed he does, with help from the other people energized by the exchange Murphy has helped realize for himself and everyone else at Folsom. In the next shot, we see a hawk floating above tall grass, seemingly free with endless horizons until another presence intrudes, telephone wires that cut the skies with diagonals, representing the world of technology, artifice, and informatics seeming to intrude upon the world of nature. Beneath these skies Murphy trains with his trainer, a new mentor. As they interact, we see that indeed all is not lost for Murphy. Rain asks the trainer, "What are you getting' out of all this?" The coach explains to him that he had mastered all of the techniques of running, but "I couldn't *be* fast." As a result, he is drawn to Murphy because, "I been waitin' my whole career for someone like you to come along." Like the men in the yard, he identifies with this man who is a natural athlete. He gives Murphy what nature cannot give—lessons based on experience. Murphy provides what only nature can give—talent. Together the men represent an unbeatable combination and an inspiring counterpoint to the failed parental relationship Murphy painfully described. Mann has used the image of the hawk and telephone wires to initiate a new realization on our part: namely that Nature and artifice can work together in a symbolic exchange that benefits men who pay debts by owing them. What could be more natural for human beings, Mann seems to imply, as he ends the scene with a shot of the sun setting behind a tree and then dissolves to a shot of the completed track, the result of a cooperative dialogical exchange process that must now seem as natural to the men as flight is for the hawk. Here, as in later films, Mann seems to suggest that the exchange is indeed natural, that resisting the unnatural tendencies of the system is as necessary and as inevitable as the conflicts that have drawn Murphy out of himself and into the competition. Above all else, Mann appears to be arguing, we must stay in touch with this natural process if we are to resist the de-naturing effects of the current political and economic system, if we are to communicate and use art and technology in ways that mutually benefit everyone involved in the exchange.

When Murphy later wins the race, he completes this trope of symbolic exchange in the moment of triumph that everyone shares in at Folsom. In this humanized space, created by the tribal exchange between Murphy and the men, Rain Murphy and the inmates can resist the oppressive forces that have otherwise dominated and fragmented their lives. This is initially shown comically at the final track meet when an immaculately dressed OAU official, absent-mindedly walking backwards as he snaps photographs with a 35 millimeter camera, and completely unaware of his physical environment, smudges one of the running lines on the track. A member of the power lifting Brotherhood, outraged, picks the official bodily off of the ground, physically tosses him away from the line and bellows: "Say man, where you walkin'? That's the track!" This is not the kind of disembodied space that the OAU people, with their digital clocks and cameras, have come to master; this is a physical reality that the men have defined collectively with their verbal and physical social presences via shared time. This is time that moves forward chronologically but is not digitialized and disembodied, for this time exists only in the moment of mutual reciprocity, time that is used immediately in exchange for a shared goal. It belongs to all of them, as is clearly shown when the race begins and they chant, not Murphy's name, but "Folsom, Folsom, Folsom!" And when the race concludes with Murphy running his own best time, beating his opponent with a supreme physical effort at the last second, the crowd surrounds him and lifts him off his feet. This shared space extends even to the man Murphy has beaten. He nods to this athlete, a black man, to recognize the value of his sacrifice as the digital clock records the time and makes it all official: 3:52:09. In a very real sense, Mann is saying, everyone has won here because of the physical sacrifice made by all that enabled them to share this space in real time for a shared purpose. Murphy's victory makes all of them more human; they are all victors.

But, as is so often the case with the Mann protagonist, the victory is only temporary, because Mann insists that beating the system is harder

2. Sympathy and the Devil

than appearances would suggest. At the Warden's Office, Gulliver, Janowski and the trainer discover that even though Murphy ran "the fifth fastest mile this year," according to the official time, a question is being raised about his participation in the Olympics. The trainer muses that they probably just want to get more "pictures," and in a manner of speaking he is right. Image, perhaps the most dangerous and often most abusive form of disembodied informatics in Mann's world, is what this athletic competition is really all about. A meeting is staged with Murphy's three mentors and the OAU officials in Los Angeles. Murphy's people sit on one side of the polished table, the OAU representatives on the other, but the perfect symmetry of the image (a grotesque parody of when the Brotherhood united with the Chicanos beneath the graffiti in the yard) belies what is about to happen. Murphy awaits his sentence as a well-dressed secretary enters the room to deliver a document, and even Murphy feels the seductive force of the culture that has objectified her as he stares at the first woman he has seen in years. It is a portent of things to come; the outside world is about to win. This is not a dialogue but a monologue attesting to the power of image and money, the avatars of the simulacrum and its politicized disembodied informatics of coercion and greed.

This is made apparent immediately when the head OAU official says, "We get our funds from private individuals ... and it is important to keep our image clean." The private individuals he refers to are those that maintain the fractured isolating status quo represented by the opening montage, just as this official does as he monologically dominates the conversation and invades Murphy's private space with repeated questions about his "rehabilitation." The man's facial expression is frozen; he does not talk *to* Murphy, but *at* him, does not listen to the objections made by Murphy's mentors, but continues to drill him with the clear purpose of pushing him to the breaking point.

And he succeeds. Murphy attempts to answer honestly when asked whether he would commit the crime again, saying, as he did to Janowski, "I don't know." But this will not satisfy the prosecuting official who will force Murphy into the status of either a rebellious antisocial subject or a compliant object. These are the only options in the kind of oppressive space the OAU man presents, the options that Baudrillard implies, as we saw in chapter 1, result from the epistemology of the simulacrum, options that do not free anyone. The official cannot understand Murphy's assertion, "All I got is my name and my face," the assertion of the tribal ethos that allows individuals to be distinct yet socially integrated and thus avoid the two equally disempowering categories of subject and object. Eventually, the OAU man wins: Murphy, enraged, shouts, "You are running a game down on us," accusing the OAU man, rightly, of already having decided the question "Before breakfast." The official has robbed Murphy of his time and his status as a human being, evincing the same criminality as Dr. D., which is implied when Murphy says, as he is being taken from the room, "You wouldn't last ten minutes in the yard, not ten minutes." Deprived of the kind of social space and shared time that he and the other inmates created in the yard, Murphy cannot beat the OAU official as he did Dr. D. The machinery of the disembodied simulacrum outside the prison is too powerful and far-reaching to be beaten on its own court (here, the city of Los Angeles)—and it is Mann's awareness of this that has led him throughout the film to express his optimism about resistance with considerable caution. The vast simulacrum system can discriminate against the individual and succeed: *that* is the power of capital and image.

Things look pretty bleak after this scene as we cut to a shot of Murphy running in a now darkened yard under the watchful eyes of a guard, and then dissolve to a shot of the yard in daylight. Initially, the final sequence appears to be a complete recapitulation of the film's opening montage, as if to suggest that Murphy's defeat is complete, that all has been lost and no resistance against the system can last or succeed. The same prisoner is walking with his boom box there, and a montage of shots seems to suggest that the men have segregated themselves again as they did before. The Brotherhood, behind the turnstile again, refuses to let a white inmate into the weight lifting area. All seems to be lost, as if we have cycled back to where we began, as if the purposive linear time the inmates once shared has been reversed, rendered cyclical and pointless again. It was all for nothing; the socialized humanity they fought for is gone.

But Mann and Murphy have one last game to play. Things are not quite as they were before. The man with the boom box is not wearing headphones—everyone can hear the speakers—and a report is coming over about Davies' winning time in the Olympic finals. The same group of men who watched that icon of capitalist American dreams, *Let's Make a Deal*, listen intently to the news as Murphy laces up the running shoes that his mentors gave him.

And he carries another gift—the stopwatch they gave him with the Jericho inspired inscription on the back: "'Til the walls come tumbling down." Shirtless, he bends over the starting mark, cradling the watch in his hands, as if he were a discus thrower from the ancient Olympic games.

As he begins his run, Dr. D. (wearing an eye patch now after his rumble) derisively says, "He's got his own Olympics." But as we watch

2. Sympathy and the Devil

Rain Murphy's (Peter Strauss, left) victory near the end of *The Jericho Mile* is a moment of liberation for all of the inmates who share in it symbolically via the exchange made possible in the humanized space created by communal effort.

Murphy, running and checking the stopwatch, it becomes clear that Dr. D., that icon of voyeurism and oppression, is as blind as ever.

Murphy is pushing himself to the limits but he is doing more than beating his own best time. With everyone in the yard watching breathlessly, he pushes himself harder and harder. And as he finishes the mile, he stops the watch, and glides in to the finish. The crowd gathers, they regard the watch, and Murphy's victory is declared by someone in the crowd: "You beat Davies!" Murphy takes the watch, hurls it at a blank white wall, and watches as it explodes into fragments. Cut to a closeup of Murphy, surrounded by the admiring men in the yard—and the story is done.

This finale prefigures so many endings for Mann's films and his protagonists—where so many themes and gestures are involved that we are overwhelmed emotionally and cognitively, somehow grasping it but also aware of the vast complexity of all that is being said here. Murphy has made another gesture of symbolic exchange, but one more important and challenging than any we have seen before. He cannot change or destroy the globalizing system that has built walls around him, demonized him, robbed him of time, deconstructed him as an objectified subject undeserving of sympathy or understanding. But, by the same token, he has not been defeated by the informatics and economics used to deny him a place in that system. The very technology used to control the masses—in the final scene represented by the boom box—affords him the opportunity to share space and time with someone not physically present in the yard. Yet he can compete with that person physically and show that he is in truth the equal of that individual just as everyone in the yard is when they act not as spectators but as participants in the symbolic exchange. He has beaten time—the hard digital time that the machinery of the system uses to control humanity inside and outside the walls of the prison. And if that system has deconstructed the inner and the outer spaces of people, invaded their lives with the blast of the loudspeakers, the intrusive questions of examiners, collapsed the distinction between subject and object as a means of killing meaning, physical reality, and human society, Murphy has countered successfully with a dialogical trope that performs similar functions but to different ends. He shares internal space and external space with his fellow inmates, he shares his own (psychological) time and objective chronological time with them; and the inner and outer merge in the yard as do identities and shared agendas. These happen through acts of sacrifice and exchange that consume polarities deconstructively but in a manner that allows members of the tribe to simultaneously exchange information and goods as a group without destroying their integrity as members of society enriched by the intangible quality of the gifts they share. Space and time become malleable but not in obedience to a paradigm that achieves this by abstracting the real and denying physicality. The measuring device of the watch is no longer necessary—a socialized cognitive paradigm of shared space and time is all that the men will need. At least in this moment in time they have successfully destroyed the simulacrum of oppression, even if it still exists beyond the boundary of their new society.

Mann, in short, uses the double aspect of the film medium—sound and sight—to overcome the shortcomings of film and television as mass media. At times the viewer seems to "float" and respond not as an idle spectator but as a participant much like the men in Folsom. The film's chronological emplotment (quite deliberately and self-consciously recapitulated in the organization and development of this analysis) captures the audience and involves us with the momentum of the characters' lives.

2. Sympathy and the Devil

This, of course, is not what modern films about the oppressive nature of informatics are supposed to do. Whether we are watching Fellini's critique of the paparazzi culture in *La Dolce Vita*, or an early masterful deconstruction like *The Cabinet of Dr. Caligari*, typically we are asked to detach from the characters even as we succumb to the hallucinogenic effect of the disaffected mind-numbing images. Mann will have none of that. He uses suspense, he uses dialogue, he engages us in the lives of the characters whose situations may be fictional but whose existential situations are no less real and no less meaningful (potentially) than our own. He engages us with the kind of narrative power and intimacy that we might more typically associate with an oral storyteller. We identify as if we are part of the tribal gift exchange. We respond to the authenticity: real prisoners (Steensland 2002, 19) are interacting with actors in the actual location of Folsom. Question: did the track exist before the film was made? Is it still there? Was this the gift of exchange left for the people who gave time while doing time during the making of the film? Could you ask this type of question of any other film like this one? Your answers will testify to the unique use of symbolic exchange in the film. Only Mann's films work this way. We sacrifice time inside and outside of our minds as we watch the film; inner and outer spaces converge meaningfully as we share in the symbolic gift of the filmmaker, the actors, and the inmates who were involved in the film. On any level of appreciation, the rewards are great—the first of many Mann projects that would capture attention but seldom return the investment at the box office.

And yet—the film's time too is finite. Though its effects may extend beyond the screen and we may share Murphy's victory, that too is finite. Time has come today, but the global system still exists. The victory for all of us is localized, even if it is a shared socializing experience, because this alone cannot change that system. Hope is sustained here, of course, but it is a very cautious hope. And it is one sustained because Mann has only begun his analysis of the divided nature of his protagonists and the wide-ranging dangers of informatics. Deeper investigation into informatics and human psychology will amplify and expand Mann's understanding of the postmodern situation. As information technologies evolve, complexify, and become more pervasive (and invasive), Mann's perception of the human condition will present new obstacles for him and his protagonists. The task of socializing humanity will grow more difficult and more problematic with time.

3

It's a Criminal World: Artifice, Nature, and Humanity in *Thief* (1981)

Nothin' means nothin' to me.
[Frank explains himself
to Jessie in *Thief*.]

In *The Jericho Mile*, Mann had asked and answered two important questions: What causes the divisive nonsocial quality of modern life and to what degree can the system causing this condition be opposed? The answer was that the cause was an oppressive, acquisitive culture created by digitalized capitalism and informatics feeding on human selfishness, and thus the antidote was a self-sacrificing symbolic exchange that could be marginally resistant on the local level. In *Thief*, Mann expands his inquiry as he expands his focus, and while the questions asked are fundamentally the same, the answers become more elaborate in detail and more pessimistic in tone with the shift in focus. Here he has a protagonist, Frank (James Caan) who, unlike the federal inmate Rain Murphy, has physical and emotional needs that can only be answered by his personal industry, by integrating himself directly into the economics of the system. These needs are characterized as social and physical and hence, natural, human. Mann's query thus is modified slightly. Can the individual preserve any of the integrity of symbolic exchange if forced to integrate fully into the economics and informatics of acquisition? Can physical and social needs be met when the informatics of the system seem to consume the reality base of society? Survival and even the happiness of the individual would seem to depend on the individual's capacity to synthesize the artifices (culture, informatics, and technology) involved in production with the natural processes embodied in the dialogics of exchange between human beings and their environments. Mann, however, insists that this cannot happen. The postmodern urban world and its oppressive economic based codes are far more treacherous than what lies within Folsom.

The opening shots of Chicago in *Thief* present an image of city life that unexpectedly anticipates the world Ridley Scott would create on film later in *Blade Runner*: rain pours down relentlessly on a blackened streetscape that would be invisible if not for the electric lights and automobile headlights that imply the presences of concrete and steel. This is not quite the indirect light that Paul Virilio writes of (and that will be discussed in full in the chapter on *Manhunter*), but it is close; in one shot, girders of a fire escape are mere shadows outlined by the electrical luminescence shining coldly behind them. Electrical technology creates this black landscape that seems already to precede the consumption of substances and physicality. The physical immediacy of Folsom is behind us—Mann has placed us squarely in a technologized empty space where his protagonists will struggle with the elements of this environment that seek to deny the subject any degree of freedom, any sense of a stabilized identity.

And yet, as in the opening sequence of *The Jericho Mile*, there are elements present that seem to be in conflict with the negative elements of this vision of the simulacrum. The screen is completely black before we have the first establishing shots, but we know something must be present because we hear the rain before we see where it falls and what it falls upon. As in his first film, and perhaps even more pointedly, Mann is alerting us to aural presence, calling attention to its significance. Sound is a physical presence, and points to the physical and substantial nature of the world that the simulacrum has not completely consumed. The rain also suggests the conflicted quality of this world: it is a product of the natural world that interacts rather violently with this high-tech city, perhaps even dangerously, given the way the city harnesses energy in the form of electricity. This is the world of *Thief* and its protagonists, a world where the physical presence of nature collides with the disembodied world of urban technology and informatics and places irreconcilable and conflicting demands on human beings. Artifice and nature, image and sound already point to the film's thematic conflicts while also establishing a major motif in the film, water.

And other motifs and themes are established as we see men in this downpour who seem involved in a desperate and dangerous struggle. Their struggle points to the importance of information technology in this cityscape and to the importance of controlling it. Frank and his partner Barry (Jim Belushi) work to hack their way into a building's security system, an information grid composed of telephone lines that are linked to the alarm system, while another partner, Joseph, acts as sentry in the car outside. Joseph listens intently to the police scanner to ensure no one has detected this security breach that can be successfully completed only if the men master the information grids that define interior and exterior spaces, protecting the booty inside the building's interior vault. In short, a war is being waged here where information technology is pitted against information technology. Nevertheless, physical industry is important too: our first close-up on Frank occurs when he drills his way into the vault. But as the electronic score of *Tangerine Dream* booms on the soundtrack, it is nevertheless clear that, if they are to win, his success depends completely on Barry's proficiency with the phone lines and Joseph's capacity to cut into the police information network. This is Frank's gamble: that he can synthesize physicality with disembodied informatics, blend natural energies with artifice and technology to declare himself as an empowered subject in this context. And it is this conflict that Mann will examine in detail to make his ultimate point in this film: you cannot cooperate with the simulacrum without losing much, including your connection to nature and your sense of identity; and even though you can reject the system, you cannot fully resist it in this environment.

The conflict Mann sets up through Frank's struggle is symbolized by Frank's objective as a professional thief: cut gems, the only objects in the vault worthy of his industry. Every other object within is thrown on the vault's floor, so much useless junk. But the gems, shown eventually in close-up, stand in metaphoric relation to that industry. They are produced partly by nature, partly by human artifice, and as they reflect the light they recall the cold city lights outside. They have physical presence but evince a beauty that is intangible and unearthly in its perfection. Their value is in part monetary but is also based on something more than that—stones that require this exchange of shared time and energy between these thieves (a kind of symbolic exchange), who are craftsmen as skilled as those who cut and polished the gems, are clearly precious in many ways. The stones have economic exchange value while pointing to the significance of symbolic exchange value and teamwork in Frank's life. They seem to promise Frank what he needs to survive and to find dignity as a human subject—a synthesis between the worlds of commerce and symbolic exchange, between the world of artifice and the world of nature.

But simultaneously, a troubling visual motif also emerges in the opening shots of the film—the vanishing point, an image that will recur throughout the film and usually just as this crew seems to be achieving success with their craft and their industry. As the men drive toward the mission objective and as they drive away from it, we see them heading into avenues that are defined by electrical lights on either side of the street, lights that create converging diagonals that merge into a vanishing point somewhere beyond in the darkened space of the *mise-en-scène*. This type of composition is present even when Barry drives Frank through the underground parking lot where he has left another car. These shots are disturbing because they place the film's principle subjects in a *mise-en-scène* that is closed and implies a kind of determinism—there is no place for them to go except where the electric lights point them. The implication is that these men have not necessarily achieved a liberating synthesis here. Technology is dominating their movements, just as it does the viewer's perceptions, just as the electronic musical sound track wipes out the sound of nature's presence, represented by the rain. And the image also calls to mind Baudrillard's argument that meaning in the postmodern world disappears into a "vanishing point" as part of the implosion of significance and social structure in the hyperreal simulacrum (*Simulacra*, 1997, 31). Mann uses the image, as we will see in the analysis below, at significant moments in the unfolding narrative to imply that the powerful forces of technology and informatics are swallowing up these men, denying their capacity to operate as independent subjects.

To elucidate this thesis, Mann introduces a counterpoint, taking us in the next scene to the opposite kind of environment, where nature (again symbolized by water) will dominate and where a form of symbolic dialogical exchange will take place. A long shot reveals the cityscape against the dawn's sky and beneath it, the shoreline where lake waters mingle with the urban world. Frank is a tiny figure, marginal on the left of the screen, as he makes his way along the shoreline toward the camera until he is a dominant element and comes upon an old black man fishing. Frank kneels beside the man and the two create an interesting scene: Frank in his sharp urban dress, breakfast in a brown bag, talking to this man who, by contrast, seems to be making his way in the world via an exchange with nature. This recalls the liberating spaces of *The Jericho Mile*: status and race do not matter in this kind of exchange, as if to imply that the potential for symbolic exchange

3. It's a Criminal World

and the denial of the simulacrum's oppressive boundaries still exist. Frank, already occupying a subordinate position to the old man on the screen, spontaneously joins the exchange, offering the old man a Danish, expecting nothing in return but, apparently, the pleasure of his company and conversation.

As the Danish is accepted, Mann cuts with a one hundred eighty degree violation, and suddenly we are *with* the men, behind them, looking out over the water, illuminated not by city lights but by the natural light of the rising sun. And here the symbolic exchange is further consummated:

Old Man: Look at that, huh? That's Magic. That's the Sky Chief. Ain't that Sky Chief somethin'?
Frank: Yeah, you bet!

We hear only their voices and the water lapping against the shore. We cannot see the city; we cannot see the speakers, except as silhouettes against the water. It is a purely oral exchange that seems to ignore station and race, since both men now are on the same level in the frame and both are the same color. Even the old man's reference to God seems to reflect a primitivistic orality—his Sky Chief recalls the epithets used to describe God in Anglo-Saxon warrior society that produced poems about symbolic gift exchanges of rings and shirts of mail in oral traditions long before being recorded in written literary texts such as *Beowulf*. God, in such clan and tribal societies, was seen as a chieftain who rewarded men for their commitments to clan and king. Such exchanges, Mann seems to suggest, still exist in the world, as these two men share a kind of spiritual awareness of humanity and our debt to nature and society. But to show us this, Mann must visually isolate Frank from the urban environment—and by having Frank respond to the exchange with a phrase reflecting his gamble and his connectedness to the acquisitive— "You bet"—he shows us that even in a moment like this Frank, unlike Rain in *The Jericho Mile*, cannot completely (or even temporarily) divorce himself from the world of artifice that has been subsumed by an oppressive economics. Oral exchanges and people who have a genuine gift for sacrifice can be contaminated, especially if, like Frank, and unlike the old fisherman, their survival is completely dependent on the artifices of the ruling system represented by the city. Mann is thus distinguishing Frank's environment from the meaningful territory defined by symbolic exchange in *The Jericho Mile*.

Later in the film, when Frank meets with his mentor Okla (Willie Nelson), Mann reemphasizes his point that Frank's dependency and his terrific desire to somehow bend the system to his will to meet his human needs, makes problematic his approach to gift exchanges. Essentially, Frank desires to meet his own and others' needs, simultaneously make him inclined to make promises and commitments before he can be sure that he can meet his obligations or realize his plans. Mann illustrates how these promises disrupt exchanges, endanger their ends, and make it difficult for someone like Frank to establish stable individual and social identities. As Frank speaks to Okla, he indicates that he has "pulled the plug" on his marriage because he made the mistake of revealing his profession to his wife after the bond was consummated. But, as if to assure Okla, whom he later indicates to his girl friend Jessie (Tuesday Weld) is like a "father" to him, that he will become a father figure like his mentor, he indicates that he is "gonna marry" Jessie and "have some kids." The urgency with which he says this seems to indicate that pleasing Okla is the same as pleasing himself—something emphasized by the visual arrangement of the shot where Frank and Okla speak through a glass window suggestive of a mirror (indeed, in some shots, Frank's reflection on this glass is visible as Okla speaks). It is the first clear visual representation of the doppelganger motif in Mann's films; here it suggests Frank's need to identify himself through others via symbolic commitments. But it also points to his complexity, his potential for psychological divisiveness as he attempts to reconcile symbolic with economic exchange, a gesture complicating his attempts to stabilize his identity socially.

Hence, unlike Murphy in *The Jericho Mile*, he tends to have unquestioning faith in and a strong need for a father figure who will help him achieve status by using artifice and technology to answer natural needs by acquiring the kind of capital he hopes can synthesize the conflicting elements of his world. Thus, when Okla asks him how he is doing, he presents a prized possession, an expensive wristwatch, which both links him to and differentiates him from Rain Murphy in *The Jericho Mile* who would never hold up such an object as a symbol of financial success. Frank, as we will see, is in some ways an even more deeply divided character than Murphy—and Mann's examination of Frank in his environment will show why, especially when the double motif later indicates that Frank cannot stabilize his sense of identity because of his connectedness to irreconcilably different types of exchange. Rain Murphy exists in an environment that is small enough for him to reject the narcoleptic world represented by Dr. D. and Murphy's alcoholic father while embracing the symbolic exchange his father offered him but never fully applied towards his own liberation. Murphy can successfully resolve his conflict in a localized, less technologized space than Chicago. Frank cannot do this in this urban environment.

Hence, Frank's exchange here with Okla, even more so than that with the old fisherman, is troubling. He assures this father figure that he will marry Jessie when, at this point in the movie, he hasn't even had a first date with her. Worried over how he should reveal his profession to this woman, Frank asks what he should tell her and he accepts Okla's advice: "Lie to no one." And yet Frank has already dissembled in describing the relationship with Jessie and perhaps dissembles even to himself in terms of projecting his wishes on others. When Okla asks him to get him out of prison so that he won't die there of heart disease, Frank responds with a smile and little hesitation: "You got it." It is a noble gesture; like Rain he will give time to this man who is running out of time, losing control over his life because of time and the way the larger system has used it as a weapon against him. But he is committing himself before he has really considered how he can do this or whether he can do it at all. Frank has internalized many contradictions from the world he lives in and, because he is not aware of these contradictions, and the mutually exclusive nature that Mann perceives in their concomitant polarities, he is, without realizing it, overextending himself, setting himself up for a disaster. The potential exists here for Frank to betray a self that is too eager to answer the conflicting demands placed upon him by his culture and by others who increase the urgency of these demands for Frank due to his intense identification with the significant others that define him even as they potentially threaten to alienate Frank from himself as a man with face and integrity. Frank seems as self-assured as Murphy in the final act of Mann's first film, but Mann is clearly demonstrating through this film's narrative in time that Frank cannot resolve this conflict. He will, instead, be torn apart by it and enable the director to show why the world of the simulacrum, more often than not in Mann's universe, emerges as a dominant force in human lives.

Frank's confidence stems from his belief that he can use capital and informatics to secure the symbolic exchange; Mann's point throughout the film is that this cannot happen. Real justice and happiness cannot be bought because they are both based on principles of exchange that are destroyed by the acquisitiveness and inhumanity that instantly corrupt the deal whenever the components of capital and the informatic market are brought into the bargain. They drain the life of the exchange, all the more quickly in the urban environment that, by virtue of its constitution as an information matrix, consumes whatever it touches as it deconstructs the inner and outer spaces of these characters, and hence their integrity as ethical agents.* Rain Murphy's symbolic gestures at the end of his film do not require capital; in fact they result and succeed as a result of Murphy being denied capital to run. Frank is not so lucky; without capital he cannot protect or support the people he seeks to connect with through sacrifice and symbolic exchange.

Thus, ironically, his commitment to Okla renders Frank vulnerable to the corrupting power of Leo (Robert Prosky), the gangster he meets to secure the stones wrongfully taken from him when Leo's people killed Frank's courier and middleman. Leo plays the same role as Dr. D. in *Jericho Mile*: he *is* the system. The only difference is that he is a vastly more powerful version of D. for he has access to the economic and information systems that will enable him to exert far greater control over Frank than D. could ever exert over Murphy. This initial meeting shows Frank suspicious of Leo, perhaps fearful that he threatens his freedom as a manifestation of the evils of the commercial world standing poised to subsume nature, the body, meaning, real society. Frank's dialogue with Leo certainly allows Mann to establish Leo as an icon of these evils when, in response to Leo's invitation to "work indirectly for me," Frank replies, "I am self-employed.... I don't deal with egos. I am Joe the boss of my own *body*." But he nevertheless listens as Leo presents himself as if he could be a substitute for the critically ill Okla who has only ten months to live: "Whatever you need, you see me. I'll be your father from here on out." Leo emerges here as someone capable of dissembling to people in such a way as to gain their confidence—he again has greater facility with information than D. and is all the more dangerous, Mann seems to suggest. Leo presents himself as a man of honor and an equal; after three scores, Frank can "split" because "everybody is businesslike. Everybody is an adult." But the artificial (overtly expressionistic) bottom lighting used to illuminate Leo's face in the noirish gloom belies the seeming generosity of these gestures and underscores the deception, artifice, and simulation involved.

And even more disturbing in this scene, Frank also engages in deception. His colleague Barry hides behind a sign declaring, "Here's to Fun!"

Michael Mann is not alone in his representation of the modern city as a matrix of disembodied information. Posthuman thinkers such as Bruce Sterling, Friedrich Kittler, and Jean Baudrillard all offer descriptions of the modern city as a kind of information matrix that reflects the progressive development of complex information technologies from the time of the telegraph to the time of cybernetic technologies. (Sterling, (1996); Kittler (1996); Baudrillard (1997); wherein Baudrillard, predictably, sees the city as participating in the implosive violence of the simulacrum (70–72).

3. It's a Criminal World

as he covers everyone with a machine gun. Both groups of men use signs for cover, and this foreshadows Frank's involuntary convergence with Leo and his methodologies. Again Mann's point is clear: Leo and the system he represents assert power by co-opting the individual into their coercive schemes. Mann is showing how this simulacrum of a father figure can enable the system to create a vortex for Frank and for all of us. How does one resist that undertow when one depends, like Frank, on authority figures to define one's social status and one's identity? The answer, Mann implies, is that one cannot resist this process so long as one must deal with the system.

The process is accelerated after Frank secures a pledge of trust from Jessie, who agrees to become his fiancée. As before, Frank drives from the scene with Leo to meet her with streetlights creating a vanishing point, underscoring the themes of determinism and implosion as we see another example of Frank's compulsions with his pursuit of a new significant other. He establishes a bond with Jessie that perhaps represents the most honest attempt at symbolic exchange that he makes in the film. He senses the emptiness of her life, the loneliness of it as she is just "Moving through the moves," in a parody of life, a simulacrum not unlike his own. She is only "making time" and "hiding out," hiding from herself. Like Okla, he makes a plea for himself because he is losing time and wants to have a chance to live in a real exchange of time in a more real, more natural world. He describes the experience of being assaulted in prison—and she begins to connect with him as a human being whose life has been a prolonged rape, a fall into a terrible kind of object status. You cannot "do time," he says, in such a world as he knew (and she has known) by counting days and months. Instead you have to realize that "Nothin' means nothin'" when you have been temporarily deconstructed as a subject, have no future, no past, only an empty present as an inert being—and she nods sympathetically. He wants her to help him move forward in linear time by giving him a shared natural, human social purpose: "Inside [prison, frozen in time and isolation] you are on ice, you can't even die, but here [in the real world] you die and children come after." He needs her because he has "run out of time." She is hesitant, explaining that she can't have children, but when he says that they can adopt, suggesting that child rearing is an exchange process, something more than a biological mechanism, she reaches out to him and they clasp hands over the collage of pictures with Okla's portrait in it, the fragile collection of photographic images that he says represents his life. The deal is set with no talk of money or acquisitiveness—though Mann shows us a shadowy image of Frank doubling him in the café window, a por-

Frank (James Caan) shows his watch to Okla (Willie Nelson) and thus reveals his double commitment to the mutually antagonistic forces of *Thief*: symbolic exchange and acquisitive materialism.

tent of bad things to come as this man seeks a seemingly independent and legitimate social identity.

The foreshadowing is appropriate here because ironically this agreement ensures that he will make the pact to secure his future with Leo. When next we see him, Frank is meeting with Leo on a building top, checking the next score and voicing his concern of "exposure" time with such an unusual electronic security system linked to a vault that is not like the others he has cracked. The fifth security system does not run through a telephone line and hence cannot be traced. Moreover, the vault is produced by a British firm that makes each lock unique—it can't be drilled into or hammered open because it is too tough and because no one can be sure where the lock work will be located in the vault. Leo cannot understand Frank's concern because the "money covers" the risk of exposure. But Frank is rightly worried; this system is like Frank himself; it represents a blending of two types of artifice, two types of technology. The vault is not like the other technologies in the film: it is not a serially replicated instrumentality but is one of a kind. Likewise, an unusual, at this point undisclosed, type of information technology is used to secure the vault when the alarm goes off. The two worlds of Leo and Frank are already in collision, but Frank, not surprisingly, is confident he can win because this technology in some sense mirrors himself and the capabilities of his crew.

3. It's a Criminal World

Frank seeks out another mentor figure, Sam, who agrees to build the chemical delivery system that will enable the men to burn into the vault. This meeting is important thematically; the implicit comparison between the two men is instructive and significant. Unlike Frank, Sam has isolated himself as much as possible from the world of men like Leo, and he is a more cautious craftsman who does not commit himself to an exchange before he is certain he can deliver. Sam has created a world for himself in which he makes technologies that are unique, not mass-produced or serially replicated like others in this market economy. He is a craftsman, as indicated when he complains of the presence of a white frock-coated metallurgist sporting a hard hat and goggles. Sam doesn't need that disembodied mathematical assessment of the metal; he assays it by touch and praises the British vault as if it were a work of art that is "well made and expensive," like the gems Frank steals. In short, he is much like Frank—but he is also different.

This exchange is an important counterpoint to the type Frank has often involved himself in. Sam, a modern day Vulcan, is too much the professional and the craftsman to make a promise unless he knows he can deliver the goods. He is a more experienced and much more isolated figure than Frank (although the metallurgist's presence suggests that this is ending), and he will not place himself in a double bind for Frank. He eventually does deliver the apparatus to the younger artist—but his caution about entering the symbolic exchange points to a kind of prudence that is missing in Frank's attempts to achieve his goals. His comparatively casual appearance also suggests that he is less materialistic than Frank; perhaps a bit less self-centered. Sam's world is nevertheless in a process of change and Mann suggests here that his kind of professionalism is becoming a thing of the past. Frank's world of the present, and by implication, our own, is different. And given Frank's character, his commitments both symbolically and commercially to others, he cannot pursue a path like Sam's. Hence, Frank clearly represents the contemporary postmodern norm, one that does not allow him to choose an alternative that would lead him away from Leo.

Despite this, as Frank proceeds with the project with the help of his partner Barry he seems to achieve a victory against the system when he discovers the means by which the fifth alarm system works—it combines oral with electronic information. It is a one-channel radio transmitter with a sonic detection device which, when triggered, trips the alarm that can only be disengaged if the verbal code is spoken before 10 seconds elapse. Frank orders Barry to "bug" the system so that they can record the word. And this synthetic approach appears to work: Barry hears the code word—*Mexico*—spoken and records it as he times the operators with a digital watch. This may seem to imply a victory over the system, a combination of oral presence and disembodied electronics that allows Frank to achieve the synthesis he hopes to achieve and beat the system at its own game. But Mann's style here implies otherwise. He presents Barry's hijacking of the information in a crisply edited series of tight close-ups that seem to splice Barry together with the technology he uses in a visually simulated interface. And, as before, the sequence ends with the vanishing point shot—an overhead bird's eye view of Barry descending endless series of rectangular staircases, reminiscent of the famous tower sequence in Hitchcock's *Vertigo*. Mann's characters here, like Hitchcock's, seem caught in a spiral toward a destructive end, or worse still, the kind of annihilation and disappearance of the human subject and the real that Baudrillard speaks of in his conception of the hyperreal as a black hole devouring everything (*Simulacra*, 72).

This spiral effect becomes evident in the structure of the narrative as well, as all of the protagonists are drawn into the vortex of Leo's ethos. The discussion about the code word takes place in Frank's and Jessie's dream home in the suburbs—a world alien to Frank's urban friend Barry who stands on the lawn like a new Adam naming things as if he has just seen them for the first time: "A tree! ... A bush!" Of course the dream would be here, as it is for most Americans—someplace not urban, yet not country, a world that synthesizes the extreme polarities of these people's lives, as represented by a collusion of technology (comfort) and nature (a place to raise children in security). It is the middle-class equivalent of the realm occupied by University of Kentucky professor John Cawelti's Western protagonist, somewhere between the too civilized and the too savage—the illusion of a purely human realm, the binary dream alternative to the too real harshness of the urban and the rural, the middle-class simulacrum.

But this site merely underscores the convergence between Frank and Leo in the simulacrum that will not allow Frank to disengage himself from this man whom he does not yet realize is the enemy. We see in a later scene that Leo and his family occupy a nearly identical home in the suburbs. This is doubly ironic because Frank, a true denizen of the city, in another scene, expresses contempt for the suburbs when he creates an ugly scene with a woman in an adoption agency who rejects Frank's and Jessie's request for a child because he was a convict. Frank's complaint is that he and his wife have not been judged fairly as human beings. Unable to deal with the woman's replies, incapable of explaining to her where he, a former "Ward of the state," is coming from, he finally asks

3. It's a Criminal World

her, "You grow up in the suburbs?" and she replies, "Yes," in a voice reflecting her own frustration. He seems to imply that this world of hers is somehow not part of reality, at least not his human reality, and yet, along with his precious gems, this space is for him the very icon of everything he apparently wants in life. Mann implies that the icon points to endless contradictions reflected in the conflicted cultural forces that Frank tries impossibly to answer via synthesis. The contradictions call to mind Baudrillard's depictions of the system's code that always oppose the subject to the object, the dream to the reality, in a socioeconomic dynamic where signs refer only to themselves and, as he says in *Symbolic Exchange and Death*, each term in the binary semiotic excludes the other and makes its opposite appear to be a product of the imagination (133). However one characterizes the system, it puts Frank in a tight place with little hope for securing freedom or control. Mann once again shows how Frank's identification with the system splinters his being and renders him—and presumably all of us who are part of this system—incapable of realizing basic human needs.

Mann reiterates this point as he proceeds to examine similar conflicts and convergences emerging as Frank is drawn into Leo's vortex. In the course of this examination Mann demonstrates that the suburbs are a place where the private and public do not remain separate; there is no security because security of self and family are hallucinogenic here just as they are in the city, a place where these polarities deconstruct or implode (as do the categories of savage and the civilized). Frank discovers that just as he has placed bugs to keep tabs on the score, the police who have conducted surveillance since his meeting with Leo have placed bugs in his car and in his home. The water motif emerges again—Frank runs tap water to conceal his and Jessie's conversation about the technological "bugs" that have invaded their home. Water provided cover for his first nighttime score, but as he continues to strive for a synthesis of nature and technology to combat this intrusive informatics, the implication is that Frank inevitably loses ground as he fights the system. Nature will not win the battle here, Mann implies. Indeed, nature too—human and otherwise—is losing ground to the consumptive black hole of this invasive informatics devouring the middle-class dreamscape of success that Frank so desperately wishes to realize.

Mann proceeds to show how, ironically, Frank's natural desires for love and family actually make him more susceptible to the power of the system that has co-opted familial structures in the simulacrum. Frank turns to Leo again, who, not surprisingly, uses this problem with surveillance and the situation with the adoption agency to try to secure even greater control over Frank. They meet in a darkened bar where Leo promises to take care of not only the heat but the adoption problem as well. Leo's simulation and perversion of paternalism is evident in his parody of the spiritual language shared by Frank and the old man in their exchange about the Sky Chief. Leo wants to express awe for the procreative process, but his language betrays his tendency to see creation as mechanical replication: "A little hootchie coo, drop of energy, wham bam ... that's something sacred." He presents this deal to Frank as if it were a car purchase: "you state your model ... black, brown ..." and Frank says he wants a boy. Earlier at the adoption agency he had offered a bribe for a son; now he engages in a commercial action to secure a son as if he were working at his own used car dealership. He is repeating the same mistake made by Stiles in *The Jericho Mile*, trying to secure the gifts of symbolic exchange (love, family, companionship, shared time) through capital—and Mann insists that this synthesis cannot work. Leo's focus on self and capital is what the exchange is about—and Frank is too naïve, too desperate for love to see this, despite his exposure to the same world as Rain Murphy. But unlike the lifer Murphy, Frank lives in a city of lights that seem to promise hope for a better tomorrow when in truth that environment is every bit as corrupt as the prison, indeed more so. The inside and outside worlds are the same in this simulated world, as Frank will eventually understand. Mann relentlessly drives the point home here and in other scenes: there can be no integrity in such a divided world where the catalytic element of the exchange is something not human, something based on a soulless and meaningless exchange with the economics and informatics of the simulacrum.

Mann makes this tragically clear with the death of Okla. Okla's condition worsens, as his lawyer says, just after being freed, on the steps of the courthouse, on the threshold of what he had hoped would be a new world. In the hospital, he can barely whisper his last words to Frank, his words of thanks for the symbolic exchange that is being terminated as he dies. Even the very moment of his death denies verbal exchange and physical presence. Frank is rushed out of the room as the alarm sounds on the heart monitor and Frank can see only a simulacrum of David Okla's death on the cold blue video screen. When the doctor tells Frank he didn't make it, Frank is silent. There is nothing to say, no place for the orality of human exchange in this technologically dominated environment. Okla was on ice, an inert being, whether inside or outside the joint. Mann is saying quite simply: in the world of the simulacrum, no matter where you are, it is all the same. The system denies life and humanity everywhere. Nothing in Frank's arsenal—neither his money

3. It's a Criminal World

nor his technology—could change that. You cannot fight the system with its own weapons. You cannot buy justice.

Frank cannot see this, however, in his naiveté and in his blinding devotion to the new family that he is trying to create. Mann is illustrating here how difficult it is to disengage oneself from a simulacrum that seems to promise the very kind of meaningful life that it in truth denies. Hence Mann shows Frank continuing with the mission and naming his son after Okla. Frank sustains hope even after being beaten by the corrupt police officers who conduct their surveillance on him with information technology to profit from his earnings. (Ironically, during the interrogations, one of the officers even hits him with a telephone book. Earlier he is arrested by an officer who kicks out his car's taillight and informs him he can't drive legally without this signaling device. The police, the ultimate authority figures in the world Mann represents here, are part of the corrupt and corrupting technological information game too.) He responds defiantly and uses his own knowledge of information technology to defeat their bugs and make it to the score undetected. This, of course, is nothing more than a reiteration of the pattern Mann institutes throughout the emplotment of the text. Frank succeeds only to find himself in worse shape than he was before. The victories are only apparent. They involve us sympathetically in the narrative, they make us cheer for Frank, but only because Mann wants us to experience the full bitterness of Frank's disappointment when he finally and inevitably fails. The structure of the text sets us up for a shock, just as the simulated world of urban Chicago sets up Frank for Leo's final trap.

Hence, the heist succeeds and later there comes a celebration on a beach—but in both cases Mann's visual style hints that something is amiss. The break-in to the building is filmed from the bottom of a shaft that creates the same vanishing point effect as before—here, pieces of the roof the crew tears out falling down the shaft onto the camera until the operation vanishes in the blackness. Again, the deterministic lure to the score is associated with the disappearance of the subjects involved, implying that any association with what Baudrillard would call the hypermarket of capitalism destroys freedom. The beach scene returns us to the water motif, and here even Barry in his swim trunks seems at home in this all-natural environment as he frolics with his wife in the surf. Frank seems a little out of place here, however, his long pants stained with sea water, his eyes covered with sunglasses. And later that evening, when he and his wife make love in bed, things somehow look out of place. Despite their passion, Frank and Jessie still wear their clothes, and as the camera steals away from their love making, it shows us the ceiling which is white and streaked with the shadows of the foliage outdoors beyond the electric lights. The presence of the natural is immaterial in their lives, suggesting not a synthesis but perhaps a deconstruction or, more pointedly, an implosion of life into some kind of simulacrum, a shadow land, the dark insubstantial and disembodied world of their actual patron, Leo. Frank's victory is no more real than the world he lives in.

And via the film's horrific conclusion Mann confirms this. In the comfort of Leo's suburban home, the deal goes sour as Frank recognizes this simulation of a father for what he is. Leo has short-changed him money for the heist and has invested it in his shopping centers. Frank's language shows how he immediately begins to disengage himself from Leo's acquisitive culture as he tells him to "Count me out." He rejects the unreality of the man and his violation of the deal: "You are *dreaming*. This is pay day." Leo interprets it as ego and equates this moment with his rejection of the policemen's offer to take a cut from his scores. Frank tries to explain that the exchange should allow all parties to maintain their dignity and integrity: "They [the police] don't own me and you don't own me." Leo tries to bring him back into the deal by saying that he gave him his family: "Where is the gratitude?" But Frank counters by saying that the original deal was only for one score and "now the deal is over." Ironically, Leo invokes the visual metaphor for his world and actually speaks the truth: "You can't see day for night."

Indeed, the acquisitive has overruled the symbolic exchange, the vortex of darkness has consumed light. Frank tries to bring the deal back to the original terms and invokes time as the instrument of exchange: "My money in twenty-four hours or you will wear your ass for a hat." But Mann's visual style has already made implicit the reality of the situation: there is no way to fix this, there is no way to bring the conflicting elements of Frank's life together in a symbolic exchange, and the inevitable result will be the releasing of the implosive violence that has always lurked beneath the exchanges we have seen throughout the film.

This is illustrated in the film's final act. The more experienced and deceitful Leo is ahead of Frank's game and, using time to his own advantage, has sent two henchmen to capture Barry at the dealership and use him as a lure to capture Frank. Frank meanwhile drives in the darkness, the hood of his car visible only as a reflector of the city's neon lights, attesting to the dark immaterial place in which he now finds himself. And as he enters his car dealership, he is depicted once again under the lights strung up above his cars creating a vanishing point, the site of the implosive violence about to come. Frank has lost his freedom under the influence of Leo in this place of business where he first established the

3. It's a Criminal World

sign of his "legitimate" economic success. The low-key illumination in the scene also underscores the victory of the simulacrum over the human protagonists. Barry, abducted and held at gunpoint in the darkness, cannot reveal himself to this man who has been like a brother to him. Instead, he is forced to violate the bond between them by calling out Frank's name in the darkness. Attempting to break free in the darkness, he is slaughtered with two shotgun blasts and Frank is taken prisoner to be presented to Leo.

Mann can make his indictment of Leo and his world clear as he provides Frank and the audience with the opportunity to recognize his enemy for what he is. Leo, by this point, has become Frank's dark double, a simulacrum that parodies the noble father figure David Okla whom Frank strove to identify with through symbolic exchange. David was the leader whose word was his bond, a once living embodiment and testament of the power of the spoken word like his Old Testament namesake. Leo, by contrast, is a self-serving predator who consumes light, matter, energy, and the kind of meaning that can only be established in exchanges such as those with the old fisherman who conveys in words the living presence of the munificent Sky Chief above the waters. Leo is a consumptive disease linked with acquisitive consumerism and coercive informatics as he threatens the dazed and immobilized Frank with these words: "Your kid's mine because I bought it. ... I'll whack your whole family. People will be eating them for lunch in their Wimpy burgers and not even know it." This inhuman monological diatribe is filmed with Leo's head eventually depicted upside down in the frame, emphasizing its denaturing of human verbal discourse as Leo concludes, "*There is no discussion.*" Frank must work for him until he is broken—and to emphasize this point, Mann shows Leo's henchmen dumping Barry's frozen body into the water that, like everything else in this grotesque scene in the meat packing plant, is divested of any potential for natural life-giving or life-sustaining properties.

Cut to a shot of Frank running water into his bathroom sink where he stands before the mirror washing away the blood, but is clearly unable to wash away the stain of what Leo represents or his threat to the life of his family that neither the water nor anything else in his world can now sustain. He regards himself in the glass as if for the first time, coming closer to his image until he connects suddenly with the mirror. He opens his eye, regards himself, and then something very unexpected happens. Mann freezes the frame for about three beats before cutting to total darkness.

Mann's unexpectedly reflexive stylistic intrusion on an otherwise naturalistic (albeit highly expressive and formalistic) presentation is startling but appropriate. Up to this point the film has appeared to be a transparent representation of Frank's world but now the freeze frame points to the movement in his life toward the simulacra and his awareness of this. Mirrors, after all, at once bring us to ourselves and alienate us from ourselves. They present an image that reverses the real and parodies it even as it appears to represent it without distortion—hence it is real, not real, perhaps more real than real, like the simulacrum. And this is what Frank has become, through his interaction with his dark parodic father—untrue to the self that he thought he could define through the honest exchange with Okla whom Frank could not save from the devouring darkness of the simulacrum. Frank has betrayed that self, has lost it, and must find a way to deal with the annihilation of self and family without ignoring the injustice done to his friend, his wife, and child. Debts must be repaid honorably—but ironically, this can only be done by destroying every vestige of his inauthentic socially constructed self. Mann makes Frank (and the audience) face up to the difficulty of recognizing the artificial and constructed nature of identity in modern culture while recognizing that even at a moment like this there are still obligations and duties to perform that cannot be met honestly and honorably as long as any vestige of the false identity gets in the way.

The final two scenes illustrate that process in all of its troubling ethical and epistemological ambiguity. Awakening his wife from slumber, Frank explains to her that the original deal has been changed. His actions here point to the painful nature of the double bind he still finds himself in. He gives her $410,000 to pay Joseph, one of his partners, to take care of her and the child, insisting that she is "going away" immediately. The money is inadequate to the debt he really owes her, but is the only way he can ensure her survival and the child's. He will allow her no personal possessions and no dialogue. When she protests, "I'm your woman. You're my man," he uses the same monological method as Leo. "To hell with me. To hell with you, with everything," he insists, despite her insistence, "I made a commitment." There is no discussion. It is the only way to save her. And the price is the ultimate sacrifice—their lives together to save the life of the child. Frank must make the ultimate symbolic sacrifice; he must destroy himself in order to save them. And the significance of this gesture is as difficult to discern as the other gestures Frank makes as the film climaxes in the next scenes. Indeed, as the film progresses, the ambiguity and the complexity of each gesture seem to increase dramatically, for Mann intends to show us how difficult it is to combat or to make sense of the simulacrum and of the human lives trapped therein once symbolic exchange has been compromised.

3. It's a Criminal World

Frank destroys everything in his public and private world with demolitions—his home, his business, even the pub where he associated with friends. It is all gone, even the collage of images with Okla's pictures left on the burning tarmac of the used car dealership.

All that is left after this is a terrible vengeance against Leo and his two henchmen in the privacy of Leo's suburban home, which Mann uses to dramatize the disorienting, meaningless world that is left where, at least for the moment, the possibility of symbolic exchange has been destroyed. This place where the final battle occurs creates an environment that intensifies the ambiguity and complexity of the finale. The interior of the house is disorienting, a simulacrum of the owner's distorted decontextualized life. At one point Frank surprises a woman inside the home on the phone—she looks at the camera, then turns her head away as she listens on a telephone. Did she see Frank? Is she Leo's wife? Did she just not care about the home invasion? Or is space so distorted in this world of Leo's that there is no human contact—except for violence?

The violence comes as Frank knocks one thug unconscious in the kitchen and then shoots Leo who attacks after lying in wait in the living room. It is a bizarre scene. Frank fires, standing beside a houseplant (the only natural object in the house). The first hollow point from Frank's .45 knocks Leo down without complete penetration or expansion. Leo seems dead. But then he stirs, gathers himself with pistol in hand, as if in some grotesque hyperreal parody of resurrection, as if you cannot kill a man like this. But the second hollow point does the job, and a shower of his blood splashing against the wall testifies to the fact that he can be destroyed—though Leo's exaggerated death expression seems oddly more animate than his face did in life. It is the paradox we have come to expect from this monster: in death and in life he is a simulation of a human being. And it is the portent of more paradoxes and the deepening ambiguity to come in this extremely unsettling finale in a simulacrum unmitigated by any kind of humanity.

Cut to a shot of the first henchman rushing out the screen door. Is he chasing Frank or fleeing the scene? We cannot tell in this denatured space until we see Frank rush out of the door and realize that this man, Attaglia, is running for his life. Frank guns him down on the darkened green lawn under the street lights and then is hit by two shotgun blasts from the second henchman he thought he had dispatched just a moment earlier. Frank is down but returns fire from the prone position, killing the second henchman.

And then Frank seems to stage his own resurrection. Lifting him-

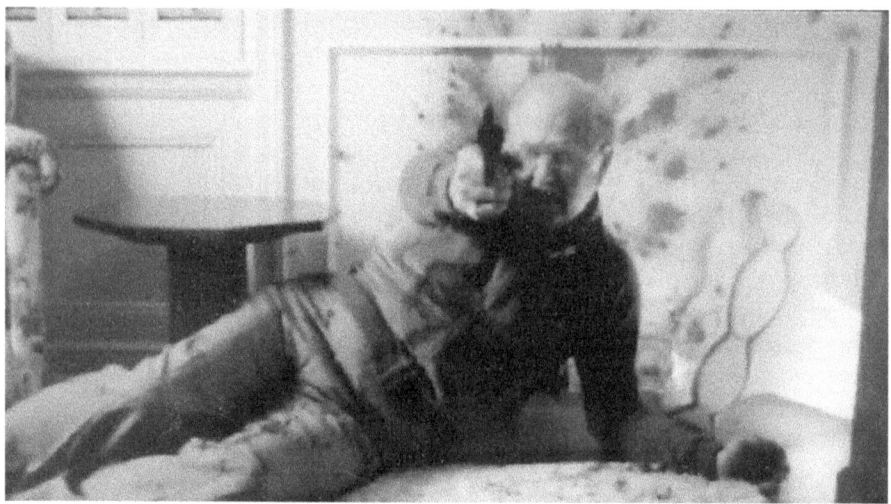

In death as well as in life, Leo (Robert Prosky) seems a hyperreal parody of a human being—even as Frank's bullets strike him in the climax of *Thief*, he is somehow not real, not human.

self off of the ground, he reaches inside his clothes and undoes a bulletproof vest. Professional to the end, he has used technology to fight and win the tactical situation once again.

But this finale continues and recapitulates the contradictory nature of the gun battle that in turn recapitulates many of the contradictions of Frank's life and the gestures he is making toward the end of the film. Frank seems to be the only stable point of reference in the fight—we know what is happening and where we are only when he steps into view. And yet he still seems caught between two worlds as he associates himself with natural objects and still uses technology to wage war. His parodies of Leo's monologism and resurrection are equally disturbing, even if they represent the only means for Frank to repay the debts to Barry and his family. What is Mann saying here?

One might be tempted to say Frank has achieved synthesis and subjecthood in the final confrontation. The style Mann implements in the final shots of the film implies something more complex, however. Frank leaves the scene and finds himself walking down a sidewalk that intersects with a driveway or another sidewalk—in the street lights it is difficult to say—but a crossroadlike pattern emerges. The frame is defined by a natural object—foliage of tree branches that surround the final image. Frank moves toward the top of the frame, the portion of the frame that

3. It's a Criminal World

implies empowerment. Yet, as he moves, he seems to follow a vanishing point arrangement in the *mise-en-scène* as he so often does. He could, of course, turn to either side on the crossroads, but instead follows the lines that will eventually cause him to disappear from view. Just as he reaches the top of the frame, Mann cuts to total darkness.

The stylistics of this final shot, in other words, thus underscores all of the contradictory forces that compose and discompose this man's life, and by extension, all lives in urban postmodern civilization. He could turn away from this path, he is still a creature endowed with the power to choose, but in this pattern, it is as if he finds himself in a world where alternatives are not apparent to him. He still follows the deterministic path of the world created in the simulacrum. This is ironic because the elements in the natural world (tree branches in the foreground) are proxemically more dominant—yet his path is away from them toward some kind of oblivion, something we associate with Leo, whom Frank parodies in his own resurrection. By contrast, as he moves along this cross pattern that Steensland (2002, 24) compares to a crucifix, this also points to Frank's martyrlike and therefore selfless sacrifice. He thus embodies an alternative to Leo but is vanishing before our eyes, as if disappearing into the simulacrum of this suburban world. And we hear no voices in this scene. When the frame goes to black, we hear nothing, even though we see the same black frame with the title *Thief* in neon blue as we did before—but this time minus the natural sound of falling rain, the aural effect that established nature as a physical presence in the film's beginning, the apparent antithesis of the city and its simulacrum. We have come full circle, and it is the circularity that, as in *The Jericho Mile*, is associated with the opposite of human progress and meaning. Like Frank, we have been subject to an optical trick that has teased us with a simulacrum of subjecthood only to reveal its conflicted, implosive, and insubstantial nature. The exchange at the end is not complete and full of renewal as it is for Murphy at the end of *The Jericho Mile*. The urban environment, as realized by the final image, proves to be a dangerously seductive and destructive environment that can be resisted only at the cost of one's identity.

But there is sufficient tension in the image to suggest that this is still only one path that human beings have created via their urban civilization. Other alternatives may exist—though their final ends are not visible in this artificial light, from this perspective. Mann thus is leaving himself other options to explore. He clearly wishes to emphasize the danger here. The postmodern condition, as it is depicted in this film, is, to borrow an analogy from Baudrillard, cancerous. Increase the flow of blood into the tumor and it grows; decrease it and it may die. The diseased landscape of the city is like that. Unlike the world of Folsom prison, it maximizes the flow of information and penetrates all realms through the capitalistic hypermarket and the hyperreal simulacrum that makes it impossible for one to survive without capitulating to its seductions. It cannot be battled effectively even on the local level in the city. No exchanges are possible without capital, and thus all symbolic exchange is doomed, plus any hope for a more naturalistic communal identity like that achieved by Rain Murphy in *The Jericho Mile*. Nevertheless, the influence of nature is not completely effaced in *Thief*'s final image, and this implies that there are still possibilities. Mann's complex epistemology will not allow him to dismiss the potential of the complex dynamics of human beings as social entities as possibly having the power to redeem and save our humanity and our capacity to have a meaningful, beneficial exchange with the natural world. The ambiguity and complexity of the final scenes of *Thief* underscore the fact that we live in a world that is sufficiently complex to preclude the exclusion of such possibilities. Those possibilities will be explored with even greater cognitive depth after Mann's next film, a descent into the even darker world of Gothic doppelgangers and Fascist informatics, *The Keep*.

4

History, the Unconscious, and Hyperreality: Gothic Doubles in *The Keep* (1983)

> *Where am I from? I am from you!*
> [*The Golem Molasar Explains himself to Major Kaempffer*]

In *The Keep* Mann explores the same themes as in his last two films, but broadens his focus still further to show that the oppressive informatics associated with the simulacrum's hyperreality are a global phenomenon linked to such evils as totalitarianism and imperialism. Moreover, he takes us back in time to show an earlier manifestation of these informatics in World War II, when the Nazis are using a temporarily less sophisticated but nevertheless equally effective means of oppressing mankind by denying them symbolic exchange and dialogism. Mann focuses on their use of iconography in order to explore the means by which the human imagination—specifically the subconscious mind—can make human beings susceptible to exploitation in mass culture. Indeed, he seems to argue that the subconscious mind, and in particular, the collective unconscious' repository of archetypes, has always represented a potential source of evil. But it is the Nazis who unleash this evil into the world as part of a globalization of the inherently not-real nature of the imagination that in turn becomes a cultural force through the oppressive use of information that enables modern humans to become susceptible, en masse, to the implosive energies of the imagination. This facilitates the assertion of the hyperreal cultural norm through the fascists' denial of symbolic exchange. The very symbol of this danger is the Keep itself, a place designed by an ancient culture to protect mankind from the demonic vortex that stands ready to devour us.

For those who know Baudrillard well, it may come as a surprise to see Mann focusing so intently on the subconscious because the French thinker, who parallels Mann in so many ways, has seemed to suggest that the subconscious does not exist. Baudrillard had indicated that the concept of the unconscious is a substitute for a territoriality lost with the implosion of the interior and exterior spaces under the influence of the hyperreal. "Animals," said Baudrillard, "have no unconscious because they have a territory." By contrast, human beings have lost any real territory and substitute the subconscious world to make up for this loss. Hence, "the unconscious is the individual structure of mourning in which the loss is incessantly, hopelessly replayed" (*Simulacra*, 139). Territoriality would represent an authentic culture of symbolic exchange where the human and the natural are bonded in cyclical sharing of goods: "The territory is the site of a completed cycle of parentage and exchanges— without a subject, but without exception: animal and vegetal cycle, cycle of goods and wealth...,—there is no subject and everything is exchanged" (139).

This no longer exists for modern man; hence as a kind of illusory surrogate, the unconscious comes into being: the unconscious becomes a place of "indefinite repetition of subjective repression and fantasies" (139). It is a place perhaps like much in the hyperreal world where serial replication has taken the place of the kind of instantiation of creative energies that can exist only in a society that believes in and thus creates an intersubjective shared realm that makes possible real metamorphosis that connects men symbolically to nature. Modern man is estranged from all that, living instead in a hyperreal subjectivity that is simulated through the site of the subconscious and in the serial cultural artifacts and artistic products induced by the hyperreality. In a hyperreal site, featuring serial replication, objects of art and individuals are transformed. Baudrillard says, paraphrasing Walter Benjamin, "in the age of ... mechanical reproducibility, what is lost in the work that is serially reproduced is its *aura*, its singular quality of the here and now." Along with this it loses its ritual function as it takes on " a political form" wherein we lose its original presence (99) as we are consumed in the mass consciousness of hyperreality.

Mann's work in *The Keep* suggests that he too sees the unconscious mind as the constructed surrogate that reflects this process; and as with Baudrillard, the trope that helps him comprehend this as an historical process is the doppelganger. Baudrillard senses the shift from a modern to a truly postmodern (and posthuman) paradigm in the new concep-

4. History, the Unconscious, and Hyperreality

tualization of doubleness that is figured in the wake of yet another manifestation of disembodied informatics, genetics, and cloning. Writing (the French version of this analysis) just two years before Mann made this film, Baudrillard said, once we lived in a world where our doubles were without substance. Unlike the posthuman clone, the old "double is precisely not a prosthesis: is an imaginary figure, which, ... makes it so that the subject is simultaneously itself and never resembles itself again ... like a subtle ... death." But genetics and cloning change this: "when the double materializes, ... it signifies imminent death." Why? Because our very attempt to "exorcise this phantasm" leads us to "materialize it in flesh and ... to change the nature of the double ... to the eternity of the Same" (95). In short, genetics leads to the serial replication of the body that leads to the hyperreal figuration of the human as a disembodied "stockpile of information" (99). Thus, historically speaking, "The metastasis that began with [mechanically reproduced] industrial objects ends with [the disembodied serial replication of] cellular organization" (101).

Mann uses an industrialized Nazi Germany and the Golem inside the Keep to dramatize a key moment in this historical process. The Golem begins his reign of terror by serially murdering Nazi soldiers to reproduce his physical body, as he is in turn constituted as the (physically present) double of their mad pursuit of power via the manipulation of the masses. The Golem also works as the doppelganger of seemingly innocent people like Cuza who still seek symbolic exchange as they attempt to combat the Nazis. But with the coming of a material, technologically induced double, with its glance at the Promethean Frankenstein trope as an early manifestation of the posthuman, not to mention the Nazi fascination with eugenics, *The Keep* makes problematic any attempt to maintain such an exchange. As Mann looks more deeply into the unconscious as a cultural force, as a manifestation of a corrupt informatics, he discovers that the materialization of the double does indeed point to the global power of the hyperreal. Resistance, in short, becomes even more difficult than it was in *Thief*, because now the mechanism of oppression is unleashed in full realization of its destructive potential. What is prefigured here is what Baudrillard called the culture of deterrence (58), of nuclear extermination depicted here by Mann as a manifestation of a cultural psychosis symbolized by the Nazis and what they release from the Keep.*

---

*Mark Steensland (2002) indicated that Mann's tendency to see Nazism as a mass psychosis was stimulated by his reading of the Walter Landon Report commissioned by the OSS after World War II (31–32).

Mann begins with a familiar gesture. We see a blackened frame but we can nevertheless hear the sound of thunder as a rainstorm begins. This testifies to the power of the aural, still a topic of interest for Mann, but it is also a trope, even a cliché in a Gothic context, and it is already pointing to how different this film is from Mann's earlier efforts. The darkened screen eventually fades to a lighter one, and suddenly we realize that the camera is in motion, tilting downward from a shot of the sky, when we see a line of fir trees outlined against the sky. Nature has made its presence known but it is not presented in crisp discrete images, motifs, and sound bridges as it was in *Thief*. Instead, as the tilt continues, and the rain obscures the images, the trees begin to lose their definition, appearing as light streaks of green. The tilt continues and arrests itself as the camera frames a German motorized infantry unit coming directly at the camera, seeming to move languidly because we can see no anticipated destination for them. Technology has also declared its presence. But this is an odd landscape: there is none of the energy that we usually see in the opening moments of a Mann film. Instead, some terrible inertia seems to have overcome things in the realms of both humanity and nature.

Ensuing cuts enhance the strange quality of the scene. Suddenly we see a match lit in closeup and brought to a cigarette; next an extreme closeup on someone's eye, side angle, as if to imply that someone is watching this convoy. But subsequent shots reveal that this eye is that of the German commanding officer, Woermann (Jurgen Prochnow) who is actually in the front seat of the lead truck. Ensuing shots show the eye opening and closing, as if he is half asleep. Another shows the sky reflected in water while others show Carpathian peasants in the village the unit has been sent to guard moving in slow motion in fog.

The effect for the viewer is one of complete disorientation, much more intense than what we see in the ending of *Thief* during Frank's confrontation with Leo. This is the kind of Gothic realm described by Rosemary Jackson (1981), where the potential of the uncanny realm of fantasy to subvert or interrogate the ruling episteme can sometimes be realized. This is the world of paraxis: "It is neither entirely 'real' (object) nor entirely 'unreal' (image) but is located somewhere indeterminately between the two" (20). It enables the artist to explore "the difficulties of interpreting events/things as objects or as images, thus disorienting the reader's categorization of the 'real'" (20). Paraphrasing Bessiere, Jackson described it as an antirational rather than irrational realm, because "It reveals reason and reality to be shifting constructs and thus scruti-

4. History, the Unconscious, and Hyperreality

Woermann (Jurgen Prochnow) is drawn irresistibly to the implosive vortex of *The Keep*.

nizes the category of the 'real'" (21).* Jackson uses the term to describe the realm between the real and the unreal wherein gothicism finds the site of its action, a site which is similar to the simulacrum that Mann and Baudrillard describe. *Para* always suggests things existing side by side; *axis* implies a central turning point. The site between the real and the unreal is the axis upon which they turn but it nevertheless allows each to remain distinct and therefore parallel to one another.

This paraxis between real and unreal allows Mann to immerse us into a simulacrum of the hyperreal more intensely and more implosively consumptive of nature and mankind than was possible or necessary in his earlier more reality based projects—and this is an appropriate use of style to configure the simulacrum here because Mann is now taking us into the realm of the unconscious mind as a construct of the simulacrum. He uses Woermann to introduce us to this world because, like

---

*"I am not the first critic to make a connection between Jackson's idea of paraxis and the culture of the posthuman. Francisco Collado Rodriguez (2002) identifies Rosemary Jackson's discussion of the thanatic aspects of fantasy with the typical posthuman interest in "bodily transgressions and the trespassing of fleshly limits" (69).

most of us, Woermann still believes himself to be living in an objective world comprehensible by reason, when in truth he is being drawn irresistibly into the implosive vortex of the Keep. He walks across the bridge that links it to the outside world, and as in *Thief*, there is the vanishing point effect, the lines of the bridge in convergence drawing him into the entrance, even as it draws the viewers' eyes. The inside space is again disorienting; as in the final battle in *Thief*, an overhead shot of the interior cannot be perceived as such until Captain Woermann enters and we can temporarily orient ourselves in space. Despite the bizarre landscape and interior, when he meets Alexandru, the caretaker of the Keep—this strange man who moves as if he is blind yet seems aware of his surroundings—he scoffs when told the reason why no one is in the Keep on a rainy night: "Dreams." Woermann assures Alexandru that the war outside in the real world is far worse than what one can dream. But the rest of this text will prove that paraxis in the hyperreal world prevents easy distinctions between nightmares and reality. The inner and outer worlds converge in the implosive energy of the Keep, just as in Mann's previous films, but with even more destructive power.

Woermann is important for another reason: he is a man who is deeply conflicted like most of Mann's characters. He is vital to showing the conflicts between the need for symbolic exchange and the desire to vanish into the dream vortex that for Mann is nothing more than the selfish lust for power. In the film's beginning, Woermann is still quoting the party line; he speaks to his young driver of duty, his pride in the Reich that will conquer Russia just as surely as it did the Low Countries. But in the course of his conflicts with his own men who seek fortune in the Keep (they are convinced the nickel crosses inside are made of silver) and with the SS unit sent to oppress the Romanians, another side of him is revealed. He believes that even a conquered people must be treated with honor and respect. He does not support the trope of empowerment for the sake of empowerment. He longs, in short, for some more meaningful form of symbolic exchange, an alternative to the hallucinogens of power and greed.

The urgency of this basic human need becomes even clearer when the other main characters appear later in the film: Dr. Cuza (Ian McKellen), his daughter Eva (Alberta Watson), and the SS Major Kaempffer (Gabriel Byrne). When the greed of Woermann's men unleashes the fury of the Keep, and a message is left on one of the Keep's walls, a local clergyman, Mikhail Fonescu (Robert Prosky), sends for Cuza and thereby liberates him from a concentration camp. Both Woermann and Fonescu become involved in acts of symbolic exchange, as does Cuza because it

4. History, the Unconscious, and Hyperreality

becomes necessary to protect the villagers, Cuza, and his daughter (both Jews) from Kaempffer and his SS men who represent a more dangerous force than greed for money. Woermann and Fonsecu both recognize the ruthlessness of the SS division sent to crush what they wrongly perceive as a peasant revolt. Both seek means to stop the violence but cannot because, like Frank in *Thief*, they have been seduced by the system in ways that they are unaware of.

Indeed, Mann shows that the efforts of all of these characters to make selfless gestures of symbolic exchange become distorted in the paraxis of this posthuman world that is neither object nor image. Mann makes this clear by the use of various motifs and symbols from religion and mythology in the film, symbols that represent the failings of the protagonists that prevent them often from engaging in meaningful and effective symbolic exchange. One of the most important of these symbols is the cross. The Keep is covered with crosses that are unlike a Christian crucifix: they lack the top part of the cross, forming what looks like a capital T. This is the same shape as the talisman Cuza will later remove from the Keep to free the Golem. Another cross appears when the SS men invade the village sporting black swastikas on red arm bands, what Woermann later contemptuously refers to as the "twisted cross" of Nazism. And finally, there is the Latin styled cross that Fonescu gives his friend Cuza to protect him and his daughter from whatever dwells within.

Mann's protagonists try to use the crucifix as the sign of genuine selfless symbolic exchange; all the other crosses are associated with the distorted counterpart of the gesture as manifested by an archetypal sign from the repressed subconscious that emerges as a result of the death of territoriality defined by true exchange. These signs help us chart the failures and successes of these characters who, like Woermann, are conflicted, but in different degrees. Woermann shows much promise initially but is in truth doomed; he does not disengage himself fully from the system and is destroyed. He has often struggled with the politics of the Reich, and tells Cuza that if he had fought in Spain like Cuza's dead son, he would have fought on the side of the Germans against fascism. This explains why he defends the peasants, why he wants to protect Eva from being attacked by his men, why he can honestly say that he wants Cuza's help so that he can prevent more of his men from being killed. He is capable of sacrifice, and it makes sense that he accepts the cross from Cuza (who by then is already in the process of making a deal with the demon in the Keep). He is, like so many Mann protagonists, making up for lost time. But, Mann insists, it is too late. When Kaempffer accuses him of being "sentimental" in order to feel superior to others, Woermann replies, " For once you are right; I am half a man. All that we are is coming out in the Keep." As he hears his men being slaughtered by the creature outside, Woermann lunges for the crucifix, and he is shot to death by Kaempffer.

It is a disturbing sight. Woermann seemed to have potential for something more, but the gesture to the cross shows that he is indeed a selfish man afraid for himself. He has spoken contemptuously to the SS commander about fear. Kaempffer sees it as the key to control for it shows dissidents "the price their actions cause them to pay." But, says Woermann, if what he battles "is like you, then does your fear work?" In the long run, clearly not, but something has prevented Woermann from acting in accordance with his conscience—he hasn't the courage to even attempt to disengage himself from the system—one can't imagine him striking out like Frank in the finale of *Thief*. He calls to mind what Baudrillard (1997) said about the sentimentality people voice for such marginalized entities as animals and ethnic minorities: "In particular, our sentimentality toward animals is a sure sign of the disdain in which we hold them. ... Sentimentality is nothing but the indefinitely degraded form of our bestiality, the racist commiseration...." (134)

Woermann is guilty of this. When he defends the people of the village, it is always on the grounds that they are not soldiers, somehow less than capable of defending themselves. His expression of compassion is based on a sense of superiority, like that he shared with the now dead soldier with whom he also shared his dream of a Russia falling to the Reich. Woermann also did not hesitate to dangle a promise for freedom before Cuza to motivate him to help save his soldiers from whatever dwells within the Keep. In short, he cannot make the symbolic gesture because, like everyone else in the film, he cannot fully disengage himself from the fascist system represented by his dopplegangers, the beast in the Keep and the SS man Kaempffer.

Kaempffer's encounter with the crucifix and the Golem are equally illustrative of this principle. He is a conflicted and hypocritical character whose allegiances are questionable. Kaempffer, who has shown complete loyalty to the brutal Reich and all it signifies since his appearance in the film, nevertheless snatches the blood-stained cross from Woermann's dead hands as he prepares to engage the Golem outside. He exits the room where he killed Woermann only to find himself in a landscape of destruction that brings to mind the horrors that humankind will survey only four years later in Hiroshima and Nagasaki. It is as if the soldiers have been melted down into one inert mass; the sameness of serial

4. History, the Unconscious, and Hyperreality

death represented by the hulks of the industrial age of warfare, burned out halftracks, cannon, and soldiers all made the same. Walking backwards, disoriented by this unearthly hyperreal landscape, Kaempffer turns suddenly to confront the now completed automaton, his physical double the Golem (this is the ancient Hebrew word for *embryo*, in this context significant as the sign of the beginning of cellular reproduction) now made flesh from all the soldiers it has serially assimilated. The formerly fearless Major now seeks sympathy for himself, and falling to his knees pleads, "Jesus protect me." He holds the cross before him, but there can be no hope: it is broken at the top and now represents the same iconic talisman of the Keep and the Golem itself. The sign that might point to genuine compassion and symbolic exchange is now appropriated by the archetypal symbolism of the subconscious and the hyperreal associated with the Keep. Fittingly, it is now that the major asks the creature what it is and where it is from, and the Golem, taking the now useless symbol from his hands tells him "I am from *you!*" just before killing him and assimilating his life energy through his eyes. The major, who has so often turned dialogues into monologues by using fear to silence all opposition, is assimilated through the very means by which his icons and gestures destroyed exchange, the windows of his something less than human soul. His death testifies to the destructive power of the simulacrum inside the Keep—it devours its proponents as well as its enemies.

The most significant gestures toward symbolic exchange in the film are made by Cuza and his daughter as they interact with Trismegestus (Scott Glenn) who, because he is unlike any other character Mann has created, will require detailed discussion later. Cuza is an agonizingly conflicted character who ironically fights against the anti–Semitic Germans even as he identifies with their mechanistic, serially productive culture. This becomes evident in his conversation with the clergyman Mikhail Fonescu who gives the cross to his secular, seemingly skeptical and rationalist friend Cuza, who is suffering from a disease that accelerates the aging process. Cuza complains about his intelligence being placed in "One of these decaying bodies." Mikhail wishes to know where else could "the soul" be placed and Cuza replies, "In a desk. Maybe in a streetcar. It wouldn't be so bad. Something breaks down, you get a new part." Mikhail wants to believe that this is only his friend's eccentricity but still calls this "blasphemy." Cuza's next remark points to an attitude that may explain how the two men could be so different yet still engage in the exchange of friendship: "You believe in gods, I believe in men." Perhaps these different forms of exchange are but different sides of one coin, different ways of expressing faith in the value of sacrifices, spiritual and human, that are still part of the symbolic exchange. Cuza accepts the cross as he and his friend both express their sympathy for Eva who will not desert her father or let anyone else take care of him.

Nevertheless, her father shows potential here for desecrating the bonds that allow humans to believe in men or God; he is part of a rationalism that is indeed a construct, as Rosemary Jackson would say, and one that is part of the informatics of disembodiment. Hence he can accept the existence of the Golem when it appears after rescuing his self-sacrificing daughter from assault at the hands of the Germans, and he can make a Faustian deal with it. It does not require a leap of faith or desertion of scientific rationalism to do this; the Golem represents what Cuza's episteme is all about. What is tragic about his involvement with the Golem and its informatics is that his motives are a combination of selfishness and selflessness. He clearly wants to avenge the death of his son at the hands of the fascists; he clearly wants to protect his daughter and the other Jews who suffer at their hands. As Trismegestus says later, only someone not yet corrupted by the world could be enlisted by the creature to carry the talisman out of the Keep to the rest of the world. But this contract is like the one Frank makes with Leo in *Thief*—the selfless quality of the exchange and its aims cannot coexist with a means that is as corrupt and vicious as that represented by the Golem.

Hence, the pact whereby Cuza also hopes selfishly to have his youth returned to him, to have time reversed and brought under control, cannot be made successful as, to some extent, it was for Rain Murphy in his more tribal society of exchange in *The Jericho Mile*. This is made apparent even in Cuza's first conversation after the pact when the more wary Eva rejects the idea. He wrongly asserts that the creature is merely a tool, like a "hammer," an object made like others in their industrial culture. But, as if she can sense its perverse connection to the serial hyperreal culture the Nazis are creating, Eva says, "It was a dream, a nightmare.... You are dealing with a Golem, a devil." Still thinking he is living in a world where things are either images or objects Cuza wrongly asserts that the real devils are men like Kaempffer. He is only half right, and like Woermann, because he lets his beliefs prevent him from seeing the world for what it is, he is only half of a man.

Hence his conflicted tendency to make Eva his other, his better half, in a gesture that at once points to and away from self: "Live a full life and live for me," he says to her. He will protect her by moving her from the Keep and offer himself as a sacrifice, even as he succumbs to the influence of that which he wishes to destroy.

In the end, fortunately, he does not follow through on the contract

4. History, the Unconscious, and Hyperreality

with the monster—and it is because he cannot obey the order of the Golem to kill his own daughter who is preventing him from taking the talisman out. When Cuza wrongly asserts that the talisman of the Golem "is *power*," Eva rightly counters, "It's corrupting. It's changing your soul." She fills him with doubt and the doubt deepens in his mind as the Golem dares to place Cuza in a parody of the sacrificial exchange between Abraham Isaac and Yahweh. He reasons that if the Golem truly is an agent of good, then Trismegestus would be wrong; the creature would not need an innocent to take the talisman into an unsuspecting world. But if it does need such a courier, then it is indeed evil, as Trismegistus and Eva have said, or as Cuza puts it, "you are the same evil as outside this place." The creature cannot comply and Cuza is successfully defiant, despite the fact that the demon strikes him with an electrical bolt and robs Cuza of his recently restored youth.

If this were all that is involved in the climax, one might be tempted to say that the selfless love of Eva represented a form of symbolic exchange that successfully resisted the damning influences of the demon and the Keep. But Mann has something far more complex and troubling in mind, as is signified by the role of Trismegestus in the end. He too helps resist—but his presence points to the futility of these efforts at the same time. Through this bizarre character Mann illustrates the principle of precession (where models precede the real in the simulacrum) and the overwhelming power of the simulacrum, as described by Baudrillard in *simulacra* (16–17).

Trismegestus, like the Golem, is not entirely human, and yet he has humanlike traits. This is to be expected given his name which, as Steensland says, is the Greek word for *harvest* (35). But in that context its resemblance to the name of the god of the old Greek, Roman, and Egyptian fertility cults, Hermes Trismegestus, is also significant. As Mead explains in his three-volume study of these cults (1964), Hermes Trismegistus is the lord associated with *logos*, the cosmic law of order and reason that is made flesh and reincarnated in Greek myths via Demeter (the fertility goddess) and in Egyptian inspired mystery cults, via Isis, the bride of Osiris (232–237). In this mythology, Osiris, the fleshly descendent of Hermes is dismembered by his brother Seth (Typhon in the Greek version, a deity associated with winds) and then is resuscitated through the birth of his son Helos, the sun deity, via the sister bride of Osiris, Isis.

As Barton Levi St. Armand (1974) said, such Eleusinian tropes are common in Gothic literature because they reflect the post–Romantic search for a monomyth begun by writers like Anne Radcliff who traced "the momentous connection between the life of nature and the life of the mind which made Romanticism," and later experiments in Gothicism such as Poe's, a true revelation of ... consciousness" (68) as they explored "the subterranean level of the subliminal and the archetypal" (69). Mann is exploring the same territory but with an end that eschews the sublime monomyth for something more monstrous and more frightening. Trismegestus is like the Golem, partly human and partly something else. He has an affair with Eva who falls under his influence just as she feels the influence of her father of pure flesh and blood. Trismegestus is introduced as a being with unearthly powers, but he is drawn to Eva's humanity saying that he needs, "To dream and touch as only mortals do." This is clear in their scene of lovemaking where the motif of the cross reappears: the two nude lovers extend their arms outward and compose a living crucifix of flesh. He is something abstract like the Golem yet bonds with Eva as a human being.

In the tradition of such figures as Jesus and Osiris, he is destroyed and resurrected. Taken prisoner by the Germans just before Eva and her father make their way to their final meeting with and temptation by the Golem, he is machine gunned by the Germans and cast into a crevice where he lies, covered in green blood that has an oddly unnatural, almost artificial (technological) appearance. As Eva and her father are threatened by the creature, Trimegestus resurrects himself and makes his way to the Keep to do combat with the Golem. Using the talisman as a weapon against the monster, he gradually loses his human appearance—his eyebrows disappear (making him seem demonic) and his blue eyes (which appear brown sometimes when he is with Eva) become grids, matrixes that look like mathematical graph paper. And although he defeats the creature, turning its own technology against it, he cannot leave this place, but instead is sucked into the hyperreal implosive vortex created by the death of the creature. He disappears as Eva impotently screams "No!"

The ending conforms in many ways with the ancient sacrificial gesture here—as Mauss and Hubert (1964) noted, heroes often die with the demons they slay in symbolic sacrifices because these doppelgangers are the result of a cultural process whereby a single sacrificial god was split into two (86–87). Such sacrifices unite tribal communities in symbolic exchanges that allow votaries to identify with the god(s) that bring renewal via death that can be comprehended through shared social belief (101–103). But that is not what is happening here. Mann clearly implies that Trismegestus is ultimately part of the Keep and its repository of hyperreal archetypes from a constructed unconscious. When asked by Eva where he comes from (the same question always asked of the Golem), Trismegestus replies "everywhere." By implication he precedes

4. History, the Unconscious, and Hyperreality

the release of the Golem from the Keep; he says he has awaited the event for a long time. Indeed, the first time we see him in the film is when the first soldier is killed by the creature in the Keep. This would point to some model of precession: the positive archetype has already been released but this is merely a precession of the demon that in turn is a precession of the destructive potential that will be released eventually in Yucca flats and Japan when nuclear fission hastens the implosion of reality and meaning. And like the Golem, he is linked to the technologies of destruction with his dehumanized, almost robotic appearance as his eyes and face are transformed when he merges with the Golem in the final battle. Hence Trismegestus and the Golem are linked as disjunctive opposites in the hyperreal archetypal semiotic code of the unconscious stored in the Keep. And since the Keep represents everything that is opposed to the natural regenerative powers of symbolic exchange once shared in the territoriality it established for humans, animals, and nature deities, the film's finale suggests that no real regeneration has taken place. Indeed what we see here is a parody, a simulacrum of regeneration, made possible by the agency of the archetype and the technologies that have unleashed it.

Mann, in short, uses these archetypal figures to make deeply unsettling suggestions here. The only characters who seem capable of genuine symbolic exchange and sacrifice are Eva and her father. Yet both are marked by their encounter and identification with these ultimately inseparable archetypal figures. This is especially true of Eva. As the film ends, she helps the villagers take her father away from the now silent and sealed Keep. The community at first seems to be restored—although it is odd to see Mikhail Fonescu part of that process. Eva had said he was driven mad by the events of that night, and in an earlier scene when Mikhail is angry with Cuza, he damns all "heretics" and the "gypsies"— an ethnic group we saw imprisoned earlier with the Jews. This man, who has shown compassion toward his Jewish friend, now seems as divided and conflicted as Woermann and Kaempffer in the wake of his interaction with these forces of the unconscious. Meanwhile, Eva herself cannot keep her eyes off of the Keep. Perhaps even more so than her father, she is deeply affected by her brush with the power of the archetype. She clearly longs for Trismegestus, as is indicated by the final shot of the film where she is frozen in time, held in a freeze frame. The depth of focus makes her seem oddly isolated, separated from the peasants who with Fonescu are helping her father behind her. It is as if for the first time in the film, she does not care what is happening to Cuza, she is focused only on her desires. Like the broken and divided Fonescu, who earlier

Fonescu (Robert Prosky) stands beside the iconography he thinks he is defending from the coercive informatics of the Nazis. But in the world of *The Keep*, the paraxis of the real and the nonreal robs saints and sinners of any distinctive kind of substantiality.

attempted to engage in symbolic exchange and failed, she is not a genuinely socialized creature. Nor, by the same token, can she move in the direction of the Keep. She is immobilized, as is our gaze, between the polarities of human society and the fantastic archetypal realm of the Keep, frozen between the worlds of human exchange and exchange with the oppressive machinery of the unconscious.

With this image, Mann can sum up many of the points he makes in the film. First, he can use Eva as testimony of the power of the archetype and the unconscious. His depiction of its power calls to mind Jung's own critique about identification with archetypes that he saw as the main source of evil in the Nazi regime. Archetypes, like people, are inevitably double-sided. To fall in love with the angel is also to risk falling in love with the demon that is its doppelganger. Such identification, said Jung (1959), will always lead to "terrifying consequences" (104). But Mann's point is even more unsettling than Jung's. Eva's identification with the archetype, her love, stems from the very thing that makes her

4. History, the Unconscious, and Hyperreality

perhaps potentially more capable of symbolic exchange than someone like Fonescu. She is a deeply compassionate person, able to connect with people without the self-congratulatory condescension of Woermann. But the very foundation of her humanity can still be turned into a weapon against humanity, can lead her toward identification with the archetype and away from society.

The full implication of this is made evident in the frozen frame at the end. Like the one used to depict Frank in his moment of alienation as he looks at his image in the mirror at the end of *Thief*, it evinces the intrusion of a reflexive medium. We are made aware of the medium as a medium that is creating the reality that we might normally assume that it only represents. This, in short, is the simulacrum. The flatness of the frozen image denies any meaningful distinction between the real and the unreal, between the world of social action in the background and the now unseen world of the Keep. Eva is trapped, frozen as it were, between these two worlds. The Gothic paraxis of the real and the unreal, by implication, is equated with the simulacrum that threatens to devour Eva's humanity as it does our own. In such a zone, the recovery of society that Fonescu and the others try to effect after the cataclysmic battle between the Golem and Trismegestus is merely another gesture without substance in the simulacrum.

Moreover, this simulacrum consumes the very historicity that Mann presents to us only to show it dissolve in the nonrationalism and cessation of logic and causal relations that inevitably happens in the simulacrum's precession. Even as the soldiers enter the town, we see life-sized saints with halos drawn on the walls, seeming to stand right beside the villagers who also seem out of touch with the real world. The film, in short, ends very much as it began, in the paraxis of the simulacrum that destroys distinctions between material object and phantasmal image. Whether the convoy comes toward us or the villagers walk away from us, it is all the same. And the implications are startling. How can the localized moments of symbolic exchange exist in such a world where the unconscious allows the simulacrum to consume all spaces? With each film, Mann's assessment of the situation grows darker and potentially more pessimistic. Each hard investigation into the culture shows why the corrupting side of informatics prevails, and the conclusions make the earlier more optimistic case of Rain Murphy seem all the more exceptional. Mann searches relentlessly for answers that continue to cast doubt on the capacity of humanity to successfully resist the oppressive system and the technologies it exploits and continues to develop to assert control over humanity.

But with typical courage and determination, Mann examines these new aspects of the problem, the complexities of the unconscious and its connection to media, in even greater detail, in even harsher light. His vision does not desert him as he pits cops and criminals against their doppelgangers in the masterful *Manhunter*.

5

Renewed Dialogue: Indirect Light, Complexity, and Exchange in *Manhunter* (1986)

> *Have you ever seen blood in the moonlight, Will? It appears quite black.*
> —Hannibal Lecktor*

The darkness of *The Keep* represents what we might expect from a director at the latter stages of his career; for Mann it represents a juncture and an opportunity for reconsideration and renewal of his epistemological quest regarding the relationship between society and informatics. With *Manhunter* he shifts focus once again and considers the impact of what Virilio would call *videoscopy* on our culture (Virilio and Camiller, 1990). Mann also examines in detail the technological and stylistic basis of informatics in film with the kind of intensity that Friedrich Kittler (1999) brings to that medium in postmodern (and post-televisual) times. Mann's analysis thereby pursues aspects of the simulacrum that could not be revealed by his examination of technologically less sophisticated use of iconography by the Nazis in World War II. The result is a masterful reconsideration of the place of symbolic exchange and dialogics in a postmodern culture that, as Jeffrey Sconce said, "allows simulation to replace reality, information to become consciousness" (199), at least to all appearances. Nevertheless, Mann will voice some extremely cautious optimism in this film, mainly through his female protagonists, as he argues that dialogue and symbolic exchange do represent realities

---

*Mann uses the spelling "Lecktor" in the screenplay and film, as opposed to the "Lecter" spelling used in Thomas Harris' novels.

that, if nothing else, allow us to understand the dangers inherent in a culture of voyeuristic intrusion and the concomitant forms of violence and oppression that Mann insists we should recognize and vilify in our culture.

Manhunter's opening frames help bring all of these themes on information to light in a sequence that surpasses all of Mann's earlier beginnings in its capacity to surprise and challenge the audience. The first shot appears, initially, to represent nothing at all. Visual noise with no apparent structure or referent, a purely abstract shape that may require multiple viewings before the reference, or the emergent form, is at all clear. It is an establishing shot that disestablishes the naïve expectation that the medium is a mode of representation. We are seeing the top of the murderer's van, with its row of red (egg-shaped) lights that feature a glow that seems neither natural nor unnatural, as if illuminating themselves instead of casting illumination as both natural and artificial lights normally do. In the wide screen director's print (where this image is not cleaned up digitally and "restored" for a "visual clarity" that Mann never sought here), we perceive the other factor contributing to this disorienting effect. This is video, not film. All of the opening shots before the title sequence are video. A slow walk up stairs, beam of the flashlight seeming to make shapes appear out of nothingness, children's toys on the steps, and then the entrance into a bedroom, the unsuspecting woman sound asleep in the seeming safety of her interior bedroom space until she stirs slightly, opens her eyes in the unearthly gloom, sits up slowly, as if awakening from a dream into what, we already know, will be a waking nightmare.

Nothing exists outside the frames; this plays before our eyes and one must ask the question: is this live? Is it happening now? There is no screen boundary framing the video. No shots tell us who records this. The camera records for itself; the image itself appears to be a type of consciousness, one with which we merge in this voyeuristic simulacrum of invasion and terror. It is the world of videoscopy.

Virilio and Camiller define it thus: "not a more or less up-to the minute 'representation' of the event, but live presentation of a place," the "constitution of an instantaneous, interactive, 'space-time' that has nothing in common with the topographical space of geographical or even simply geometrical distance" (58). It effectively destroys reality space: "For the sudden *commutation of perceptible appearances* is ultimately only the herald of a general derealization resulting from the new illumination of perceptible reality—a reality not just 'apparent' as before but transparent" (62). Videography is thus not a passive optics like cinema, but

5. Renewed Dialogue

an active one, where "commutation of emission and reception of the video signal ... indicates *mutation-commutation* of distances (topology) into *power* (teletopology), that is, into light energy" (59). This changes the nature of observation and subject-object relations because the "interface of observation" is no longer "the visible result of direct solar or electric lighting" as it results from a new kind of "indirect lighting by the radio-electrical field of a Herzian system or an optical fibre cable" (60). In a world where all of the globe's surface is under constant surveillance from "meteorological and other satellites," a "mysterious 'tele-bridge' is established between an ever-growing number of surfaces, from the largest to the most minute, in a kind of sound and image feedback which triggers for observers a ... 'telereality' ... expressed by the concept of real time" and thus the "electrico-optical environment wins out over the classical 'ecological' environment" (61). This works to "the detriment of the real object and subject—a phenomenon so indicated by the primacy of image over thing resulting from the new supremacy of real time over real space" (62).

Hence, video and television contribute to the primary elements of what Baudrillard would describe as the hyperreal, since real space and physicality are once again consumed by a bizarre manifestation of informatics. Mann thrusts us into the midst of this realm and forces us to recognize it as a collective nightmarish experience that is intensified by a technology that can exploit human beings even more viciously than what was released from the Keep. This videoscopic indirect light does not merely invade the mind through the subconscious that appears as territoriality vanishes with real space. Rather, it represents a kind of consciousness that suddenly makes itself known to us in the opening sequence that is all the more unsettling because of the utter lack of sound (except for the electronic musical score). Mann suggests videoscopy makes possible all that is wrong with the hyperreal culture, a culture that, in this indirect light would seem to have even greater and more threatening claims on us now than in his earlier films.

Mann, by reproducing this videoscopic simulacrum on celluloid, also points to the potential complicity of cinema in this destruction of real space and the threat this poses to human security, a topic of major concern in this film about home invasion. In this first scene, Mann has depicted how the serial killer Red Dragon (Francis Dollarhyde, who imitates a dragon depicted in a painting by poet William Blake) videotapes one of his first victims, Mrs Leeds, so that Mann may eventually link the serial killers in the film to the horrific dehumanizing aspects of the cultural simulacrum enhanced by the videoscopic technological revolution.

(The Red Dragon is the perfect focus for Mann's examination of this new kind of terror: the killer is obsessed with the visual—a fact also made apparent when he views himself in bits of broken mirror glass that he puts in his dead victim's eyes.) Mann thus returns to the theme of denaturing and serial replication explored in *The Keep*, by using the serial killers Hannibal Lecktor (Brian Cox) and Francis Dollarhyde (Tom Noonan), who are working together as a team to dehumanize and destroy the Red Dragon's victim, as representatives of the hyperreal culture that undermines physical presence and the human capacity for symbolic gesture through its complicity with an informatics that reduces humans to disembodied information. The culture accomplishes this via the creation of modes of industrial production and serially replicated art that replace ritual with mass produced art that subsumes, as Walter Benjamin implies, the consciousness of the individual as it creates a mass audience: "the distracted mass [audience] absorbs the work of art" (749). Mann examines the visual media that links these killers with the man who hunts them, Will Graham (William Petersen), in order to define these modes as disembodied instrumentalities that exist solely as modes of empowerment that lead to the oppression of everyone, including those who seek power.

Ultimately, Mann characterizes the serial killers as people who wrongly perceive themselves as using archetypal symbols and disembodied media as a means for returning to a primitive ritual state that will allow them to use real time to catalyze an apotheosis. Mann reveals in them the same will to power he recognized in the Nazis, something that corrupts humans and their instrumentalities. He does this by contrasting the serial killers' use of time, archetypes, and visualizations with types of genuine symbolic exchange offered by the more marginalized women and children in the film. Graham is a man caught between these two worlds—the videoscopic and the dialogical—and his story shows us the difficulties involved in resisting a culture such as ours, especially for men who seem especially susceptible in our culture to the hallucinogenic lure of power in the videoscopic world. *Manhunter* is an essay on how what seems to be characterized in the film as a masculinized desire for control in an information culture featuring noise and chaotic complexity, blinds men to the real nature of complex dynamics in culture and nature, and leads them to forsake better means of comprehending complexity and finding security that should be sought only in dialogue and symbolic exchange.

Mann alerts us to the problematic nature of cinema with unusual editing techniques that have often been mistaken by fans of the film,

5. Renewed Dialogue

sharing views on it via the Internet, for continuity errors. These techniques reflexively point to the dangerous yet powerful capacity of visual media to subsume the subject. Editing is the key here because, as Kittler (1999) indicated, it is via "film tricks, montage, and cuts that the recording of optical processes began." As "Daguerre's photographic plates" were replaced by celluloid, images could be linked so smoothly that today, "A cut has undercut its conscious registration" (115). In this way visual media record differently from audio media because "Instead of recording physical waves" as vinyl and analog tapes do, the visual medium "only stores chemical effects on its negatives." Film thus is a stream of doppelgangers that seem through editing to "reproduce the continuities and regularities of motion" when, in truth, they are only so many "phantasms before our deluded eyes" (119). Thus film is not "directly linked to the real" (119), and we have a medium creating a double of reality, where "Film doppelgangers film filming itself" (149) and "film and video cameras as mass entertainment liquidate the real event" (133). Kittler linked mass entertainment to serial death and destruction also, as is evident not only in the violence associated with the medium but also in film's link to the earliest technologies of mass destruction. The Gattling gun and the camera utilized identical mechanisms to serialize images, entertainment, and gunfire (124). Hence Mann's focus on and reflexive use of editing here is appropriate in the context of his examination of video and film that link serial death and visual media.

Mann's occasional bizarre applications of editing simultaneously alert us to the phantasmal nature of the serial doppelgangers in his film while they confirm the irresistible hallucinogenic lure of the medium they use to create themselves in their simulacra. The most unusual method is the skip frame where Mann removes a very few frames of film to disrupt the continuity of motion for a fraction of a second. He does this twice as a means of linking Graham and Dollarhyde to each other and to visual media. In the first instance, Graham is studying films of the murdered families transferred to videotape that he replays in his room. The *mise-en-scène* already indicates that something odd is about to happen: Graham is on the right side of the screen where he barely establishes enough visual weight to counterbalance the huge black shape of the television and VCR to his left. He seems to be making little progress as he studies the tapes; suddenly he gets up and crosses the room with the black set dominating the foreground until he picks up the phone, calls his wife, and, finding she is in bed, instructs her to "Go back to sleep." The soundtrack music rises to suggest impending danger to her (though none is apparent) as the camera dollies in on Molly Graham in bed, bathed in the unearthly glow of a blue light that seems to have no direct source. Cut back to Graham who returns to the screen and asks a question he might just as easily asked of Molly: "What are you dreaming?" He studies the movements of the deceased Mrs. Leeds and again asks a question that oddly seems to conjure up the image of Molly: "God, she's lovely, isn't she?" But it is clear that he is addressing the killer as he says, "It was maddening to have to touch her with rubber gloves on, wasn't it?" And it is at that precise instant that the skip frame occurs. Graham's head moves forward and downward suddenly, almost as if he is nodding in assent to his own question, a question he does know the answer to, as is evident when he calls up his colleague Jack Crawford (Dennis Farina) and instructs him to have Agent Price dust the corneas of the victims' eyes.

What has happened here? Mann is using the editing and the action to suggest that the psychic link between Will and the Red Dragon (Dollarhyde, murderer of Mrs Leeds) is the result of the destruction of space that is facilitated by the medium that both hunters use to stalk their prey. Longing for the physical presence of his wife, much as Dollarhyde longed to touch Mrs. Leeds, Will seeks an aural link with the wife via technology and cannot maintain it. He is then cast back to the videoscopic world with its version of the woman of the house, a virtual substitute. The skip frame occurs just as the visual link allows Will to see what the Red Dragon sees for a reason that he will discover only at the end of the story—these are indeed images that Dollarhyde developed and studied; for all intents and purposes, they are his consciousness, his visual perceptions of the victims, preceding his own videotaping of their deaths. The skip frame interrupts the flow of doppelgangers on film to underscore the technological link between the two men. And, more importantly, it points to the visual nature of our link with Graham, its phantasmal quality that allows us to merge with the consciousnesses of both men simultaneously.

The skip frame technique also occurs in the film's violent finale in association with Dollarhyde, and this makes clearer the irresistible power of these doubles and their media even if we are aware of Mann's reflexive technique. A skip frame occurs at the very instant that Dollarhyde is first shot by Graham who, temporarily disabled, was previously lying on the floor unconscious. We have been told that the bullets, blue glasers, will explode on impact, and the anticipation level is high as the first shot is fired in the wake of Dollarhyde's killing and wounding of more than one officer on screen with a shot gun. But our expectations are delayed for a fraction of a second; we see Dollarhyde bend over in reaction to the shot (in a visual parody of Graham's nodlike motion in the other scene), but we do not see the moment of impact as we do with the several other shots Graham puts into Dollarhyde before the Dragon succumbs to the final headshot.

The film has seduced us with the voyeuristic implosive undertow of hyperviolence, and it is at this instant that Mann chooses to interrupt the flow of energy and imagery in the thunder of the moment. It is as if he is saying that we can recognize the startling artificiality of the medium and its terrible effects, but even if we see the skip frame, we cannot disengage ourselves from the action. Like Graham and the Dragon, we are part of the show, accepting the bizarre violation of real space as we seem to live in the hyperenhancement of real time in the videscopic immediacy of it all, even as the skip frame points to the fictive manipulation of time created by cuts that no longer register on our consciousness, regardless of whether we attempt to note their "presence" or not.

There are other examples of unusual cuts in the film that allow Mann to point to other aspects of the hyperreal nature of these characters' existences within the context of the videoscopic destruction of real space. Graham, Dollarhyde, and Lecktor all exist in a world where this destruction of reality spaces, and the kind of cause and effect logic we associate with them is consumed by precession whereby events are modeled in hyperreality "before" they take place. Lecktor seems strangely in tune with this; he is amused and frustrated when Graham comes to visit him to regain the "mindset," because, as he points out to Will, "We're just alike" and so it was unnecessary for him to come and "look at me." Every act precedes itself in these men's shared consciousnesses: videotapes of home movies have already given up the murderer's mindset which was preceded and prefigured by the consciousness of Lecktor whose capture likewise preceded and prefigured Dollarhyde's defeat by Graham. As if to prove this, when Lecktor says, "You came here to look at me," Mann cuts back and forth between the two men who are identical distances from the bars between them, and filmed at identical angles emphasizing their sameness. Will, of course, cannot allow himself to recognize this consciously and rushes out into the zigzag maze of stairs that simulates his vacillation between recognition and denial. Outdoors, he can scarcely focus on the grass lawn before him; he unbuttons his collar for relief. And then in the next shot, the collar is buttoned again in closeup, as if to emphasize that he is where he was previously, just as before, just as he feared, just as Lecktor knew, for nothing has changed, he still participates in the forgone conclusiveness of the madness he shares with Lecktor. Cut to the invasive avatar of informatics, yellow journalist Freddy Lounds, taking Will's photo and exclaiming "Gotcha!" as if the camera were a deadly weapon. And that is just the point Mann is making as he cuts again to Graham's picture in the *Tatler*, the picture that will draw Dollarhyde to Graham and the private space of his family life. Lounds has taken Graham's picture like this before, and the cycle of his pathological consciousness repeats itself. Mann is also clearly emphasizing the connectedness between the serially replicated medium of the photo and the newspaper and the serial violence that it helps perpetuate (a theme he will explore more deeply later in *The Insider*).

There is at least one other noteworthy instance of this extraordinary editing style, but the discussion of it must wait until we have engaged another topic, the significance of dialogue and symbolic exchange in the film. Immediately after the opening video sequence, we are presented with the conversation between Will and former FBI colleague Jack Crawford who is saying they should have spoken earlier and is indicating that they don't have to talk if Will does not wish to. The visual arrangement and proxemics here are striking. The men are in a naturalistic setting in the first shot, seated on a large piece of driftwood, yet they are at opposite ends of it and facing in opposite directions: Will faces toward us (and his home) and Jack out to the vast ocean. Already there is the suggestion of something less than honest happening here, and subsequent shots help underscore Jack's alternations between manipulation and despera-

The decay of dialogue in the age of the videoscope. Will Graham (William Petersen, left) and Jack Crawford (Dennis Farina, right) are out of touch despite their physical proximity in this early scene from *Manhunter*.

5. Renewed Dialogue

tion. Midshots bring us close in, but we can see only one man's face at a time (and never more than the other man's shoulder) in a series of over the shoulder shots that reveal that these men still share some intimacy but are also separated from one another.

It is a disturbing scene: the men's dialogue seems tainted by the videoscopic indirect light of the opening sequence that establishes the epistemological frame of their world. The visual arrangement suggests that these men do not communicate well dialogically, that their honesty has somehow been compromised. Jack's use of the pictures of the victims to motivate Graham is grossly manipulative, and Mann suggests here that the videoscopic world of the yellow journalist Lounds and the serial killers has somehow colored the discourse of Jack and Graham. By contrast, Will's wife, Molly Graham, who also appears in the scene, seems to communicate in a very different manner. Interestingly, when Jack speaks to her here, she refuses to talk, as if to imply that her linguistic exchanges are not as easy to secure as her husband's, especially if manipulation is involved.

This becomes evident in the next scene as she watches Will and their son build a fence to defend a turtle egg nest, the first inhabited ecological space we see in the film. We see them from her over-the-shoulder shot that significantly presents her point of view with a more naturalistic proxemic than we saw in the first conversation (she is not as close to the camera as the two men were earlier in their over-the-shoulder shots and we can see her face) that allows us to perceive her point of view without having a purely subjective POV shot like the one the videocamera gives us in the very beginning. Her spaces thus seem different from those of the men; the perspective somehow makes her seem intimate with her boy and her husband even though they are dozens of yards away. Her world is one of intimate and direct interaction (with the other characters and the audience), not isolation. Mann's style thus conveys how singular her discourse is, and in ensuing scenes she emerges as one of the film's truest exemplars of symbolic exchange.

She turns to Jack and says, "You were supposed to be his friend, Jack. Why didn't you leave him alone?" She suggests that Jack's obligation to the unarticulated but still binding symbolic contract of friendship outweighs obligations to duty and profession. Jack responds with a gesture that we might regard with suspicion initially but which nevertheless speaks to his double obligation to his friend and to his professional commitments: "If he decides to do it, Molly, I'll keep him as far away from it as I can." The lighting is identical to that in the Sky Chief scene in *Thief*: striking natural light of the sun setting over the ocean with

Molly and Jack silhouetted in the foreground as they sit in the dining room. Less space separates the two of them than in the conversation between Jack and Will, suggesting that this verbal contract represents something different from the earlier meeting between Jack and Will, perhaps mainly as a result of Molly's presence. Mann clearly wishes to represent Molly as an effective agent of symbolic gesture—even if Jack is still committed to supporting the system, he is nevertheless reacting to her discourse and remembering his obligations to Will that go beyond professionalism, obligations that will make him stand by his friend's side to the bitter and horrifying end.

In conjunction with another conversation just prior to Jack and Molly's, one between Graham and his son, Mann also takes the opportunity to set up important themes concerning gestures of promise in the context of the world they live in, themes that further differentiate the men from Molly on epistemological grounds. Graham previously makes a gesture similar to Crawford's when he says to his boy Kevin that there are forty to fifty turtle eggs in the beach hatchery and "These are all gonna make it. Guaranteed." People often make promises like this in the film; when an agent later issues Graham the Charter Arms forty-four special, he says the blue glaser bullets are "guaranteed" to produce one-shot stops. These are interesting gestures because, as it turns out, all three of the men guarantee something and fail to deliver the goods as completely as they promised. In the film's end, most of the turtles survive, but not all. Jack Crawford is indeed dedicated to protecting Graham, so much so that he runs into a shot gun blast from Dollarhyde as he attempts to help Graham in the film's final gun battle. But he clearly fails to protect Graham—Lecktor gives Dollarhyde Graham's address and Graham assaults the Dragon's hideout despite Jack's protestations to let the SWAT team handle it. And certainly it takes more than one glaser from the forty-four special to kill Dollarhyde. All of these gestures are sincere but reveal a weakness—these men all underestimate the complexity of the world they live in, even more than Frank does when he overextends himself in the acquisitive world of *Thief*. Both the natural and the human world prove to be much more complex and more difficult to control in *Manhunter* than these three men in the film realize. Theirs is a naïve probabilism, a game of chance based on an assumption that the world is much more deterministic and predictable than the film shows it to be. They all believe in control, something they share in common with the serial killers. But the question is: why does Mann establish this pattern with the men?

The answer is that he is contrasting their epistemologies with those of the women in the film in order to elaborate on an important related

5. Renewed Dialogue

topic: the need in these men's lives for control. Molly clearly does not perceive life as purely deterministic or purely random. Rather, she embraces the idea of what chaoticians like Hayles (1990) call *complexity* or *pseudo-randomness* (9)—the world may feature some deterministic rules at some level, but it also features a certain degree of unpredictability. This may make the world seem purely chaotic, noisy, and potentially meaningless; and it could thus provoke the urge to control (a theme that, as we will see, Mann studies in even greater depth later in *The Last of the Mohicans*). Nevertheless in such a complex world there can exist what Hayles and other chaoticians call an *emergent form*, patterns of order within disorder that in the form of coincidences and synchronicities, create opportunities from which, in certain contexts, meaning can be made. And, at least in Mann's universe, that meaning can only exist between people who share ideas dialogically and honestly through self-sacrificing acts of symbolic exchange that provide meaning and temporary security even in a videoscopic culture as invasive and as terrifying as that created by the Lecktors, the Dollarhydes and, yes, even the Freddy Loundses of this world.

Molly articulates this point of view in her unique and subtle way. She is a very astute interpreter of language; when Will promises her his minimal involvement in the case and asks her what she thinks he should do, she responds with her characteristic mixture of bluntness and sensitivity: "I think you've already decided and you're not really asking." And when Will says what if he *were* asking, her reply is interesting: "Stay here with me—but that's selfish and I know it." With this reply she establishes herself as one of the few people in this world of duplicity who can stand aside from herself and connect with herself simultaneously. She recognizes her double motives—she wants him for herself but she is also deeply concerned for his welfare—and that of her son, and the potential victims. We see the fear in her eye after she and Will make love in that strange blue (indirect) lighting of their bedroom—she has no illusions about the isolation that she fears could result from Graham's promises that she must already sense cannot be kept. Her linguistic bonding is grounded in an epistemology that is not like his, and it allows her to channel signals in two directions without the bizarre commutation of the videoscopic realm that we later witness when Graham's consciousness merges with Dollarhyde's visually. Molly is oriented toward self and lover because she grounds herself in a reality space, a territoriality that is based on a presence, the spoken word, the bonds of real flesh in real space, constituted by the symbolic exchange of their love for each other.

Her orientation in time is also different from Graham's, as is evident in the speech she makes on synchronicity. She and Graham meet later in a hotel where the topic is the time that is running out for the next victims. She initiates the discussion with a question suggesting her different focus from Will's: "So where are we?" As he discusses his fears about the case, she asks him whether he remembers their first meeting where they first shared time and space together, where she could not believe how easy it was to talk to him. He recalls what he said then: "This is too good to be luck." Luck for him means pure randomness; such a good thing must be destiny, something predetermined—his deterministic reading of complexity, which is nothing more than a translation or commutation of the precession in his life into a conceptualization that fits in with his desire for control. His mechanistic approach sanctions the precession that results from the videoscopic hyperreality of his life where the present moment attains urgency, seeming significance, in a site where real space no longer exists.

Molly counters with her own dialogical rebuttal: "Time is luck, Will." She insists that we must "know the value of every day." This is more than a caution to stop and smell the roses. This is her bid to make Will focus on being, rather than becoming, for like the serial murderers he pursues, Graham focuses on becoming. Lecktor and Dollarhyde's fullest moments always point to the visual object of the apotheosis they wish to merge with as videoscopically conjured archetypes ("God's a champ," says Lecktor in admiration of "His Majesty" killing parishioners with a tornado, which cannot, of course, be an example of random or pseudo-random violence in Lecktor's deterministic reading of things). The present moment for these men is forever eluding their grasp in the videoscopic vortex that swallows real space. It is an expression of the will to power, for control, to fix the object of desire with the gaze that objectifies the physical subject as an image in a hyperrealized real time. To this, Molly says no. Real time is shared in real space by real people with the exchange of language and love. It happens when you appreciate that the complexity of life can serve up moments of synchronicity that are not prefigured by determinism or precession. Those alternative conceptions of what luck means drink the life from life via the serial event that denies true individuality and shared meaning. Time is not measured by endless series of doppelgangers on film and video that deny presence, shared meaning, and voice. Time is measured by the word, by the genuine sacrifice like the one she is making by coming to him, by sharing him with the victims who deserve their time together in a place that secures such interactions. Real time and real dialogue are the only reality space left. Real time is love. But even as Molly finishes her dia-

5. Renewed Dialogue

logue, Mann cuts to the reflection of the couple in the window, and like all of the reflections we see of Graham in the film, it points to the strange attraction of the videoscopic for Will that propels him into his collision course with Dollarhyde. Mann shows us here and elsewhere in the film that Graham has not fully differentiated himself from the killers he seeks.

Dollarhyde's life is parallel with Graham's, for, like Will, he too is drawn to a woman who represents the alternative to his videoscopic power play, the blind woman Reba (Joan Allen), his co-worker with whom he will eventually fall in love. Before meeting her, Dollarhyde lives in a purely visual realm. Graham, toward the film's conclusion, says of Dollarhyde, "Everything with you is seeing, isn't it?" for it makes Dollarhyde's "dream live." The dream is a simulacrum of what he desires, love and acceptance, which Dollarhyde achieves by arranging the dead families before him with a means to commutation made possible not only by his electronic optics but by the use of mirrors placed in the victims' eyes. As Graham says when he achieves full commutation with Dollarhyde, "I see me desired by you. Accepted. And loved. In the silver mirrors of your eyes." The mirrors give Dollarhyde immediate information feedback, immediate commutation, where he becomes the only image of consciousness in the eyes of the people who now reflect his narcissistic dream. He destroys their reality space to subsume them in the hyperreal fantasy life where a different kind of chronological time from what Molly articulates becomes like a narcotic, provides the rush, the escape from the unbearable isolation and meaninglessness of his life. He is en route to becoming the Red Dragon of Blake's painting, a gesture toward a visual archetype from the subconscious poised to consume the lady wrapped in the light of the real world. This hyperreal subconscious fantasy will replace the reality space of a lost territoriality in a false gesture toward primitivism. Dollarhyde makes no distinctions between humans and animals; he kills pets and their owners in his parody of a symbolic exchange through which he hopes to identify with a deity. Mauss and Hubert (1964) described such sacrificial rituals as part of social exchange in primitive societies (103), but the gesture here is not that, for it destroys the social fabric as it violates the communal space and consumes the lives of the families he destroys.

And one cause of this is the silencing of Dollarhyde earlier in his life—an aspect of his life that Mann uses to indicate how Dollarhyde has lost touch with orality and embodiment and has thus become an icon of the evil associated with the disembodied videoscopic realm. Initial shots of him in his work environment show the harelip that makes it difficult to communicate orally. When he eventually makes love to Reba, he places her hand over his mouth as she sleeps and weeps uncontrollably. This part of his life, his orality, has been severed in a castrationlike gesture that will make him seek an interface with technologies that can become prosthetic devices for him. In terms of informatics, he is a cyborg. Significantly, when he kidnaps and abuses Freddy Lounds, he uses his prosthetic teeth to seal their pact of communication with "a kiss." The prosthesis is a substitute for what he has been denied, and it is used by Dollarhyde in his role as the "Tooth Fairy" to seal all of his silent accords with his victims. As Baudrillard (1997) would say, it represents a link to the posthuman technologies: "The prostheses of the industrial age are still external, exotechnical, those that we know have been subdivided and internalized: esotechnical. We are in the age of soft technologies—genetic and mental software." (100)

Dollarhyde uses both types of prostheses: the exotechnical teeth and the esotechnical software of the videoscope that helps him relive the experience of becoming godlike (so he thinks) in the eyes of his victims. As Baudrillard says of the clone as ultimate high tech prosthesis: "Delirious apotheosis" of technology (97). It is the logical extension and terrifying consequence of what the Nazis sought in the subconscious nonreal world of the Keep.

Reba, however, poses a challenge to all of this. She is blind and cannot see Dollarhyde's physical (oral) deformity. She has training in speech therapy, recognizes his impediments but compliments him for the directness of his speech. She communicates only by touch and sound. She does not lose her orientation in real time and real space as long as she has her cane, a prosthetic device, but one which works differently for her due to her nonvisual participation in space. (It is a device that Dollarhyde significantly denies her when he eventually attempts to destroy her in the hyperreal space of his home—television with the fluttering unstable images beside the unearthly landscape of the moon reflecting the now indirect light of an invisible sun, a hyperreal site for Dollarhyde's disembodiment and psychotic evil). She is confident in the space of the dark room and welcomes him with the kind of gesture we might expect Molly to articulate in her home: "Come in, it's safe."

In the beginning of their first chance encounter and conversation, Dollarhyde studies her carefully, and seems surprised by her inability to see. As the conversation progresses, he stops looking at her and only listens. It is a moment of synchronicity as Molly has described it—they are sharing time in a verbal exchange. Here is a woman who will not judge him with her eyes but who offers him the kind of intimate space that thus far he has only parodied via the simulacrum he creates with his victims.

5. Renewed Dialogue

Fascinated, he takes Reba to the zoo for a "surprise," an encounter with an anesthetized Bengal tiger. But it is Dollarhyde who is in for a surprise. The tiger is not the emblematic gesture toward the archetype of the unconscious he may remember from Blake's poem but instead becomes a tactile and sonic resonance of ritual shared time and space, a means to symbolic exchange. We seem to participate in the exchange as the aural and tactile qualities of film are emphasized. Reba's hands push through the tiger's thick fur, against the grain, move on to the ears, then down over the animal's blinking eye, down further to the whiskers and teeth, and then to the hot breath of the animal, while we and Dollarhyde watch. Next, in an unexpected gesture, she places her face against the animal's rising chest and listens to its heartbeat. She closes her eyes as the beat grows louder in her ears and ours, and the camera reveals Dollarhyde too closing his eyes in bliss, as the three of them, and we, share in the aural and physical presence of the animal that is not a flat icon but a living thing sharing time with us with each beat of the heart, like the ancient gods Baudrillard (1997) has said we once believed in when there was no gap between humans and animals in the shared ecology of our territoriality (133). Humans once had territories like animals, defined by ritual and exchange, but after our loss of those territories, "animals are the nostalgia for it" (140). But the tiger here is more than an icon making up for loss, he is the means for realizing Reba as a special kind of erotic presence who promises an alternative to the disembodied simulacrum that has possessed Dollarhyde, the world Mann's analysis decries as his plot unfolds in time.

When Reba later goes to Dollarhyde's home, he watches films of his next intended victims and tries to fix Reba with the same gaze he implements on the wife in the film clad only in a swimsuit. Reba is oblivious to this visual eroticism and quickly converts the exchange into a physical sharing of space. She takes him and makes love to him in a scene that inverts the territoriality and proxemics of his beloved icon, Blake's painting of the Red Dragon with the woman. It is Reba at the top of the frame and the Dragon Dollarhyde at the bottom, completely in her power as she draws him into her space. In the bedroom later his tears and silencing gesture show that his soul is still conflicted, but later in the morning when he sees her in the full brilliant direct lighting of the dawn, he compliments her for how she looks in the sun and begs her not to go back inside the house. He wants to follow her into the world of direct light and real space, leaving the videoscopic world of indirect light behind him.

He cannot do this, however, and in subsequent scenes Mann shows how powerful the undertow of the videoscope really is. When Dollarhyde sees her with a colleague from work who attempts to remove some pollen from her eye, his visual imagination responds to the threat of an intruder invading the reality space of his relationship with her. Mann simulates this with the bizarre overexposed backlighting used to illuminate Reba and the coworker in a point of view shot presenting Dollarhyde's indirectly illuminated view of the event. Dollarhyde is not prepared for this challenge from his visual imagination proceeding from so many years of perceived inadequacy in his voiceless isolation. With the musical soundtrack booming "See Me as I Really Am," Dollarhyde waits until Reba is back in her home's interior space and shoots her colleague as Mann cuts with a one hundred eighty degree violation implying that Dollarhyde, like the other manhunter Graham, has merged with the intruder through his visual imagination. Francis Dollarhyde follows the vanishing point lines of her walkway to her home, as if accepting the predetermined (preceded) destiny of his becoming. And when Reba opens the door for him, he announces, "Francis is gone." He thinks he has rejected the seeming illusion of being that she presented to him, that now he can return to becoming the Red Dragon. He is proven wrong. For Mann also wishes to show how difficult it is to divest oneself completely of one's humanity, regardless of the power of the hyperreal videoscope.

Dollarhyde discovers this when he kidnaps Reba and then attacks her in the gloom of his house where, deprived of touch and sound as "In a Gadda Da Vida" replaces dialogue with the electronically induced noise of Dollarhyde's world, Reba cannot oppose his intrusion, cannot even connect physically when she tries to slash him with her finger nails. But it is actually Dollarhyde who is at a disadvantage now, not Reba. He attempts the old simulacrum routine, smashing the mirror image of himself, choosing a piece that will fit her eyes (surely a futile and ironic gesture in her case), selecting a long shard that will be the prosthesis for slashing her throat. She fights back, lying on her back as he leans over her, but already the iconic stances of the Blake painting have been betrayed. Yes, he is above her, but she wears the bright pink color suggesting power, while he is in dark blue. She fights him physically until she has no strength, and we, like Dollarhyde, expect this to be the moment of her death (unless Graham, lurking outside, intervenes). But it is not to be, for this is Dollarhyde's moment of weakness, not hers. Fully in contact with her, he looks, purely by chance, into the glass, and all of his predetermined plans are foiled. Reflected in the glass is a face torn by guilt and human grief—*his own*. She can still define his physical space for him, and so it is all over for him. There is nothing for him to do—until he sees the dark figure

5. Renewed Dialogue

hurtling toward the window, the phantasmal other who could perhaps help him complete his becoming, Will Graham.

At this juncture, one might well ask where precisely Will's mindset is at this point in the film, and the answer is, in a place much like Dollarhyde's—neither completely given to the videoscopic realm nor completely given to the real space the women have defined for these men. The situation is even more complex for Graham because he feels the presence not only of his wife but his son Kevin who engages him in a conversation that shows how divided his life is, even as it continues to evolve. Graham has learned that Kevin has seen the Lounds *Tatler* article on him, one that describes Will's pursuit of Lecktor and the mental illness that resulted for Graham after identifying too strongly with the killer. Because Kevin is now uncertain about leaving Molly alone with his father, Graham takes the boy shopping in a grocery store where he faces a difficult rhetorical situation. He must answer the boy's blunt questions—"This guy's gonna kill us?"—but he must be careful how he presents the truth. Graham has previously had an encounter on a plane in which he unwittingly shows pictures of the murder victims to a little girl who is traumatized by the event. This episode occurs while Will has a disturbing dream on the plane where he fantasizes about being at home but nevertheless stares at Molly in the dream and fixes her with his gaze, as if her were one of the serial killers. This is the vidoescopic realm he shares with Dollarhyde, a world he must somehow translate honestly into words for Kevin without the same effect he has had on the little girl.

As Will and his son walk down the produce aisle, however, Will is already showing the positive benefits of his conversation with Molly on the nature of time and luck. His answer to his son's inquiry about the future is unlike the guarantee he gave at the turtle pen. Pressed to answer the question of whether Dollarhyde will kill them, Graham answers: "We don't know that." He evinces awareness of the complicated and unpredictable nature of their world that helps create a more open exchange with the boy. Even at the end of the conversation, when the boy asks when they can go home, Will shows this new sensibility by replying, "I don't know."

It is a remarkable conversation; both Will and Kevin are discovering themselves, attempting to understand themselves better as they try to understand each other. When Will asks the boy if the report on his stay in the hospital bothers him, Kevin answers, "I don't know." There is much that Kevin does not know about himself, and perhaps Graham's surprising encounters with such different people as Molly, Jack, and Lecktor are opening doors within that make him appreciate Molly's dialogical uncertainty principle that much more. He also comes to recognize his strange divorce between body and mind as he explains to Kevin the nature of his illness: "After my body got okay, I still had his [Lecktor's] thoughts going around in my head." Graham next points to the most significant symptom of this. Like Dollarhyde, he was silenced, lost his orality, isolated in the nonreal space of a mind that shared a consciousness with Lecktor: "I stopped talking to people." But he assures Kevin that eventually he "was okay again," something he knows is not quite true in the way he previously thought.

At this point Kevin—whose physical resemblance to his similarly blond and tan mother is quite noticeable—rises unexpectedly to the occasion, saying, "And the way he thought was that bad?" Graham, without hesitation, responds, "They're the ugliest thoughts in the world"; and he is rendered so vulnerable by this moment of honesty that he must turn his head from the boy. Kevin understands immediately what the gesture means, can feel the depth of his father's pain without being shown the terrors he has dealt with. In his next gesture, the boy recognizes his bonds with his father and mother simultaneously, saying, "So what kind of coffee do you like? You like that Folger's stuff, right?" And when Will replies yes, the boy says, "Mom likes it too." In other words, Molly is right. They share time here in a way that strengthens their bond, simply because Kevin accidentally read the *Tatler* article. They make the best of the moment, just as Kevin does when he notices that they have wandered together into the coffee aisle, the place where he can end the awkward moment of silence following his father's moment of vulnerability. They leave the aisle in an embrace, the kind of physical gesture with which Molly often ends her conversations with Will.

This does not mean that Graham is healed, however, as Mann indicates with one more odd trick of editing. When the part of the conversation on Will's illness begins, he and Kevin stop to talk, and Kevin is clearly standing before a shelf of Carnation Milk. They do not walk as they come to the close of the discourse, but when Kevin makes his move toward the adult world by asking, "And the way he thought felt that bad?" he is suddenly standing before shelves of coffee. This looks like a continuity error but is not: clearly the conversation is meant to conclude at the coffee shelf or Kevin cannot make his gesture of empathy and complete trust to his father. Graham's background has changed too—he has moved from shelves of cereal to an aisle of canned fruit without walking one step. Mann's point is clear: even as Graham shares this space with Kevin, he is still in another kind of space, the deconstructed space of the posthuman that he shares with the murderers, one that still

5. Renewed Dialogue

Graham's (William Petersen) efforts to connect dialogically with his son are undercut by the shifting background that denatures the context of communication in *Manhunter*.

impinges upon the world that he and Kevin make together dialogically. He is not free.

But this is not to say that he is not changing, as is apparent in at least two other scenes before his confrontation with Dollarhyde. Right after Dollarhyde has his blissful exchange with Reba and the tiger, the camera dollies in on Graham who, surrounded by crates of evidence from the crime scenes says to the Dragon, "You think that what you do will make you something different. ... What do the mirrors make you dream you're becoming?" And as he does this, he touches for the first time physical evidence from the crime, clothes of one of the victims. Earlier, during his painful departure from Molly, he has said, "This killing, it's gotta stop." In the next scene, he looks at his reflection in the window of a diner, and when he hears Mrs. Leeds' voice on tape saying, "I'm sorry I can't come to the phone right now," he replies to her (something he did not do earlier when he heard the same voice in her home) by saying, "I'm sorry too." A waitress thinks he is talking to her and to cover his embarrassment he orders a coffee. He is in both worlds now, the aural and the visual. The former, impressed upon him by Molly and Kevin, allows him to identify empathically with the victims in a symbolic gesture of self-sacrifice. The latter places him in the world of the killer. This is his double bind: to protect his family and other families defined by the rituals of dialogical embrace, he must share the consciousnesses of those who would destroy such places.

And the strategy, in that conflicted field of contexts, is effective. An angry but revealing dialogue with Lecktor over the phone allows him to enhance his cognitive distancing from his visual simulation of Dollarhyde's consciousness when he visits the murder scene again. Later, when he views the home movie tapes again and argues with Jack Crawford, who is testy, guilt ridden, and anxious over Will's obsession with the images, he invokes the synchronicity principle with Jack. It's not just noise and chaos they are seeing here, Graham insists in the face of Crawford's arguments that the computers' objective processing of the information links could not have missed anything meaningful. "All the women," Will observes, "had a bloom on them; he didn't win them in a lottery." It's not purely random: there's an emergent form here if they can just seize on the right clue—and Will at that point notices what has gone unnoticed, the padlock. The bolt cutter was not a meaningless detail. Nor was it pure coincidence that Dollarhyde knew that the dog belonged to this family even though it did not wear a collar. Now Will knows—he and the killer have both seen these films.

But would Graham have realized this without the frustrating presence of Crawford and his verbal resistance? Almost certainly not. Graham also talks to the Dragon here as always, but does so with a rhetorical focus in mind, one prompted by Jack's skepticism. Duality of the discourse has presented Will with a context for the images. We actually see the videos on two separate screens; their boundaries are clearly visible, not at all like the skip frame scene in the hotel when either the videos or Will filled the screen. Dialogue and human interaction do make a difference for Will.

Nevertheless, the climax and denouement of the director's cut show that Will, like all of us, is still in jeopardy. He destroys Francis Dollarhyde in the end but still makes possible the killer's dream of becoming the Red Dragon. Lying on the floor, his arms extended above twin pools of blood that have given Dollarhyde his dragon wings at last, Francis has merged with the archetypal icon, though the price was his life, his total divorce from his body, as was already evident when the SWAT team's .357 magnum slugs and Will's glasers penetrated him without effect. Only the headshot entering the seat of his consciousness could stop him, but this is all that remained for him after losing Reba. It was the destiny that he believed was inevitable, a destiny that, ironically, only Graham who shared and even helped complete his dream consciousness, could help him fulfill.

And as for Graham and his family, their condition, like the condi-

5. Renewed Dialogue

tion of all families, all social units in Mann's world, remains precarious. Graham embraces Reba at the end but does not affirm his identity to her in the director's cut as he does in the theatrical version. And again, unlike the theatrical version, Will goes to visit the next family of intended victims and utters this disturbing line to the wife and husband: "I just wanted to *see* you." It is as if Dollarhyde is still a part of him. Graham may not be a unified subject; there can be no such thing in the simulacrum that still makes a claim on his identity, despite his attempts to find alternatives in his shared life with his family.

He does reunite with his family in the end, but the gestures here are mixed and difficult to read. In the final scene Kevin shows concerns for his father's wounds (slash marks, traumas inflicted with the mirror shard Dollarhyde wields as a weapon) and Graham says, "*Looks* worse than it is pal." Then he asks him to "See the turtles." His wife comes to him, unable to wait for him after hearing about it on the news. She is so full of emotion that, like Will in the supermarket with Kevin, she must turn her head to hide her moment of vulnerability. They embrace, she asks how many of the turtles made it and he replies with the honest truth: "Most of 'em." Red 7's song "Heartbeat" rises in the background as the family shares this moment of synchronicity, of shared time marked by the heartfelt relief they experience in this natural space they share with the brood of sea turtles that have somehow survived.

But Mann is not yet finished. They move to the beach and look out over the ocean. Mother and father move to the right of the frame; Kevin joins them, then moves to the left side and skips stones across the water. And a few beats later, we are left with a freeze frame image of them, the boy's arm raised in a violent gesture that seems aimed toward the mother and father.

Mann often leaves us with complex equivocal images like this as if to tease us into thought, to suggest that the resolution of the plot does not necessarily point to resolution of questions raised in the text. Surely Graham, like everyone, benefits from the presences and the voices of his loved ones, but the question remains: is that enough? The final two scenes suggest that the world he shared with the serial killers is still with him. By the same token, so are the oral presences of the family that has partaken in a ritual sacrifice of exchange with other living creatures in the natural world, something the serial killers of the videoscope could not do. But much of Graham's dialogue with his son focuses on the visual, and the frozen image of the son's (unintended but perhaps subconscious) gesture of defiance is disturbing. Have the tensions between the father and the son been resolved in this world where the repressed subconscious can subvert the more open social exchanges between human beings? Does the boy harbor subconscious fears of the father, tendencies to compete for the mother's attentions? One might interpret the final shot many ways, and perhaps that is Mann's concern—how will you interpret it? Dialogue? Monologue? Visually? Aurally? Stylistically, he points to the inevitability of all of these things. And in the mean time we must ask ourselves, can Graham protect his son from a hyperreal culture that is so invasive when it is part of his own consciousness? Will the dialogue with Molly and Kevin in turn protect him? In a world as complex as this, there can, of course, seldom be any guarantees.

6

Translating Ritual Time and Symbolic Exchange: Colonialism and Nationalism in *The Last of the Mohicans* (1992)

> *The whole world is on fire, isn't it?*
> Cora Munro

In *The Last of the Mohicans*, Mann repeats the gesture he made when he visited *The Keep*; after examining and summarizing the state of the present culture, he looks to the past to better explicate the circumstances of what has created the troubled society his characters find themselves in. With *Mohicans* he can offer even more precise hypotheses than before. He can turn the clock back to a time when a ritualistic culture of symbolic exchange still existed among the Native Americans of the mid–eighteenth century but was nevertheless in collision with the rising nationalist culture associated with a colonialism that opposed the dialogical epistemology necessary for creating a society of shared value. What emerges here is a historically based critique of modern societies that allows Mann to describe in greater depth the causes of what makes today's informatics such an oppressive, dehumanizing force in modern life.

In *Mohicans* Mann is describing the antecedents of something he had touched on in *Manhunter*, what has sometimes been called by scholars of the posthuman the *control revolution*. In *Manhunter* we saw various characters reacting to their complex information-rich culture with their attempts to control and make predictable their reality by attempting to assert dominion over a world that, in the face of increasing complexity, seemed less controllable and all the more oppressive due to their often misplaced attempts to achieve power. Hayles, in *How We Became Post Human* (1999), indicated that such attempts at control are part of a seriated history in which each stage reflecting human attempts at control recapitulates, while it progresses beyond, earlier stages in the process:

> For us, in the age of information, it may seem obvious that communication should be understood as requiring control and that control should be construed as a form of communication. Underlying this construction, however, is a complex series of events, with its own seriated history of engineering problems, material forms, and bureaucratic structures—a history that James Beniger has written about so well in *The Control Revolution: Technological and Economic Origins of the Information Society*. In broad outline, the forms of control moved from mechanical ... to thermodynamic ... to informational.... As each new form of exchange came to the fore, the older ones did not disappear.... The new forms are distinguished not by the disappearance of the old but rather by a shift in the nature of their control mechanisms, which in turn are determined by the kinds of exchanges the machine is understood to transact [90-91].

With the mechanical stage of exchanges, "determinism and predictability loom large," but with each successive stage, "probability necessarily enters the picture," and finally, with the coming of the information stage, probability "moves to becoming a fundamental attribute of the communication act" (90).

Mann's villains often seem to react to this increasingly probabilistic state with a psychotic obsession for control and a nostalgia for determinism: witness Hannibal Lecktor's assertion to Will that we cannot fight our natures because they are issued to us like our pancreas. The Nazis of *The Keep*, in their desire to use fear as a device for absolute control, ironically seem to do so, at least in part, because of their fear of the very chaotic culture and paranoid society they create via the implosive vortex of totalitarian informatics. Mann is tracing a seriatic history here, describing the strangely recursive and fearful symmetry of informatics past and present. And, unexpectedly, like some modern eighteenth-century scholars, he makes the assertion that we can trace this probabilistic informatics back to the time period when *The Last of the Mohicans* takes place.

It is an astute observation on Mann's part. We may associate the period with a kind of mechanistic, "Newtonian" determinism, but as Robert Markley (1993) has said, the scientific revolution forced eighteenth-century thinkers such as Newton to recognize that the cosmos is "irreducibly complex, beyond the explanatory power of the var-

6. Translating Ritual Time and Symbolic Exchange

ious semiotic systems ... he uses to analyze it" (10). In such a context, in a world influenced by the increasing complexity of an England on the brink of an industrial revolution, it is not surprising that the English would seek greater control with the semiotics of abstract mathematics; as John Brewer said (1990): "The object of applying mathematical science to 'useful knowledge' was to make accurate decisions, to reduce the elements of chance and caprice in what was perceived to be an unpredictable world." This would "produce precision, certainty and security out of seeming chaos and disorder" (229). Roy Porter (1990) described the phenomenon manifesting itself in eighteenth-century economics and culture. "The hurly-burly of life was taken under control in new attempts to stabilize the environment, predict the future and protect investments" (283). This desire for control was evident in attempts to shape the natural world both physically and through aesthetic systems of representation: "The desire to extend control was implemented in many walks of life. Landscape gardening exemplified dominion over nature," for "Landowners could redesign corners of creation, making it 'picturesque,' like a picture." Even in urban areas, parks were "laid out," rivers were embanked, and bridges were built with this purpose in mind. Not surprisingly, in this age of optics and the picturesque, Jeremy Bentham "described his panacea for all social ills, the Panopticon, a total surveillance institution, as 'a machine for grinding rogues honest'" (283).

Perceptions of time changed too. At the beginning of England's industrial age, time became a means of driving serial production:

> Entrepreneurs imposed factory discipline upon their workers, Wedgewood hoping to make "such machines of men as cannot err." Task-orientation gave way to time orientation.... Keeping good time mattered more—"Everybody has a watch," observed Mission in 1719—for 'in a commercial country,' as Dr. Johnson reflected, "time becomes precious" [282].

Mann links these new perceptions of time, order, and panoptics to the abstract disembodied community of the nationalist state in *Mohicans*, and again he has drawn an intelligent conclusion. Benedict Anderson (1991) discussed the rise of such states in *Imagined Communities* where he described the emergence of new perceptions of time and materiality as nationalist states replaced the old hierarchies based on monarchies sanctioned by divine texts and cosmology. The old monarchies died with the rise of the middle class, new scientific discoveries, and "the development of increasingly rapid communications" that "drove a wedge between cosmology and history." Not surprisingly, "the search was on, so to speak, for a new way of linking fraternity, power and time meaningfully together," with the help of "print-capitalism, which made it possible for rapidly growing numbers of people to think about themselves, and to relate themselves to others, in profoundly new ways" (36).

Essential to the rise of such a state, said Anderson, is a sense of chronology and simultaneity different from that of medieval culture, "what Benjamin calls Messianic time, a simultaneity of past and future in an instantaneous present." This is completely unlike what replaces it, what Benjamin called the idea "of 'homogeneous, empty time,' in which simultaneity is, as it were, transverse, cross-time, marked not by prefiguring and fulfillment, but by temporal coincidence, and measured by clock and calendar" (24). Hence we see that "The idea of a sociological organism moving calendrically through homogeneous, empty time is a precise analogue of the idea of the nation, which also is conceived as a solid community moving steadily down (or up) history." Members of the nation-state are like characters in a novel: they exist in an imagined system with or without physical contact with each other simply by virtue of the fact that they are suspended in an empty chronological site made possible by synchronous time. Hence a member of a nation state may have "no idea of what" others are doing at any given time. But he or she "has complete confidence in their steady, anonymous, simultaneous activity" (26) as participants in an imagined community made possible by print culture and continuing evolution and revolutions in informatics.

This facilitates the birth of colonialism and imperialism because colonies can participate in the imagined communities as parallels of the old world communities—they are doppelgangers of one another tied by the trope of filial bonds. Hence the appearance of so many place names pointing to duplication and serialization: "New York, Nueva Leon, Nouvelle Orleans, Nova Lisbon, Nieuw Amsterdam." "What is startling in the American namings of the sixteenth to eighteenth centuries is that the 'new' and 'old' were understood synchronically, co-existing within homogeneous, empty time" (187). "This new synchronic novelty could arise historically only when substantial groups of people were in a position to think of themselves as living lives *parallel* to those of other substantial groups of people—if never meeting, yet certainly proceeding along the same trajectory. Between 1500 and 1800 an accumulation of technological innovations in the fields of ship building, navigation, horology and cartography, mediated through print-capitalism, was making this type of imagining possible." The new communities would be "subordinated to the older" (188) but through the trope of filial bonds and common genealogy, disputes could be managed. "The revolutionary

6. Translating Ritual Time and Symbolic Exchange

wars, bitter as they were, were still reassuring in that they were wars between kinsmen. This family link ensured that..., ties could be reknit between the former metropoles and the new nations"(Anderson, 192).

Hence, under the influence of an information revolution, a new imperialistic nation-state arose with a new sense of time and history: nations and their colonies "began the process of reading nationalism *genealogically*—as the expression of an historical tradition of serial continuity" (195). The products and informatics of these states all were made serially in a new time continuum that made possible conceptualizing serial reproduction:

> Serially published newspapers were by then a familiar part of urban civilization. So was the novel, with its particular possibilities for representation of simultaneous actions.... The cosmic clocking which had made intelligible our transoceanic pairings was increasingly felt to entail a ... serial view of social causality; and this sense of the world was now speedily deepening its grip on Western imaginations [194].

The resulting colonial nationalist state created a "style of thinking about its domain." The "'warp' of this thinking was a totalizing classification grid, which could be applied ... to anything under the state's real or contemplated control: peoples, regions, religions, languages, ... monuments, and so forth...." Meanwhile, its "'weft' was what one could call serialization: the assumption that the world was made up of replicable plurals" (184). Ultimately, as a manifestation of the control revolution's antecedents in the eighteenth century, it was "the magic of nationalism to turn chance into destiny" (12)—or, more specifically in the Americas, Manifest Destiny.

Mann exposes the oppressive quality of this manifestation of serialization and informatics in the eighteenth century in *The Last of the Mohicans* by contrasting a naturalistic tribal culture of symbolic exchange with the dehumanizing exchanges wrought by the machinery of the imagined community's empty, valueless, simulacrum of love and family as a manifestation of the serialized imperialist enterprise. Interestingly, Anderson sees the original Natty Bumpo stories with their depiction of "blood-brotherhood" as examples of the "striking nineteenth-century imaginings of fraternity, emerging naturally in a society fractured by the most violent racial, class and regional antagonisms" reflected in the "brutal eight-year war against the Seminoles of Florida" taking place when James Fenimore Cooper originally published them (202–203). Mann's attitudes concur with Anderson's readings. In his AFI *Directors'* interview, Mann called Cooper's novel "politically evil" and "highly revisionist." And in his interview with Graham Fuller he decried Cooper's love of "static hierarchies" and fear of "miscegenation" (3). Hence, in *Mohicans*, Mann completely inverts the politics of the original stories by making clear that the Europeanization of the colonies is a detestable thing, a terrible precursor to the world of serial death and oppression that he has depicted in the videoscopic world of *Manhunter* and the serial slaughter of *The Keep*. By the same token, the white fathers from Europe are no more real fathers or brothers than Leo was a real father to Frank in *Thief*. This is where the horror of the simulacrum in all human relations started for Americans.

The opening sequence quite pointedly takes us as far away from the world of such warped filial relations and oppressive economics as possible. What we will see and experience here, briefly, is the world Mann describes in his interview with Cynthia Rose: "a time when, just for a moment, people knew how to live with each other. They knew ... the day-to-day language of coexistence" (5). We hear drum beats; we see a darkened screen that announces that it is 1757, and titles bring us from our world to theirs; we are moving backward to another time and a different kind of culture:

> The American colonies.
> It is the 3rd year of the war between England and France for possession of the continent.

Then fade from this abstract, chronological synchronous contextualization of the world of imagined communities to a more intimate focus of men sharing what we will soon see is the end of a kind of mythic and ritual time:

> Three men, last of a vanishing people, are on the frontier west of the Hudson River.

After the titles, another fade and we are seeing the mountains of this frontier in a steady pan that moves eventually into a tilt bringing us from sky to the wilderness these men share just beyond the border of civilization. They are chasing something in this place that we will learn later is near Albany, New York, but that colonial name has no place here even though there is a tension; the larger context is 1757, but we are drawn into this special time by the pounding rhythms of the score and the racing movements of the men in pursuit of something near the river, a deer, the sacred animal they have tracked and run down until the moment is right and Nathaniel (Daniel Day-Lewis) can take it *with a single shot*. These are the last moments of the archaic world before the serialized slaughter of nature and humanity can begin.

6. Translating Ritual Time and Symbolic Exchange

Their relationship with this animal is made clear by the ritual words they share with him in thanks for its sacrifice. Chingachgook (Russell Means) speaks in the dying language of the Mohicans: "We're sorry to kill you, Brother. We do honor to your courage, and speed, your strength."

According to Baudrillard, (1997) this relationship of symbolic exchange between humans and animals was once common to all human cultures: "Once, animals had a more sacred, more divine character than men ... only the animal is worth being sacrificed, as a god, ... Men qualify only by their affiliation to the animal" (133). Thus, "Even murder by hunting is still a symbolic relation" (134). This "violence of sacrifice, which is one of 'intimacy' (Bataille), has been succeeded by the sentimental or experimental violence that is one of distance" (135). This is all a result of "The imperialism of reason, ... of difference" (137). If Anderson is right, it could be no other way; the matrix of imperialism fixes lesser beings in categories of inferiority as serial entities that we can destroy at extreme distances.

But in this forest things are different, at least for the time being. All three men and the deer share in this moment. Their community is defined by a shared space and time that finds its rhythms in ritual speech, the voice of the gun, the meandering pathway of the running river that brought them to this place by chance but in a meaningful way because of the shared value implicitly there; we are brothers as Chingachgook says to both his white and his Mohican son. (Uncas is Chingachgook's natural son but he has adopted Nathaniel as his white son after Nathaniel's parents were killed in a battle.) Synchronicity is not the same as empty synchronic time. The community is not shared in the abstract; they know each other through physical ties: the word, the river, their blood. Death is life: all three share and exchange what made the event happen and have meaning, the shared gifts of courage, speed, and strength.

Nevertheless, as the opening titles imply, this world is not untouched by the world of the Europeans, and this becomes clear when these men find themselves in the next scene at John Cameron's lodge. They are there to share time; as soon as the two groups see each other, they are speaking of "another year [that] has passed." And there is much sharing here and talk of raising the young; Camerons' wife is concerned that the young Uncas has not found a woman, and Nathaniel jokes of finding him a Delaware woman as the Camerons' child is passed around the table, a lively communal tiding of the bonds of love that bring these people, white and Native American, together. But these are not the only types of exchange we come to know here. Nathaniel and his brothers have taken furs for trade, but they will not deal with the British and French who offer only "wampum and brandy." They prefer the Dutch who offer "silver." It is, after all, better than the purely exploitive exchange that the British and French offer, but by the same token it is nothing like the exchange with the deer. A new kind of materialism has entered their world, and with it a new kind of time. When the Camerons' high-spirited little boy says that Uncas should have a child like him some day, Uncas says, "You're too strong, you're going to be old too fast." And the mother reflects the same perspective: "That's what he's doing to his momma." Time is running out for all of these people, and even their good-natured raillery shows that, somehow, they know it.

When the British, the first Europeans we see in the film, are introduced, we come to know why their time has run short—the British are for the most part the antithesis of what the dying tribal culture is about and they are consuming it under the banners of nationalism and colonialism. A young English lieutenant is recruiting men to fight against the French, invoking the familial tropes that seem to affect whites and Native Americans alike; he calls them to fight "for your homes, for King, for Country." Already a representative of the Mohawk Nation has said he and his people formerly had "no quarrel with Les Francais" but will fight them now. Meanwhile Jack Winthrop, a friend who had shared the table with Hawkeye and the Camerons the night before, evinces similar support: "I believe that England is still our sovereign," so he will join as soon as he can arrange "terms" with General Webb. Like Frank in *Thief* he is setting himself up for a fall; later in the film when the colonial militia's homes are under attack they will not be granted permission to protect them. It is the precursor to the world of *Manhunter*: under the aegis of nationalism private boundaries will be consumed in the vortex created by the voracious needs of a new public system of oppression. No one can be safe under this system. Only Hawkeye and Uncas seem hesitant of involvement here; when the officer asks, "You call yourself a Patriot? A loyal subject to the Crown?" Hawkeye replies, "I do not consider myself subject to much at all," and his younger brother laughs.

The brothers will not be able to resist the attraction of the larger system much longer, however, for the pact made with the British will affect them all. Mann demonstrates that the social bonds that are opposed to this system will nevertheless be exploited by it even as they are destroyed by it. Briefly we see Nathaniel and the other Native Americans playing a game, but then we cut to an initially disorienting shot—the screen divided by perfect symmetry and balance, an abstract shape, purely geometrical and mathematical, as peculiar a sight here as is the opening image of *Manhunter*, featuring the geometrics of Dollarhyde's van roof. Patches of green within the design; horses and men moving at

6. Translating Ritual Time and Symbolic Exchange

The British have built a bridge that links the worlds of civilized order and natural flux, but clearly the implication of this shot is that the former seeks to absorb and dominate the latter in *The Last of the Mohicans.*

the top of the screen. This is a bridge over green water and a bridge between two worlds. Major Duncan Heyward has arrived above the river that earlier meandered freely as a tributary of the Hudson, but now is fixed by the neoclassical architectural design that shapes the landscape into a garden, one controlled and ordered instead of obeying the more natural principles of flux and turbulence. Without a speech community like the one the three Mohican brothers share, this is the only way to deal with nature's complexity and unpredictability. Not surprisingly, the interior shot reveals Heyward studying the image of Cora Munro (Madeleine Stowe), the object of his affections fixed inside his opened pocket watch. He is from the world of abstraction and geometrics—everything that runs counter to that must be objectified, controlled by borders and boundaries that are fixed not by shared symbols of ritual exchange but by the cold inert reality of mechanistic exchange. He is looking for a significant other in this New World that he seeks to make a double of the old world. As he says to General Webb when he reports to him, "I thought British policy is make the world England—Sir."

His exchanges with Cora Munro confirm this. He approaches her in full uniform on horseback from behind, framed in the long shot by the balanced brick columns of the entrance as the camera moves downward in a crane shot until she is revealed, eyes averted, wearing a straw hat trimmed with fresh wildflowers. Cut via a one hundred eighty degree violation to her happy reaction as she turns to him. Behind her a fruit press where a man leads a horse as his partner pours more apples into the action of the simple machine. And above the press in the far background, bags of grain await similar processing. This is Cora's world: physically instantiated technologies operated by people cooperating and taking full advantage of the rhythms of nature, a type of exchange unlike that represented by the linear columns behind Duncan Heyward that recall the bridge that has brought him there.

He has come to negotiate terms of agreement regarding their relationship, but she is as hesitant to agree to them as Nathaniel and Uncas are to accept General Webb's. Like Molly in *Manhunter*, she believes that the main requirement for the relationship is love. He does not. Respect will be enough to begin with and they will become the "most marvelous couple in London." This disembodied image of them is all he needs. She needs more but agrees to think about the terms that she will nevertheless reject after Nathaniel makes available the world she is really seeking, the world of symbolic exchange.

She, her sister Alice, and Duncan make their way to her father's fort through the wilderness, and by chance, Nathniel, Uncas, and Chingachgook, following the river, find the tracks of the Huron party that plans to meet up with their secret ally Magua (Wes Studi). The river has clearly emerged at this point as a symbol; it is the world of flux that unites these characters together in a mazelike dance, which affords the characters opportunities to achieve tone with complexity according to their preferred forms of exchange. A battle ensues in the woods, and the characters behave in ways that reflect these orientations. The British form a square, firing massed volleys of musket fire, their version of serial murder before the advent of the machine gun. These prove ineffective against the nonserial tactics of the Hurons who seem to realize that this type of serial slaughter is only effective if you are foolish enough to play the game in the same manner. They kill as Nathaniel, Uncas, and Chingachgook do: no death at a distance or en masse when one should be using musket and tomahawk at close range and scalping one's enemy as he dies. All except Magua, whose character emerges here with his distinctive commutation of both worlds; his main weapon is deception, simulation. Simulacrum of your friend one minute, he is hitting you with a tomahawk the next. A clear target one second, as the Long Carabine, Nathaniel, draws a bead on him, he is gone the next, disappearing behind a cloud of gun smoke, a demonic, insubstantial phantasm playing one world against the other, unaware of the implosive vortex opening before

6. Translating Ritual Time and Symbolic Exchange

him, ready to consume him as he becomes the New World double of his much hated enemy, Colonel Munro, Cora's father.

The stage is set for Cora Munro's discovery of her genuine sense of being as she falls in love with Nathaniel and the world he represents. This process is Mann's main method for demonstrating the process of translation highlighted in the film whereby he shows that people in this preindustrial imagined community can still make the crossing to a more archaic and, for Mann, a more humane mode of discursive transaction. An arduous journey up the river that takes them to where the Camerons have been murdered senselessly, the place where she will be able to understand the New World. Nathaniel, Chingachgook, and Uncas are stunned by this new impersonal form of killing; the Hurons took nothing from inside, not even the mirrors. As they survey the crime scene, Duncan complains that he cannot hear what they are saying, but this is merely his incapacity to connect with them orally and understand their sense of alienation from this violence brought to them from the world of the imagined community that does not distinguish between warrior and civilian.* Cora, however, is determined to become involved in the verbal exchange and insists that these people be given a "Christian" burial. She cannot understand the nature of Nathaniel's sacrifice here when he refuses and moves into her territorial space forcing her to back up. But she will back up only so far; her eyes meet his and she clearly wants to understand what this world of his is all about. She will enter the world of dialogical territoriality and eventually steps away from the simulacrum of the imagined community—with Mann taking the audience along to enlighten them on the differences between these two worlds.

At the site of a Native American burial ground, she comes to an understanding of the New World (as a manifestation of an archaic one) as Nathaniel explicates for her the world of symbolic exchange, a world where events of the past prefigure those of the present meaningfully in a culture where humans and all living things make exchanges with the complex natural world rather than imposing an abstract order on it. As in previous films, the moment of the most honest exchange focuses on the *spoken* word; it is night and Cora and Nathaniel can barely see each other. When he tells her that he left his friends the Camerons where they lay in order to protect her and her sister, she now realizes the sacrifice this ges-

---

**In his interview in the AFI's* The Directors, *Mann implies that, to some degree, this kind of violence "waged against the people" qualified the war between the French and the British as the first modern war where "civilians" were deliberately made targets in the first of many world wars to come.*

ture required of him and apologizes. When he tells her that his Mohican father warned him about people from her world, she is shocked because she does not yet understand his conception of kinship. This, however, begins to change. They are interrupted by intruders, and she pulls out the flintlock pistol she had the presence of mind to lift off of one of the dead men in the woods. He offers his powder horn to prime the pan and she accepts. The mode of symbolic exchange, in short, is being demonstrated verbally and through other types of gesture. The war party leaves and Nathaniel explains that it is out of respect for the dead. He also explains why the Camerons would live in such a place as this so they would not bound by "another's law." She pretends skepticism but is obviously listening intently, taking it all seriously. We see her thinking and can consider how the translation process is beginning to work for her. So this is what this place is all about. In the face of an unpredictable world where death can happen at any moment, genuinely protective boundaries are created via shared beliefs to help people cooperate in accordance with a law that does not need to be written down because it is alive for those who share in the sacrifice. Everyone shares, the living and the dead. Everyone is distinct yet the same. It is all beginning to make sense.

And it makes still greater sense when Nathaniel shows her, with the help of the stars, what it means to live in a world where no wedge has been driven between history and cosmology. It is a place where the feminine has special mythic significance and physical presence. The star field tells the story of all people and of particular people who share in a kind of mythic time where the past has special significance for the present, as it always shall. Nathaniel interprets these signs for Cora:

> My father's people say that at the birth of the sun and his brother the moon, their mother died. So the sun gave to the earth her body from which was to spring all life. And he drew forth from her breasts the stars. The stars he threw into the night sky to remind him of her soul. So there's the Cameron's monument. My folks' too, I guess.

Nathaniel has spoken worlds here. In the beginning was the feminine and from her comes love and life, her gifts upon the masculine that she creates in accordance with those forms of exchange that she and her progeny have embodied. Procreation is her gift, not serial production but genuine life, which exists because of exchanges between the masculine and the feminine and the values they both share and embody through the exchange. The stars embody the soul that engendered all this. And this is here for everyone, regardless of the empty categories of rank and privilege formed by the mechanical exchange of the imperialistic infor-

6. Translating Ritual Time and Symbolic Exchange

mation grid. It is shared by the Camerons and Nathaniel's white parents, just as it is by Chingachgook, Uncas, Cora, and himself. All that has come before has prefigured this moment of exchange and other sacrifices, this moment where Nathaniel reveals his respect for the feminine and the place in his heart that, long after his natural parents' death, should be filled by a woman. It is the antithesis of Duncan's world, a world like that described by Annis Pratt in *Dancing with Goddesses*: "A world in which women and love have become abstract symbols is a world of estrangement from nature as well as from our own bodies" (123). Cora (like Mann) will have no part of that disembodied picturesque world of the imagined community; she prefers the wilderness that "is more deeply stirring to my blood than any *imagining* could possibly have been." The moment of honesty and revelation has arrived for her, and, as is always the case when this happens in Mann's films, it is overwhelming, and so she must turn her face from Nathaniel.

This is the path she will choose as she makes her way past obstacles in her journey along and over the waters, obstacles laid down by her culture, by Heyward, by her father, and by the extraordinarily dangerous and conflicted Magua. In the process, many of these characters will become involved in processes of translation wherein the New World and the Old will meet as sign systems. For Cora, her father, her sister Alice, and even Duncan, the symbolic exchange system will become more persuasive as these characters eventually move, in varying degrees, toward a deeper understanding of sacrifice. Once again, Mann shows that the power of the dialogical community has not vanished and can sometimes enlighten even those who, unlike Cora, initially show little to no inclination for embracing the significance of the exchange. Unfortunately, Mann must also show once again the power of the globalizing information systems of oppression. This he demonstrates through Magua, who also translates between the systems but always in such a fashion that the European informatics and exchange with the machinery of oppression wins. He shows that even if one can win the local battle against Magua, he is part of an implosive vortex that will eventually consume the tribal cultures we see represented by the film's protagonists.

Magua's mortal enemy Munro plays a vital role in setting up the theme of translation and its consequences. When we first see Cora's father, he clearly is a part of Duncan's control revolution culture. Both of them count down the time it will take the fort to fall ("three days") with deterministic certainty. They are part of the early industrial age warfare being waged outside the fort where cannons and mortars belch fire and rain death down indiscriminately on its inhabitants whom the

French soldiers cannot even see. Munro dominates the discussion with his monological rhetoric of control and ignores the pleas of Nathaniel and the scout to let them return to their homes in honor of their agreement. As Nathaniel says later, Munro "does not even want to hear" what happened. He represents the written law that does not guarantee freedom or fair exchange. In the second debate on the issue, Mann presents him in a perfectly balanced long shot where he and Duncan are on one side of the room and Nathaniel and the now betrayed Jack Winthrop are on the other. It is the neoclassical equipoise* we saw when Hayward's carriage crossed the bridge, an equipoise maintained until Nathaniel steps forward, disrupts the balanced frame and angers Munro with his first rebellious denial of Munro's dominance: "Your judgment is not more important than their right."

It is the first time Munro's world has lost its equilibrium, but it will not be the last. Even Duncan initially voices some support for Nathaniel, saying in the first meeting, "Things were done. Nobody was spared." Eventually Duncan's jealousy over Cora will prevent him from siding with Nathaniel, but Munro also sees his own daughter supporting this man whom he considers guilty of sedition. Munro seeks justice via the abstract legalism of the system and is surprised by Cora's defense of a different standard of what she calls "justice" based on symbolic exchange; all that matters is the fact that Nathaniel "saved us." She is involved in a commutation he cannot understand; she considers herself equally guilty of sedition. Still, another side of Colonel Munro briefly appears when Hayward embarrasses her by suggesting that her defense is based only on infatuation. Munro looks at his daughter with genuine concern for her feelings. He is being quite honest when he says he would do anything "to protect her from being hurt." He simply doesn't realize that he supports a system that makes such protection impossible, no more than he realizes that his daughter no longer requires his protection.

Shortly, however, his experiences lead him to recognize that the system he represents does not work as he imagined. He finds himself at the mercy of a man who understands, internalizes, and exploits imperialistic informatics much better than he, the French officer Montcalm. The British oppress through direct application of technology and language as brute force; the French couple this with the weapon Baudrillard fears

---

In the Graham Fuller interview, Mann indicates that he researched paintings from the eighteenth and nineteenth centuries to create the look of eighteenth-century America in the film. This seems to have informed the way in which he recreates the imperialist simulacrum of the imagined community in this film, if only to disrupt it as the British world is challenged here and elsewhere in the film (Fuller, 5).

6. Translating Ritual Time and Symbolic Exchange

Competition between the nation states will undermine the balance of power as implied by the precarious Neo-classical equipoise (note the disruptive diagonal especially clear in the center of the composition) in this shot from *The Last of the Mohicans*.

more, seduction. Montcalm parleys with the unsuspecting Munro, compliments him for being a gallant opponent who has done all that he could "for the Honor of your Prince. But now I beg you to listen to the admonitions of humanity"—a topic which, by Mann's standards, Montcalm knows nothing about. He pleads with Munro to quit the fort in this seeming gesture of sympathy and honor, when in truth he is setting Munro up to be taken out by Magua and his warriors. Still regarding all of this from his panoptical imagined site of cultural superiority, Munro asks Montcalm if "the General's spyglass can reach as far as the Hudson," to discern Webb's approach, only to discover from Montcalm that Webb will not come. Montcalm is winning the game of control.

Initially, the meeting is presented in long shot with the neoclassical balance we have seen earlier—gallant opponents, French and British, on opposite sides of the screen—but the balance seems questionable as the officers move closer to talk, and then it is lost entirely in medium shots relating the shock of this news. Munro has been betrayed and his deterministic sense of certainty has vanished, as he makes clear when he says to his officers: "I've lived to see something which I have never expected—a British officer afraid to support another." The irony is especially deep; in his first meeting with Duncan, Webb had said there was no reason to fear the French who were naturally inferior to Englishmen because of their Gallic constitutions. It is the same bias that Webb shows toward Munro whom Webb typically refers to as "the Scotsman." In the grid of the imagined community there are categories for every ethnic group, categories that keep conquered peoples like the Scots in their place. Munro, becoming dimly aware of the inhumanity of it all seems to see into the emptiness of the imagined community's values. "Death and honor," he says, "are thought to be the same—but today I have learned that sometimes they are not." Like his daughter he is learning, translating experiences as he listens to the Frenchman and his officers and chooses protecting the lives of his men and his family over this false sense of honor. But for him it is too late. The militant double Magua that he has created blindsides him on the battlefield and, surrounded by the protective ring of warriors who have replaced the circle of Magua's family destroyed by Munro, Magua cuts out Munro's beating heart and promises to wipe his seed from the earth. And here Mann has shown how the doppelganger cultures on either side of the Atlantic, participating in a vast global imagined community, unleash implosive violence and destruction of human values through men like Magua.

Magua, however, is also the catalyst for acts of sacrifice that bring Duncan, Alice, Cora, and Nathaniel together in acts of symbolic exchange and acts of translation. For Duncan the process is both retarded and made possible by his feelings for Cora. When, after the battle in which Munro dies, Nathaniel makes another sacrifice by leaving Cora and promising to find her as she had promised herself to him when he was imprisoned at the fort, Duncan wrongly calls him a coward. It is in truth an act of bravery of a kind that, surprisingly, Duncan later proves capable of performing. When Magua takes the captive Munros and the Major to the great Huron leader Sachem, Magua at once makes necessary this sacrifice and unwittingly makes clear its greater value. Magua, up to this point has commanded perhaps some sympathy; we too can recognize the impact the Europeans have had on his life and his world; it makes sense from his perspective that he would hate the Grey Hair Munro. But as he speaks in many tongues—Huron, French, English— other motives emerge. There is a degree of selfishness in Magua that runs counter to what is honored in the symbolic exchanges described by Mauss and Hubert (1964) and Bataille. He is not seeking justice as Cora earlier defined it; he is seeking self-promotion. He offers the captives to Great Sachem and seeks his "acknowledgment" of his skills. When Nathaniel arrives on the scene, after selflessly suffering a beating from the men and women of the tribe, still other motives for Magua's behav-

6. Translating Ritual Time and Symbolic Exchange

ior become clear as Duncan translates for Nathaniel in a gesture prefiguring their exchanging of places in symbolic sacrifice.

Through Duncan, Nathaniel is able to reveal the truth about Magua who only appears to stand between two worlds and translate them equally when in reality he belongs to the Europeans. Nathaniel accuses him of breaking the peace with the English and offers himself to appease their anger. Magua scoffs, saying that there is no reason to worry for soon everyone will fear the Hurons:

> We do not fear the English anger.... Now the French fear the Huron. That is good. When the Huron is stronger from the fear, we will make the new terms of the trade with the French. We will become traders as the whites. Take land from the Abenaki, furs from the Osage, Sauk and Fox. Trade for gold. No less than whites, as strong as the whites.

Nathaniel sees the insanity of this plan and implements a special kind of oral and rhetorical leverage to undermine this selfish philosophy. He says, "These are the ways of the Yangees and the Francais fur traders, their masters in Europe infected with the sickness of greed." Nathaniel sees through the sick identification in Magua's mind with his tormentors, an irreversible outcome of the illness that Graham resists in *Manhunter*. "Magua's heart is twisted. He would make himself into what has twisted him," an empty serial image of the oppressor en route to becoming his double. By contrast, Nathaniel stands in the ritual moment connected to his past in the present; he offers the belt of his ancestors as proof that what he says and the sacrifice he offers is true. He *is* the Long Carabine.

Sachem is clearly moved by these words but cannot understand a heart like Magua's, offering him the young Munro daughter as a restorative to his heart, accepting Cora as a sacrifice, Duncan as a symbolic gift to the English, and giving Nathaniel his life. This enrages the psychotic Magua and distresses Duncan and Nathaniel equally. They both are willing to die for Cora. Duncan offers himself in French, never really lying to Nathaniel about this but determined to take his place as the sacrifice for Cora. It is as if the expulsion or at least the exposure of Magua's evil was the preliminary ground for the sacrifice. Mauss and Hubert described this as a dimension of some ritual sacrifices: unwanted entities can be expelled after the participants identify with them (9–10). Duncan, as he translates between Nathaniel's world and Magua's, reaches a place where he can now understand what Nathaniel represents. His love for Cora is the means whereby that translation and commutation takes place. He is not living now in Magua's horrific simulacrum of selfishness, greed, and power. Webb had suggested earlier that fear was the key for controlling the French, just as Magua had (and just as Herr Kaempffer did in *The Keep*). Within the dialogical space of this moment, Duncan lets go of fear and self-centeredness. He has become one with Nathaniel and Cora. In his moment of sacrifice, raised in agony above the raging fires that seem at times to be consuming the whole world in this film, the gift is returned when Nathaniel kills him—*with a single shot,* one that recalls the symbolic sacrifice with which the film began.

The promenade up the mountain, up to the source of the streams, a waterfall, seems to take the form of one more ritual attempt to permanently expel Magua's demonic presence. The sacrifices continue, the toll is terrible. Uncas attempts to take on Magua single handedly but is no match for the more experienced and ruthless warrior. Alice, frail and disoriented through much of the film, suddenly becomes self-possessed in light of his sacrifice. As rain begins to fall, she looks Magua in the eye and throws herself off the cliff to join Uncas where Magua has thrown his lifeless body. An enraged Chingachgook, under the protective cover of Nathaniel's guns, attacks Magua and blow for blow, wreaks the same havoc on his body that Magua wrought on his son. Magua's lifeless body falls on water rushing over the rocks, his face in the foreground of the shot, hideously twisted in his death agony like his heart. Behind him in the background, Nathaniel stands with his rifle next to the waterfall. The water can give or take life; we have seen that in two escapes earlier. And now it seems part of a final ritual cleansing as Magua is destroyed.

But is such a cleansing possible with such a foe? Immediately, the images suggest that the situation is not what it appears to be. Mann cuts to Nathaniel and Cora embracing, but as the camera lingers in long shot, she leaves; we see Nathaniel alone, and, turning his head to the right, he seems to be looking after Chingachgook. Nathaniel is clearly uneasy with what he sees, but exits in the direction of Cora. The camera stays in position; it does not pan right to allow us to share in Chingachgook's grief. Nor does it move left to allow us to see the departing couple. Instead, we see only the rock wall before which Nathaniel stood, its complex wave patterns suggesting the flux of the waters, but as if they were suddenly frozen in time. It is as if one kind of time has stopped and another begun, one marked by ritual exchange, the other by the exchange with the machinery of oppression. We know that all three characters are still there but we do not see them. They exist only in our mind's eye, by virtue of synchronous time. They and we are now an imagined community.

The demon cannot be expelled; it is everywhere and nowhere. Chingachgook's sad final eulogy, delivered in English, confirms this:

6. Translating Ritual Time and Symbolic Exchange

Great Spirit, maker of all life, a warrior goes to you, straight and sure as an arrow shot into the sun. Welcome him, let him take his place at the council fire with my people. He is Uncas, my son. Tell him to be patient and ask death for speed. For they are all there but one, I, Chingachgook, last of the Mohicans.

Chingachgook forsakes the world of being for becoming; he wishes to control time, accelerate it, for his world is gone and he is ready for death. To do this is, of course, to recognize the power of the European, to be subsumed by it. The same is true of his claim that he is the last of his people. The film began by telling us that we were about to see three men who were the last of a vanishing people. Nathaniel is his white son, but his son nevertheless. However, after he speaks, Cora, who has remained separate from the other two, approaches Nathaniel, her hair beautifully backlit by the setting sun. She and he will produce progeny of a different kind. Chingachgook is right; he is now a breed apart. The imperialistic grid is complete. To be a breed apart now is to accept the category of race, whose members are serial replications of parts comprising a mechanism in serial time. It is over. The old tribal community and its exchange system are gone. History is not cosmology. Meanwhile, like all of Mann's lovers, Nathaniel and Cora will no doubt do what they can to keep symbolic exchanges alive. But they cannot win the greater war. They have met the enemy who is now all of us.*

This is made even more apparent in Mann's revised director's version of the film, The Last of the Mohicans. Perf. Daniel Day-Lewis, Madeleine Stowe, Russell Means, and Wes Studi. 1992. DVD. Fox Video, 1999. Here the film ends with an extended version of Chingachgook's speech, where Chingachgook asserts that his people will die and that the time will come when even people like Nathaniel and Cora, who will replace his generation, will disappear when the frontier also dies. The changes in this version seem to have been made by Mann to ensure that the seriousness of his themes will be made clearer and thus lessen the chance that the film could be seen as a formulaic frontier epic. The theme of serial slaughter versus violence as part of symbolic sacrifice, for example, is also made clearer in the director's DVD version. In this 1999 version, when Nathaniel protects the runners leaving the fort to seek reinforcements, shots of him neatly taking out each enemy with a single shot are intercut with shots of Heyward slaughtering Frenchmen who march toward the well-oiled machine of the British square like so many automatons in a night attack. Note also in the final scene the omission of Clannad's love song to make the tragic ending seem darker and less romanticized.

While these changes clarify the film's themes and intent, I have nevertheless focused my analysis on the original version of the film because it is better known to audiences and features a deftness and subtlety that provides the kind of challenges that make for good critical analysis. Both versions of the film say substantially the same thing about the rise of the imagined community, so the choice of which film to discuss is less crucial here than in the case of Manhunter, *where the director's revision clearly presents a darker and more significant statement about videoscopy than that evinced in the version released in theaters.*

7

The Decay of Dialogue: Disguise and Duplicity in *Heat* (1995)

> *Our situation is absurd.*
> Justine explains to Vincent Hanna
> why she is cheating on him.

Heat is Mann's most pessimistic film to date, and the reasons for that can be explained succinctly. Two centuries after the disembodied imagined communities of *The Last of the Mohicans* have been created, and a decade after the videoscopic world of *Manhunter* has been formalized, human society and culture in the 1990's show signs of continuous disintegration and decay. The two previous films showed that real space was being consumed by hyperreality's implosive disequilibrium, and they showed that as the world of informatics invaded the domestic realm, and there could no longer be an exterior and an interior, then human beings could not be fully secure. As Hayles (1990) said of Baudrillard, when these implosions happen, they point to the constructed quality of human contexts and space and hence further emphasize the denaturing of humanity (275–276). "Consequently," said Hayles, "context becomes a construction rather than a natural result of shared activities" (272). With *Heat*, Mann points to yet another unfortunate consequence. As a result of the disintegration of space and context, dialogue cannot function. In denatured space, people seek security through deception and disguise. Ironically, this further compromises security because it kills the rhetorical grounding of dialogue and prevents an open symbolic exchange. This, of course, promotes even more deception.

When even localized speech communities are threatened, human beings are forced to face the constructed quality of their own lives and identities. Selfhood becomes a (trans) apparent lie, a disguise that cannot protect us from the soul denying implosive violence that consumes society.

The opening scenes of *Heat* show Mann's sensitivity to the increasing intensity of the problems he addresses. Typically he begins his films with one scene that features a certain degree of closure in a particular setting; even *Manhunter* ends its videoscopic teaser before moving to the dialogue between Will and Jack. Not so in *Heat*—the opening armored car heist with Neil McCauley (Robert De Niro) and his crew is interrupted by a long expository sequence concerning a police detective, Vincent Hanna (Al Pacino), his wife Justine (Diane Venora), and his stepdaughter Laurie (Natalie Portman). It is reminiscent of what Hayles (1990) has said about television—spacetime relations are constantly being disrupted as the main action is interrupted by news announcements and commercials creating "spliced contexts" in a kind of schizophrenic hyperreality (282). Even the action of the heist isn't fully set up before we meet Vincent and his family.

And the ends of that action aren't apparent immediately either because everyone involved is already wearing a disguise. Neil is pretending to be an ambulance driver. Chris (Val Kilmer) holds up a driver's license as he picks up materials for the explosives as if he were an honest building contractor. Michael Cheritto (Tom Sizemore) picks up Waingro, who is wearing dark glasses and must identify himself before he can enter Cheritto's truck. Even when the heist begins, everyone is wearing masks, making it difficult to discern who has done what until the job is over.

It is a world of incongruities and dissemblance. En route to the hospital and the ambulance parking lot, Neil first appears on a train in the cold dark morning. The train comes straight toward the camera on a deterministic path before coming to the lighted station, which resembles a flat geometric icon in the darkness, as if it had no depth, no real interior space at all, an icon of the simulacrum. In the station, all of Neil's movements seem prescribed and deterministic; he comes down an escalator on the right side of a screen split evenly between the escalator and the stairs that are empty. But on the cold dark streets, he walks against the grain; an overhead shot reveals him moving in the opposite direction of an arrow painted on the street. Then, amidst the steel and glass of the LA streets, an enormous statue of a fully lit pietà is suddenly apparent. This before Neil moves into the hospital—a place of electronics, computer screens, and antiseptic whiteness, until Neil glances in one room

7. The Decay of Dialogue

A world of incongruities and dissimulation. Neil McCauly (Robert DeNiro), the man who typically goes against the grain, seems trapped here in the deterministic mechanism of the train station in the opening sequence of *Heat*.

and we see a bleeding victim's body in closeup, first sign of what this all means, anything can be invaded, nothing is secure, and nothing is sacred in this fragmented world of incongruities.

This applies not only to the armored car heist that ensues, but also, as we will see, to the domestic privacies of Hanna's home. The heist contextualizes the home scene and the home contextualizes the heist, which is just another way of pointing to the death of context, for how can context truly and meaningfully exist when such different worlds, inside and outside the home, are virtually the same? We read meaning in context by looking at what precedes and what follows a particular lexical item or phrase; icons have contextual grounds from which they emerge and develop significance; shared values help us create a context for interpreting tone, irony, meaning in dialogue and writing. But to have those things we must have boundaries, as Mann's earlier films show, defined by a speech community that has a sense of shared space and time, a community that seeks to distinguish inner and outer, public and private. That is not what we see in the heist where the armored car is ripped open with a deafening blast, a blast that contributes to the death of the guards whose bleeding ears signify that they cannot hear the commands of a frustrated Waingro who kills the first guard in a fit of rage. In the furious noise of this world, the significance of human gestures is lost, along with meaning in general.

This is apparent in Vincent's home, which he later describes, when he is breaking up with Justine in front of her boyfriend, as "her ex-husband's dead tech postmodern bullshit home." It is indeed postmodern, or more pointedly, posthuman, a place where people seem to appear from (and sometimes disappear into) nowhere, from spiral stairways that abruptly emerge into living spaces, from hallways that seem to connect everything and nothing at the same time, much like the spaces (if one can call them that) that we see in the train station where Neil arrives during the opening sequence. Indeed, one shot of Justine coming down the staircase is framed exactly as Neil's is when he comes down the escalator in the station. Everything seems alien in this home; the opening lovemaking scene is depicted in a series of cuts that are like jump cuts disrupting the flow of their movements.

And there is no dialogue between these lovers as there is in *Mohicans* and *Manhunter*; indeed, we do not even know that this couple is man and wife as we see them here—we are given no context for this relationship, except this very disorienting home where Vincent leaves his pistol lying on the table in plain sight of wife and stepdaughter before slipping it into his pants. He and Justine speak but seldom look at each other—how can they in a home that seems to have its space deconstructed into private arcs of habitation that somehow convene in a cacophony of discontinuous living environments? The little girl Laurie appears suddenly just over her mother's elbow, deeply upset that she cannot find the berets she needs to meet her absent biological father (who stands her up). The girl is even more inconsolable after Hanna leaves, knocking a newspaper away from her distracted mother, breaking down into tears until the mother assures her they will find the berets if they "look together." Everything we see of the outside is here—violence, disorientation, no real dialogue, people who do not connect directly, except through violence, the violence that does not directly reveal the real problems even as it points to them. To adapt a phrase from Virilio's description of the indirectly lit world of the videoscope, the violence we see here is the transapparent mask of human desolation.

And there are other masks that Mann points to in order to underscore this desolate, desperate, and dehumanizing condition. In *The Last of the Mohicans,* only the villainous Magua wore masks consistently in the imagined community he helped to (de-) construct and globalize, but here it is almost everyone. People differ with regard to the mask motif mainly by degree. Perhaps the most honorable and honest character is

7. The Decay of Dialogue

Nate (Jon Voight), though he is a figure who is sheltered by anonymity—he seems to live in a site that is neither public nor private, like a phantom, someone whose job is to coordinate information. Yet, as such, he is someone who enables people to penetrate each other's covers; ironically, he helps Mann show why it is that even this degree of honesty is dangerous and cannot represent a solution to the problem of deception in this local society. It is Nate, after all, who arranges for Van Zant to buy back his insured bearer bonds at a profit exceeding his 100 percent insurance coverage investment. He does not anticipate that Van Zant will interpret this as a violation of his secure space because he believes that everyone "on the street" will think they can rip him off. Hence begins the violence that will lead Van Zant to work with Waingro to force Trejo to betray the crew at the bank robbery—an act of violence that leads Neil to forsake his lover Eady (Amy Brenneman) to kill Waingro when Nate unwittingly falls for the trap Hanna sets by dangling the location of Waingro's hiding place. Nate is the one character who never sets out deliberately to deceive anyone, yet his translucent approach to the truth causes him to promote more deception, betrayal, and violence than anyone in the film except, oddly enough, the man who seems to be his opposite number, Waingro.

Waingro is the most obviously deceptive and dishonorable character in the film, and, as such, is the one person that everyone in the film, regardless of which side of the law they are on, can agree to vilify. With his initial appearance in the film, he sets up the major trope we see played out almost every time a character steps into view—either they identify themselves or they ask someone else to identify themselves (or they do both). (Mann calls attention to this with self-consciously absurd parody when the lover of Chris's wife, Marciano, repeatedly asks Vince who he is and Vincent replies, "*Who? Who?* What are you, a fucking *owl?*") Waingro pretends to be a cool professional like the rest of the crew, but reveals himself to be an uncontrollable psychopath when he unnecessarily kills a guard after Cheritto tells him the guards are deafened by the blast. He lies to Van Zant when he promises to help protect him from the betrayed Neil McCauley and says, "We took down some major scores together." He is the source of all of the serial violence in the film and is also a serial killer; he kills a young African-American prostitute (ironically after accusing her of lying about his sexual performance) as he has killed many others, according to Rachel, Vincent's forensic pathologist. He also sports Nazi white power tattoos on his body, something that connects him (serially) to many of Mann's other power obsessed villains who use fear to control victims. He is also identified with the death of real space and context; before Neil can kill him after the first heist he simply disappears in a parking lot even though he is surrounded by Neil's crew. If this vast, deeply unsettling film on the emptiness and meaningless of postmodern culture could have a cold dark center, Waingro would occupy that place.

But there can be no such center because, in truth, what Waingro is associated with appears everywhere and nowhere; for most of the other characters participate in the deceptiveness and emptiness he is associated with. This becomes clear every time there are sustained and probing conversations between the main characters. Men and women try hard in this film to establish honest dialogue that can define the kind of dialogical reality space that promotes symbolic exchange, as we saw in the previous films. But deceptions of one kind or another always prevent this from happening.

This is clear in the relationship between Neil and Eady that begins and ends in deception despite the real need these two people have for each other. When Neil first meets Eady, he has led such a life of secrecy as a felon that he regards her overtures of friendship and attempts to establish dialogue during a chance encounter at a diner as an intrusion upon his privacy: "Lady, why are you so interested in what I read and what I do?" She has seen him in the bookstore where she works and, working off a principle of synchronicity like Molly in *Manhunter*, she has decided to take advantage of the coincidence and share time with him. He is taken completely unawares by this. They come from different worlds. He recognizes that she comes from "a tight family," something unknown to a man with no father and no mother, and a brother whose location is unknown to him. The only human contact he has known is with the "tight crew," as Waingro calls his men. After a life like this, he does what seems to come naturally, he does the very thing David Okla told Frank never to do in a relationship, he lies about his identity, telling her "I work in metals; I'm a salesman."

Eady attempts earnest dialogue here, although even she has trouble opening up. When asked if she likes working at the store, she replies hesitantly, "Sure—I get a discount and there's a whole section of books in my area." But clearly she is less than content with her life; she has moved to LA mainly for the work and she is hoping to turn her night job into a full-time career in graphic design. She is perhaps more honest than Neil who seems to have trouble being honest with himself. When she confesses her loneliness to him, he says, "I'm alone; I'm not lonely." Clearly, however, that is not the case; like Frank in *Thief* he later shows he is aware of shortness of time in his life and, as his actions in the rest of the film prove, he desperately wants to share his life with someone in some

7. The Decay of Dialogue

kind of protected space where time can be shared. Later in the film he asks her to go with him to New Zealand. He recognizes the emptiness of his life and even himself: "I'm a needle, starting at zero, going the other way, a double blank." It is as if Eady, with her familial ties (which she can trace back to the arrival of her Scotch-Irish ancestors in America during the 1700s—that mythic time of *Last of the Mohicans*) can fill the void of a life that has been about nothing but criminality and concealment. Surprised by his sudden overtures, she rightly points out, "You don't know me Neil."

That is just half the problem; the other half is the man that *she* does not know. Later, that all-seeing videoscopic eye of the TV cameras reveals what he really does with his time when, after being betrayed by one of his own men (Trejo, who does it to protect his wife Ana, whom Waingro will murder anyway), his bank heist goes horribly wrong. When he enters her home, she is standing there, no makeup on, asking, "That was *you?*" He offers the collateral damage excuse, "It rains, people get wet," and she is stunned. She runs out of the protective space of the home, into the tall weeds outside, and as he tackles her, screams, "Why did you do this to me? Who *are* you?" She is a young woman falling in love with someone who fills a void in her life and now is realizing that because she did not know him, did not perhaps even know her own motives in this, she has, in truth, tumbled into the void that Mann argues is inescapable for these characters, perhaps for all of us.

Eventually Neil wins her back, using Molly's gesture from *Manhunter:* "I don't even know what I'm doing any more. I know life is short. Whatever time you get is luck." But this is not really like Molly and her sense of luck as a shared spontaneous destiny. Luck here is pure chance, having time to share, wanting to share it to escape the emptiness created in this culture where there is no security, no sense of place. Neil wants to share time with her, but his focus initially is on himself and, as in Eady's case, the fear of the void: "All I know is, there's no point in me going anywhere any more if it's going to be alone. Without you." She will forgive the deception, still longing to escape that void. But this is a divided man who often fails to be honest with himself. When Nate later calls him and tells him of Waingro's whereabouts, Neil indicates that he will forget about him. But as he drives with the innocent Eady in the car, he seems to battle with himself and turns away from the escape route to the airport and toward Waingro's hotel. He says he has something to do quickly and she asks if there is time. He assures her that there is—and we cannot tell whether he is deceiving her or himself. In truth, Mann seems to say, it does not matter—they are the same thing. Both of these people are equally without direction, equally without place, equally divided despite their apparent differences. Deception of other and deception of self are the same in a world where boundaries for spaces within and outside, psychologically and topologically, have vanished, consumed in this culture of the simulacrum. We deceive ourselves as we deceive each other. Subject and object (other) are linked and deconstructed in the deceptive tropes of the simulacrum.

This pattern is repeated with every relationship we see in the film. Dialogue, for one reason or another, always seems to break down. Of all of Mann's protagonists, Vincent Hanna seems to be the poorest communicator. When he comes home from the crime scene where the armored car guards were murdered, Justine is visibly concerned about him, despite the fact that she is equally upset with his failure to appear at dinner at a time when Laurie is distraught over her absent father. "You all right?" she asks and cannot engage him in a conversation about himself. He is concerned about Laurie, asking if her father "has any idea of what's goin' on with this kid?" instead of recognizing Justine's double focus on the absence of two men in her life, the ex-husband and Vincent. She complains and says, "Every time I try to maintain a consistent mood between us, you withdraw." He will not address the issue, and as he says he's sorry if the chicken was overcooked, seems to show with the falling tone of his voice his recognition that the reply is inappropriate, that it wrongly belittles Justine's world. She leaves, exiting up the strange spiraling staircase that appears beside a painting of a woman, eyes averted, mouth completely covered with black paint, a sadly poignant correlative of how dialogical exchange has been destroyed here, mainly by Vincent Hanna. Hanna, meanwhile, makes another disturbing gesture: as she leaves, he picks up the remote control of the TV and turns the set on.

Television becomes a disturbing presence in their lives, as it is throughout the film, as we see especially in the final breakup of the marriage. It is a reminder of how dialogue is dying in this videoscopic culture where electronic images are commuted, instead of feelings and gifts in symbolic exchange. We see this coming when Vincent returns to a party after leaving for the crime scene where the murdered prostitute has been found, and Justine is still waiting for him. Again, he will not reveal his feelings. She says, "I'd like to know what's behind that grim look on your face," and he replies, "I don't do that." She seems to feel that an original agreement of exchange has been violated here: "You never told me I'd be excluded." He feels it has not been violated because the deal was that she would have to share him with the worst people in

7. The Decay of Dialogue

the world, but she rebuts him saying, "But you have to be present some of the time, like a normal guy. That's sharing. This isn't sharing; this is leftovers." He chides her for her belief that sharing would somehow be "cathartic" for him (which isn't what she is saying) and claims, "I got to hold onto my angst. It keeps me sharp, where I got to be." He will not allow her into his emotional life, and she responds with a diatribe to which he has no reply:

> You don't live with me. You live among the remains of dead people. You sift through the detritus, you read the terrain, you search for signs of passing, for the scent of your prey, and then you hunt them down. That is the only thing you are committed to. The rest is the mess you leave as you pass through. What I can't understand is why I can't cut loose of you.

Justine keeps trying to evoke an emotional response from Vincent, even going so far as cheating on him with her lover Ralph. But this simulacrum of a deception evokes no human response from him. She asks him, "Don't you get angry?" and he replies, "Oh, I'm angry." But the anger is directed at Ralph, not her, and he shows it by saying to him that Ralph can take his home and his wife, but he cannot watch his television. As he begins to remove this icon of the death of shared space and dialogue from the room, Justine makes one last attempt to evoke a human response from him, saying the whole situation is absurd. He defends the image of himself as a keeper of honorable symbolic exchange: "I say what I mean and I mean what I say." She deflates the claim easily with a smirk and a rebuttal: "Except none of it's about us." She says she may "be high on grass and Prozac but you have been walking through our life dead. And now I have to demean myself with Ralph just to get closure with you." Vincent will not reply. He walks out with the TV which he later throws out onto the street before a shocked crowd that witnesses the implosive fury of this man and the technology that points to the vortex created in the lives of these people in their isolation, frustration, and fear.

In truth, both Justine and Vincent are vacant people in the company of the dead; they do not realize that they have this in common until Laurie's implosively violent suicide attempt. She has been disappearing into that vortex since the beginning of the film. In an earlier scene Vincent had picked her up in the squad car when he saw her sitting alone. He asks her why she is there and though she replies, "I just wanted to be alone," he does not inquire why. Like Justine he seems to do little to help the girl resist the strange attraction of the absent father who creates this undertow, this void in her life. Laurie slits her wrists in the overflowing tub in Vincent's hotel—and Vincent actually walks over the soaked carpet as he enters, oblivious to the real space he is in, preoccupied with the defeat he thinks he is about to suffer at the hands of Neil McCauley. He does rush her to the hospital where the equally ineffectual mother, now without makeup and emotionally naked in this moment of horror, asks Vincent why the girl did this to herself. He has no answer, and neither of them considers the role they both might have played in this through their distractedness and absence. Beside Justine in the waiting area is a television set that no one watches; meanwhile Vincent's beeper goes off and he tries to ignore it. These disembodied information technologies that promise omniscience and control have not enabled them to help Laurie; indeed, they testify to how their divided attentions prevented them from giving the girl the kind of help she really needed. Laurie should have been a reason for these two people to communicate, but they were not focused on her.

Battered by the events of the evening, Vincent briefly recognizes his limitations. When Justine asks him if they can work out the relationship, he has a moment of honesty with himself and with her, recognizing the validity of her side of their arguments: "You know it's like you said, all I am is what I'm going after; I'm not what you want Justine." The angry tough guy bluster we see when he interrogates snitches and suspects with what he describes rightly as a "ferocious" demeanor is gone. The man who monologically dominates with his posturing and anger has recognized the emptiness of his life. And it is too late to amend things between him and Justine, who has also done her share of posturing and who now, as they part forever, can only ask him to call her and let her know that he is okay.

Hanna also reveals this basic emptiness in himself when talking earlier with Neil—a conversation that admits some honest exchange but which nevertheless begins and ends with dishonesty as part of the deadly cat and mouse game these two men play. Vincent approaches Neil's car to arrange a negotiation while holding a gun behind his back; Neil likewise keeps his hand on his weapon and is actually planning to give Vincent's surveillance teams the slip as soon as the conversation is over. For all that, the dialogue is one of their more revealing moments in the film. But what is revealed by the men is that they are dreamers whose dreams reveal the desperation and emptiness of their lives. The conversation confirms what Baudrillard would say: the subconscious replaces territoriality. Both men have lost that in the simulacrum they live in, where territory, space, and context vanish and take away everything that is nec-

7. The Decay of Dialogue

essary for meaningful communication. Only by revealing their subconscious desires, the simulacra that replace the gestures they would normally make in a territory defined by ritual exchange, can these men reveal anything of themselves. Vincent's dream is especially unsettling and revealing:

> You know, I have this recurring dream. I'm sitting at this big banquet table, and all the victims of all the murders I ever worked are sitting at this table and they're staring at me—with these black eyeballs, because they got eight ball hemorrhages, from head wounds, and there they are, these big balloon people, because I found them two weeks after they've been under the bed, the neighbors reported the smell, and there they are, all of them, just sitting there. ... They don't have anything to say; they just look at each other, they look at me, and that's it, that's the dream.

It's his world. A public event, a banquet; it should be a place of life and exchange, a territory where society celebrates its sense of community via ritual. But that is not the world he lives in, and he knows it. He lives in a world where there is no verbal or symbolic exchange, where death of the victim is only the confirmation of a precession, where everyone is already dead in a simulacrum of life that is a parody of community and shared meaning. He is fixed by the gaze of the dead who perhaps seem to accuse him, plague him with guilt for not saving them, for having been consumed by what consumes them; and they constitute his existence through the dead mirrors of their eyes that convene their videoscopic commutation where the gaze of death begets more death and the man assigned to save them is impotent to do so. He is his job and warns Neil that he will not let him make a cop's wife into a widow; if that happens, then, "Brother you are going *down*." He sees it as justice, but Mann implies that it is just a perpetuation of implosive violence and death.

The simulacrum of life presented in Neil's dream is equally disturbing. His reflects his fear that time has run out for him:

Neil: I have one where I'm drowning. And I gotta wake myself and start breathing or I'll die in my sleep.
Vincent: You know what that's about?
Neil: Yeah, having enough time.
Vincent: Enough time? To do what you want to do?
Neil: Yeah.
Vincent: You doin' it now?
Neil: No, not yet.

Neil's dream is so vivid to him that he could die if he does not awaken from it—he lives in the simulacrum created by his wishes and unconscious desires that take the place of any real territoriality in his life. The dream is all that he has, and he ends his side of the conversation with a warning too—if he sees Vincent at the next score, he will die. The ultimate expression of this lost territoriality, the fear of the void, the vortex, is violence.

Violence escalates and spreads throughout the world of the film as promises are violated and the implosive hyperreal world consumes lovers and enemies alike. The stunning gun battle at the bank robbery typifies this—as Thoret (2000) said, it shows how the inside and outside have collapsed, is as if the Indians are circled by the wagons as they fight the settlers (7)—a moment made all the more ironic by the fact that Wes Studi (Casals), the former Magua of *Mohicans,* is in the outer circle with the police. There is no security in this world of today, any more than two hundred years ago, and the collapse of dialogue accelerates the process whereby implosive violence consumes human space and territory.

But there are still darker ironies here that testify to the destruction of domestic space in the contemporary world. Near the end of the battle, family man Michael Cheritto takes a little girl hostage to protect himself. Cheritto was shown earlier in the film at a banquet honoring the crew's success where he gave his wife a ring and, after asking his own little girl what she wanted to be when she grew up admitted that, like his daughter, he does not want to grow up. Now he uses a little girl who resembles his daughter as a shield, another mask to protect him from the hyperreal mayhem he and the others have induced. Hanna dispatches him with one shot—but one filmed very much unlike the merciful shots that dispatched the deer and Major Heyward in *Last of the Mohicans.* The camera zeroes in on Vincent in closeup as he fires; and at that precise moment, when the bolt of the FN assault carbine explodes backward in recoil, Mann skips a frame, disrupting the fluidity of the action. In this hyperviolent moment, real space and time are not shared. Vincent's wrist chronometer is exposed as he assesses the effectiveness of the shot, and then he cradles the girl and says, "I gotcha." It is a precession of implosive hyperreal violence to come: he will say the same thing later to Laurie when he pulls her blood soaked form from the tub; and his chronometer will be exposed on his wrist as he cradles Justine in the hospital. All of these times and places are connected only by the hyperreality of destruction, the death of society and domestic tranquility.

These people do not share real time in these moments of tragedy and loss; this is instead that bizarre accelerated time exposed in the vic-

7. The Decay of Dialogue

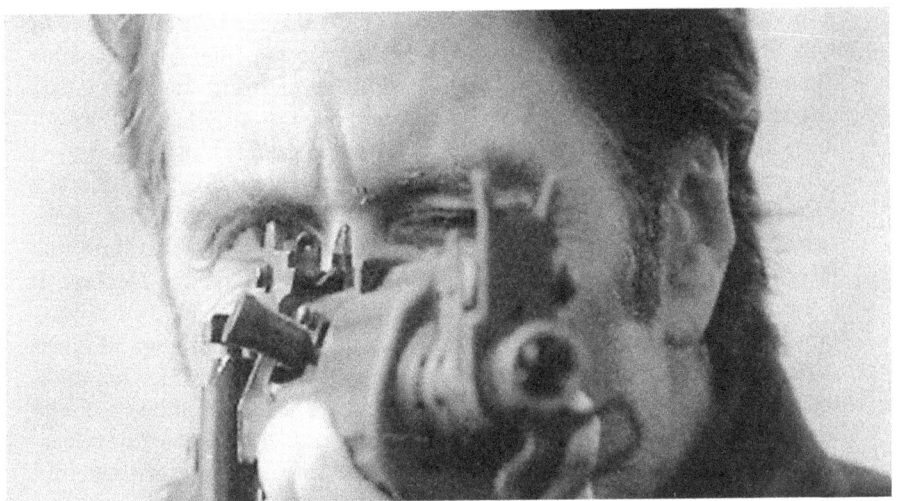

The hyperreality of violence in *Heat*. Just as Vincent Hanna (Al Pacino) touches off his assault rifle, a skip frame occurs, as if to call attention to the denaturing of space and time in the simulacrum.

timology of *Manhunter*, a parody of dialogically shared real time measured by the human heart, hyperreal time that comes with the destruction of space in the consumptive violence of the simulacrum. Precession of violence that feels like the destiny that destroys lives in classical tragedy, except it is not that. Vincent is right; there is no catharsis for there is no community to define the meaning of the pity and terror we feel for these people. It is exactly what Justine implied it was, a stark new ridiculous yet terrifying theater of the absurd.

And the violence spreads from this point like blood soaking into a carpet as more relationships are destroyed as a consequence of this gun battle and the deceptions that promoted the implosion of all these lives. Ex-convict Breedan, who drives the getaway car is killed, his picture flashed on the six o'clock news as his lover Lilly watches it all on a TV at a bar. He had told her that even though he hated his job, no one had invented the "Hard time" he couldn't handle and he would stick with the job for her sake. Now Lilly knows that he was probably deceiving himself as well as her. The relationship between Chris and Charlene has been on the rocks since the beginning: Charlene has seen Chris's gambling addiction as a sign that he (like his friend Cheritto) is just a "child grown older" incapable of handling responsibilities, only playing at being a father to Dominick and a husband to her. He receives a head wound in the battle, and one of Vincent's men, Sgt. Drucker, uses her illicit affair with Marciano to trap her and use her as a weapon of deception against Chris. It is perhaps the most heart-breaking moment in the film: Charlene must choose either to betray her husband or betray her son. Previously all that has apparently mattered to her is money—even Neil used it to get her to stay with Chris until the heist could be finished—but she makes a remarkable decision. When she sees Chris, she makes a secret sign with her hand that signifies that he must go. It is the one time that deception is used purely to benefit someone other than the deceiver. It is the noblest gesture of sacrifice in the film because it allows her husband and her son to stay out of detention. And yet it dooms her and Chris to never see each other again and ensures that her child, like Justine's, will be without a father. Certainly neither she nor the child has any visible means of support. The system that they and all of these other characters live in ensures that the attempt at symbolic exchange and sacrifice will do almost as much harm as it does good.

Everything collapses and implodes in the end. Without any ties to loves, home, or family, all that Neil and Vincent are left with in the end is the grim, meaningless, and terrible duty of destroying each other. Shedding his disguise as a hotel security man after killing Waingro, Neil leaves Eady at the hotel without saying a word to her in the chaos he has created there with his false fire alarm. The obsessive Hanna, of course, manages to pick Neil out of the implosive mayhem and they fight it out at the airport, the perfect environment for these men to consummate their pact of mutual destruction. It should have been the place where Neil would escape; all he had to do was commit himself to Eady and it would have been over. But his commitment to his dead and dying comrades is every bit as great as his commitments in his private world, so now the airport becomes a place to finish the job that constitutes his life and his destruction.

It is a bizarre, denatured, and dehumanized environment: a trackless heath filled with all of the deafening noise that modern technology can conspire to create as each plane takes off or lands, a place where you cannot hear your opponent until it is too late. Equally bizarre are the airport lights: they come up, increasing in intensity as the planes come in to land. Everything here, in short, exists for the machines; human beings have no *place* here, there is no *space* for them. A fit simulacrum for the world that these two men have always struggled with: microcosm of a simulacrum made to serve the dead machinery of the culture itself, a place where men who are already dead fight to the last. And it is the lighting that betrays Neil in the end, even as he tries to pull off one last decep-

7. The Decay of Dialogue

tion, hiding where he thinks Vincent cannot see him or hear him. Then the lights come up, defining Vincent in the darkness, and Neil thinks it is the moment to make his move—the light and the roar of the engines will efface him from view, he can destroy his opponent, save himself, escape.

But the opposite happens. The lights throw Neil's shadow on the ground and Vincent spots it peripherally, animation of the shadow partly from Neil's own movement and partly from the lights moving to meet the incoming aircraft, their intended target. But, indirectly, they cast this shadow, this phantasmal self (see Thoret, 9) on the ground, deception betraying deception, and that is enough for Vincent who turns, fires, and kills, not with a single shot, but with five, the last hitting Neil in the chest and releasing the violent implosive power of Neil's aorta to count off, in real time, the last seconds of his life.

Dying, Neil says, "Told you I'm never goin' back" to prison, reiterating the commitment he made when they met and shared their dreams. It is the one pledge he could keep, his one moment of uncompromising honesty, though it is not the way that he wanted it, and it is a betrayal of his dream, of his life. It is also the moment where Mann demonstrates once and for all the sheer soulessness and madness of the culture Neil once inhabited. The place Vincent and Neil share in these last seconds is what we would expect: a disrupted, deconstructed space in the simulacrum where Mann's cinematic style, aurally and visually, shows how human life and meaning die as they are swept into the black hole of the cultural vortex. We see Vincent in closeup on the right, then cut to Neil looking to the left side of the screen, appearing not to see Hanna, until we realize that he is in the shot with Neil and on the left hand side of the screen. Then Neil's outstretched hand and Vincent moving from the left hand side to the right hand side, and grasping the hand as Neil dies. Closeup on a shattered Vincent Hannah who cannot even look at this man as he dies when we cut to Neil and his head sags on his chest. No more speech, no contact through physical, dialogical exchange, only the contact of a living hand with a dead hand, the hand of the only human being Vincent came close to sharing real time with. Cut to a long shot of them holding hands; diagonal created by airport lights on Neil's side; lights parallel to the ground and the horizon on Vincent's side. Light disclosing a space of utter discontinuity, light that no longer seems physical, light that does not help create context; it was a shadow that betrayed them both, that thing that makes our substantiality apparent, or transapparent, and therefore not really substantial at all. Moby's musical theme, "God Moving Over the Face of the Waters," booms in the background as these men are frozen in time together, time they cannot share in this moment of mutual nihilism, of anticreation in the simulacrum that Mann exposes and vilifies here. And where *is* God in this? Where is humanity? Where is nature?

The screen goes black. They are nowhere to be seen.

8

Reviewing the Dialogue: Information as Commodity in *The Insider* (1999)

You go public and thirty million people hear what you have to say, nothing, and I mean nothing, will ever be the same again.
                                                            Lowell Bergman

    Heat teaches us that in a society where boundaries and reality space no longer persist, duplicity and concealment are the norm: *The Insider* emphasizes the flip side of the paradox that links these two films. In such a society, secrets cannot be kept despite efforts at control. Because of that, those in power absurdly extend the zone of the control revolution to information itself and use law to turn information into a commodity, disembodied bits of information in the digitalized matrix of capitalism that are used to silence any voices of resistance. The result is global terrorism: journalist and AK-47 wielding fanatic are the same. As Baudrillard (1997) has said, "the media make themselves into the vehicle of the moral condemnation of terrorism, ... but simultaneously..., they propagate the charm of the terrorist act, they themselves are terrorists" (84). Mann shows us that the media, the terrorists, and big business constitute an information network that simultaneously conceals and reveals information as a means of manipulating the public with serialized information made more potent by various forms of impact boosting that enhance their potential to use fear as a means to acquire absolute control. In their path he places two protagonists, Lowell Bergman (Al Pacino) and Jeffrey Wigand (Russell Crowe), who, by constituting among themselves a speech community of symbolic exchange, help show why this network constitutes an illusion of control. They also reveal why it is that once the sacred contract of oral symbolic exchange is broken it cannot be repaired. The result of the irreparable damage to free information exchange is a world without shared value, where global chaos, lawlessness, and terrorism are the norm.

The film's first two scenes enable Mann to contrast two different forms of information exchange in this posthuman milieu. Both Lowell Bergman and Jeffrey Wigand are caught between two worlds representing different forms of exchange. On the one hand, they are men of honor who want to see themselves as people whose word is their bond because they deliver what they promise without self-regard. On the other hand, they are men who are part of global organizations whose power is based mainly on another form of exchange—the purely economic kind, where the emphasis is on maximizing profit without loss or personal sacrifice. Both men think that both systems can operate according to a single system of obligation and honor, based on common assumptions of the worth of the individual's integrity. Both are wrong, and the first signs of this appear in the opening scenes.

The first shot, as in the case of *Manhunter*, is deliberately bizarre and disorienting, meant to take us into a world where our normal assumptions and perceptions are interrogated. This is a way of introducing us to the world of the protagonists—it turns out that this is a point of view shot of a blindfold worn by Lowell Bergman, a producer for the CBS program *60 Minutes* as he is taken to meet the head of Hesbolah—but it also works as a metaphor. Without the benefit of other shots to contextualize the image (shots which come later), we are confronted by the bizarre image of a network of intersecting lines that transverse the screen parallel to the edges of the top and bottom of the screen, except on the right hand side where they evince curvature and move out of focus. The screen confronts us with a paradox: this image seems purely abstract yet the shading and curvature point to something with extension in contact with the physical world. We hear pounding drums and a motor vehicle on the soundtrack, and the image seems to tremble in consonance with the rhythms of the drum and the car motor, as if it were simultaneously reflexive of the film as a construct and as a reference to the exterior world. Via this image, like Bergman, we have not been deprived of the power of sight, or the awareness of a referent, but we are not seeing the exterior world as an objective referent either. Our perceptions are being completely controlled. Subsequently, we will realize that this metaphor points self-reflexively to the ways in which perceptions can be controlled by various media networks in such a way as to control how human beings

8. Reviewing the Dialogue

engage and exchange information with the world they live in. In short, the medium is not only the message, it is perception, and in the world of *The Insider* perception becomes reality.

Cut to the exterior world, and as was the case in *Heat*, it turns out that there is not much difference between the inside and the outside after all. It is a world of coercion, the naked exercise of power and aggression, rule by force. We see Bergman's entire head is covered with wrappings; we see the bumper of the car as a convoy pushes along; we see one man with a .50 caliber machine gun and another with an AK-47 aboard the escort truck. And then the first shot of a city in the Middle East, a view dominated by the image posted beneath a statue of a man on a horse, the image of the Sheik who runs Hesbolah; then even more startlingly, a road bordered by seemingly endless images of an Ayatollah, serially replicated, as if to boost the impact of the Sheik's iconography in a landscape of signs that assault the mind and senses, a landscape of adults and children living in poverty, in fear. We share this landscape with Bergman in a strange way—we see and hear it while he only hears it, and we perhaps wonder if he imagines anything like what we can see. In either case, all of us see only what we are meant to see—our perceptions are being controlled by networks that work the same whether they are the

Impact boosting: serial replication of the religious leader's image is combined with the vanishing point effect to underscore the capacity of visual information to undermine the individual's agency in the opening sequence of *The Insider*.

fabric of a blindfold or the patterns created by the information systems that dot this landscape.

This is Bergman's situation: he perceives everything through a gridlike network that has been forced on him. Yet, paradoxically, when he speaks with the Sheik, we learn that he does not perceive himself as an object of coercion and manipulation. He speaks as an agent perceiving himself as a subject possessing free will, freedom of choice, and integrity. When the Sheik asks a question geared to kill the dialogue, one of those rhetorical questions that is clearly antirhetorical, namely, why should he agree to speak to the "pro–Zionist American media," Bergman makes a deft and unexpected rhetorical maneuver. Instead of going on the defensive and playing into the Sheik's aggressive stance with its seemingly unquestionable warrant, Bergman brings up the issue of *face*. He eliminates the seemingly radical stance of Hesbolah by announcing a common rhetorical ground: Hesbolah is becoming a party, they are seeking to become politicized in a respectable way. And, Bergman says, "At this time in America, Hesbolah does not have a face." He challenges the Sheik with the idea of face as sign of honor, sign of integrity, probably knowing full well that the Sheik will respond by questioning Bergman's and *60 Minutes'* face by asking to see the questions ahead of time as a proof of objectivity and journalistic integrity. Bergman does this because of his confidence in his own face and that of the colleagues he works with, and thus counters: "No, we don't do that. You've seen *60 Minutes* and Mike Wallace; you know our reputation for objectivity and integrity. We are the highest rated, most respected TV magazine news show in America." In other words, the Sheik can either have faith in the integrity of Bergman and his colleagues, or lose any chance of establishing a face in America via the integrity of Bergman and Wallace. This is how oral rhetoric works: show the common ground, the mutual advantage of exchange, and let the party choose freely what is best for them. Not surprisingly, the Sheik accepts, confirming the initial impression that Bergman and the people at *60 Minutes* have integrity, that they involve themselves in an honorable exchange of information that seems somehow apart from the kind of informatics that Mann has indicted elsewhere.

But there are elements in the scene that suggest that there is more to all of this than meets the eye, especially coming on the heels of that bizarre opening sequence. The blindfold covers all of Bergman's face; we cannot see the face of the man making this deal based on face any more than he can see the face of the Sheik who simply disappears before Bergman can take off the blindfold. And there is another disturbing moment. After Bergman offers the deal to the Sheik, he says, "So—Mr.

8. Reviewing the Dialogue

Wallace," in a tone of voice as if he were addressing Wallace *in person*, when he really means to ask the Sheik if he should ask Wallace to get on a plane. The bottom line is that this man of journalistic integrity is in a world where the orientation necessary for determining rhetorical groundings and honorable verbal exchanges just does not exist. He is being manipulated and he can't be sure who or what he is talking about. And this becomes even more apparent as the plot unwinds.

We meet Jeff Wigand under similarly intriguing circumstances. When we first see Wigand, it is in the shadow world of his place of employment where everyone in the background seems to watch his every move as he prepares to leave the building that houses the tobacco company Brown and Williamson. We do not yet know that his position has been terminated, that he is in a period of transition, but each visual element here conspires to depict his world as being every bit as confounded as Bergman's. When he is on the elevator, the camera incredibly puts us inside the right lens of his eyeglasses, establishing his point of view without subjectivity; as in the case of Bergman's blindfold we are simultaneously inside and outside his world where the lens implies that we are in a world that is simultaneously transparent and opaque. The drive to his home where we view the neighborhood through the lens of his windshield further establishes the link between him and Bergman: they are in an oppressive world where the tight shots and astonishingly intimate proxemics that defy physical boundaries create an atmosphere of fear and paranoia.

When Wigand arrives home, as in the case of Bergman, we see the flip side—Wigand as man of honor and integrity, Wigand as man with faith in the power of the spoken word. He greets his little girl, compliments her for getting a gold star in reading, and gently persuades her not to watch cartoons on TV so early in the day. The opposite of Vincent and Justine in *Heat*, he seeks to stabilize the boundaries between public and private spaces by controlling the types of information that will influence his children. The degree of his dedication to the power of the word is further revealed in the next few moments when he saves his other daughter Debbie, who starts to succumb to what appears to be a potentially deadly asthma attack. Wigand does more than hook her up to the medical apparatus; he *talks* her through the process of regaining her capacity to breathe. His effectiveness here is astonishing; he explains to her why she feels the way she feels and what her body must do to combat the attack happening as a result of her body's boundary being invaded by the deadly dust on her sister's toy. Her lungs are like "branches," he says, and "when they close up you get an asthmatic attack." She must "slow down, honey, breathe deep, breathe deep." If she does as he says, "You get better—you're better already, aren't you?" And indeed she is, as they work in concert together.

Later in the film, Wigand explains to a room full of high school students that he is attracted to science because it is "magical"—but in this initial scene we see the first instance of his association with magic as something connecting with the power of the word, with speech, with healing, with dialogical rhetoric. As Carolyn Ericksen Hill (1990) said, summarizing the work of Daniel O'Keefe and John Ward in the area of rhetoric and magic, both rhetoric and magic are "forms of social action that achieve their effects primarily through words" (143). Paraphrasing O'Keefe, Hill asserted that because the human cognitive frame is itself a social construct, "the practice of magic is simply an acknowledgement that through ... words ... that embody concepts and images, that construction can be altered" (144). Hence, she says, quoting O'Keefe, "'the quality of the words passes into the objective'" (144). This happens by virtue of the fact that the person who speaks the words is who that person says he or she is (145). The result is a "boundary-breaking practice" where "the bodily effect of words" can change the physical reality of embodied subjects (145).

But all magicians—be they witch doctors, trepanners, or faith healers—are still partly dependent on tools, and hence technologies of some kind; and here is the source of Wigand's dilemma, one that allows Mann to revisit a problem he highlighted in *Thief*: the difficulty involved when an artisan or a maker of magic depends on the system for his tools, for his livelihood. In the next scene Wigand tells his wife that he has been fired, and her first concern is for their financial security, the children's medical coverage. He says the severance package has them covered. He is not deeply concerned because with *60 Minutes* he believes he is dealing with men who will stand by his confidentiality agreement with Brown and Williamson. Like Frank in *Thief*, he naively believes he can work with the system, as if the system shared his values. Mann's point, once again, is that human integrity is not commensurate with the rampant materialism of the simulacrum. This he demonstrates by showing that Wigand's dialogical magic is dependent, like Bergman's, on a larger economic system that in truth does not mirror the system he has established at home where he takes care of his dependents with powers ensured by verbal bonds and selfless exchanges of information and care. He will face the unpleasant reality that Brown and Williamson is a shallow simulacrum of all that. They use information to control through coercion and various forms of addiction that reduce human beings to disembodied

8. Reviewing the Dialogue

information that can be manipulated without considerations of choice or free will. Their breaching of boundaries is not like Wigand's. It is not about sharing information or sustaining life. It is about perpetuating fear and using chemically induced addiction and death as a means to absolute control of an unsuspecting population. Mann here, and throughout the film, demonstrates that this control ultimately is acquired by reducing human beings to information and information to a commodity that can be owned and manipulated by big business with impunity.

Wigand's first meeting with his boss Sandefur and his corporate henchmen presents Mann with the first opportunity to make this case and to illustrate how Wigand's world and his perceptions of his role in it will, like Bergman's, fall apart because they are based on naïve perceptions of how the corporate system works. This meeting takes place after Wigand's first encounter with Bergman, and Wigand establishes the presence we would expect based on his earlier scenes, when he says, "I signed a confidentiality agreement. I honor agreements." His former employers do recognize this and attempt, as Sandefur says, "to expand our zone of comfort with" Wigand by trying to force him to sign a supplement to the agreement that he already honors. Mann seizes the opportunity to link the corporation to the hyperreal when Sandefur evokes the simulacrum of the family to justify this paranoid gesture, saying that the work Wigand and the rest did at Brown and Williamson was not meant for "public scrutiny any more than one's family matters." Sandefur's simulation of a rhetorical analogy is clearly flawed; he has invoked no exchange between himself and Wigand that would substantiate such a comparison. There is no bond of trust here as there is between Wigand and his children; quite the contrary, Sandefur has already implied that Wigand is not trustworthy: "Jeffrey," he says, "says exactly what is on his mind," which clearly implies that Sandefur cannot trust him unless he can coerce him. Wigand reacts with paranoia to match his boss's: "You're threatening my family now, too?" Then later, "Now you question my integrity." Sandefur does not recognize Wigand's assumptions about how verbal exchanges are to take place; he believes that only coercion can ensure security of his boundaries. Ironically, coercion leads to the negation of boundaries and will ensure that Wigand will resist his being reduced to object status and hit them with everything he has, eventually. In short, the more Sandefur asserts his coercive tactics, the less power he will really secure over Jeff. He is creating a kind of antirhetorical exchange where there can be no boundaries, no security, no trust. Power is indeed, as Baudrillard always said, a delusion.

But, delusion or not, it has a very palpable impact on the lives of

Bergman and Wigand who grow closer and attempt to devise strategies of resistance after Bergman convinces Wigand that he did not betray him. A process begins whereby these two men begin to win each other's trust because of their shared assumptions about the nature of exchange and the function of language, combined with their shared need to deal with an exigency that grows more complex and more threatening as Big Tobacco and their allies devise new and terrifying means to combat the two men's crusade against these coercive forces. The plan, essentially, is to force the world, despite its coercive tendencies, to recognize the integrity of their shared values, to expand the honorable exchange of information for public well-being to the global scale. Mann's sad task is to show why, in a world such as the one we live in, such a plan cannot really succeed, despite the genuine efforts of individuals like these to restore the integrity of the oral exchange that the corporate world of the tobacco companies is so eager to destroy.

The bond between these men begins with Bergman asserting his presence as an interlocutor when he denies Jeff's charges that he gave him up to his bosses. Although what he says does not seem calculated, it seems to work on Wigand mainly because it represents Bergman in a way that would appeal to Wigand's conflicted soul. Wigand is himself a paradox: he is a rational man of science but he is also a deeply emotional man given to fits of anger and unpremeditated outbursts of honest self-expression. Bergman establishes a similar presence with a degree of spontaneity that suggests that this cannot be a simulation. Despite his own anger, Bergman's language appeals to his audience on the basis of both logic and emotion. First, it is illogical for Wigand to accuse him of ratting him out because, as Bergman argues, he can't screw people who provide him with information "*before* they provided it." Second, he makes it apparent that he too is upset over this violation of trust, a concept that is essential to both men's value systems. This is evident even as Bergman's anger and frustration spill out: "Story, no story, fuck your story. I don't burn people." The gesture reveals Bergman's lack of selfish attachment and disregard for consequences—like Wigand, he sees himself and presents himself as a man for whom principle comes first, self second. Wigand, after consideration, invites him into the private space of the car he shares with his daughter whom he is driving to school. These men are beginning to share time and space together, a private place constituted by a common concern for integrity and honesty. Hence Mann characterizes them as fit agents for the symbolic exchange that will fail mainly due to the system they live in, not because of any lack of effort or sincerity on their part.

8. Reviewing the Dialogue

Wigand now reveals his private values and his concern that perhaps he has placed himself in a condition where he is now forced to violate them. He professes his admiration for the Tylenol CEO who, after his products were poisoned, pulled them off the shelf before the government ordered him to do so. Why? Because this CEO is not only "a great businessman, but he's also a man of science," who is not going to hurt people like the seven CEOs of Big Tobacco. This is Wigand's core value: balancing acquisitive economics and profit with a humane system of exchange that protects people on the basis of selfless humanitarian grounds. Bergman, however, immediately senses the conflict here and asks why Jeff forsook a culture where research is a "core value" for Big Tobacco that is a "sales culture." His answer: to make his family secure and because "mostly I got paid a lot." Bergman sees immediately that these two things do not mix: "Then you're in a state of conflict, Jeff." He must either honor the agreement or not. There is only "one guy" that can decide "and that's you." As in the first scene with the Sheik, Bergman is introducing the value of choice. No one can make the decision for him—he must make up his own mind. Choose one culture or the other. You can't have both. The one culture literally and figuratively poisons the other.

Mann is intent on showing here, however, that Bergman can establish this rapport because he too is a conflicted individual who, like an earlier version of Wigand, does not yet fully recognize how his efforts are being compromised by the system within which his human agency is embedded. The next scene illustrates this as he suggests to his *60 Minutes* team that perhaps the real solution to Wigand's problem would be a form of coercion. In the first of two unsettling allusions in the film to the hyperreal fictive worlds of Lewis Carroll, Bergman suggests that they "look through the looking glass the other way." What if Wigand were "compelled to talk?" Mike Wallace's (Christopher Plummer) sardonic reply oddly portends the shape of things to come in the film: "*Torture!* Great ratings." Bergman is not deterred: wouldn't it work if he were compelled by a state court or the Justice Department to testify? His team suggests that they would need to line up some powerful legal counsel first. But what does it mean that they are doing this? Wigand hasn't agreed to testify. And just how do you compel a man to testify and protect him from coercion at the same time? It is the kind of paradox that Lewis Carroll might have delighted in—but it also suggests that already some of the boundaries that Bergman spoke to regarding value systems inside and outside corporate America are becoming very indistinct. As one Mann protagonist after another has learned in his previous films, it is difficult to borrow weapons from one's enemies without being influenced by their ethically bankrupt value systems as well.

Ensuing scenes show how Wigand and Bergman bond more deeply, and how they and the legal team from Mississippi try (with occasional success) to stabilize the boundaries between the world of acquisitive profit and honorable exchange in their fight against the system. By the same token, as the bonds deepen, Wigand's paranoia begins to reflect doubt not only of the system but of himself and Bergman as well, doubt that shows his awareness of Bergman's own conflicted nature. It is a constant struggle for Wigand to trust Bergman; aware as he is of the capacity for the corporate mindset to influence his own behavior, he keeps questioning Bergman's honor. Wigand, a man who had once lived in Japan, spoke and taught Japanese, takes Bergman to a Japanese restaurant in a setting that is ironically appropriate for testing loyalty to duty, willingness to commit to self-sacrifice, given what is associated with that culture. Wigand's paranoia comes to the fore as he announces his fear to Bergman: "I'm just a commodity to you, aren't I?" "To a network," says Bergman, we all are, but to "me you're important." The editing in the scene is fascinating; Mann cuts back and forth between side views of the two men at table, creating the effect that they are literally changing places on the screen. They are indeed: Wigand's paranoia causes him to project on Bergman as he says, "Maybe that's just what you've been telling yourself all these years to justify having a good job." Later, in time, as the two men grow closer, these words will come back to haunt Bergman as he begins to question his relationship with the system. Mann uses their conflicted natures to illustrate just what kind of sacrifice is involved to battle the system that makes terrific claims on human freedom of thought and action. Wigand temporarily lacks a rhetorical ground for a commitment to this plan, but as time passes, his relationship with the legal team and the passage of other events in his life eventually promote a conviction that resistance is right, and the audience may share in this experience. Mann clearly wants us to be able to understand what is attractive about resistance and in what ways it may even be effective. He insists that what he argued in *The Jericho Mile* is true: resistance is still feasible at the local level when exchanges can be oral, immediate in a physical space shared by the interlocutors.

Mann makes this case as he shows the impact of Wigand's testimony on groups of individuals who are literally within earshot of him. Wigand finally speaks his piece in his taped interview with Wallace before giving his deposition in Mississippi. This time it is *his* words that move Bergman and his colleagues as they learn the nature of the modern evil that they

8. Reviewing the Dialogue

are combating. He describes the nature of "impact boosting," the use of chemicals to enhance the effect of nicotine without increasing the actual amount of nicotine in the cigarettes. As he tells Wallace, despite the denials of the seven CEOs from Big Tobacco that nicotine is addictive, the bottom line is that Big Tobacco is "in the nicotine delivery business." Wallace makes the connection Wigand wants him to make: you light up and "you get your fix." These people, in short, are narcotics dealers, and something worse. They conceal what they are and what they do (by not manipulating the level of nicotine overtly) and they also do so while taking risks that they will increase the risk of the lethality of the cigarettes. The ugliness of the corporate acquisitiveness and will to power emerges in Wigand's spoken words as he reveals that even though he charged them with ignoring health concerns, his gestures were considered irrelevant because they would "affect sales." He is released by Brown and Williamson, ironically, because of his "poor communication skills." The people on the set are stunned by the power of his words.

Mann thus makes resistance seem even more imperative after this dialogue with Wallace. He wants us to side with these men as he involves us dialogically in their first localized attempts to set the record straight. He is demonstrating how Big Tobacco has topped the Nazis in *The Keep* and the mad European imperialists of *The Last of the Mohicans*. They have devised a chemical means to introduce information to the body, in the form of an imperative (read addictive) biochemical command that makes a human being incapable of exercising free will, once they have entered the pact with the agency that would rob them of their freedom. Not surprisingly, therefore, Wigand's commitment to battle this monstrosity deepens as he is introduced to another group of individuals who wield words with power: the Mississippi lawyers who have been battling these companies unsuccessfully for years because they have had no insider information. We see this team first flying their own Lear jet en route to their next trial when Lowell Bergman calls them and asks them to call him back when they can on a land line. Without hesitation they do so—landing the plane immediately, talking to this man they do not know, and only returning to their plane after they have concluded the conversation.

Clearly these are extraordinary, committed professionals, and it is a combination of commitment and compassion that makes them strong allies for Wigand, whose cause is as much now about integrity and principle as it is about saving his family before the corporation can finish robbing him of it. Mann introduces them now as allies to the cause who will show us how the local battle against this corruption can succeed. The audience's confidence in them is won in the process whereby they win Wigand's support and show their commitment to using a humanitarian rhetoric to establish justice. Wigand shows suspicion toward these men when one of them has to leave their first meeting early, staring after him with the same hurt and paranoid expression he wore with Bergman. But Scruggs, the head of the team, shows amazing sensitivity in his attempts to secure the trust of Wigand, whose attention he finally wins by expressing his concern for Wigand and his family. Wigand listens intently as Scruggs discusses the ways this could limit his family whose future is being "held hostage" by these corporate terrorists. The bond is being made secure as Scruggs, a former combat pilot of A-6 attack aircraft says, "I do know how this is," and by implication honestly reveals that the hard fact of the matter is that even if his team will provide air support, ultimately it is Wigand who must win the battle on his own.

The ensuing scenes in which Wigand does decide to testify and his legal council defends his right to testify illustrate persuasively that resistance is feasible at least on the local level. Certainly they help explain why resistance seems to be the right course and why it is perhaps at its best at this moment in the film, despite the darker aspect of the long-term battle that emerges later on.

It is one of the most stirring sequences in the film. Wigand, in the company of many security people, Bergman, Scruggs, and others, stands before a vast empty body of water. The Mississippi? The Gulf? It might just as well be some primordial ocean it is so intimidating in its vastness, correlative of the great void, the terrible powers that threaten to destroy him. He is open and honest with Bergman. "I don't know what to do," he says, with so much at risk. And worse still, there seem to be no definable grounds for exercising choice, for knowing whether he should testify or not: "Can't seem to find the criteria to decide. Too big a decision to make without being resolved in my mind." Bergman, who has orchestrated this legal coercion to allow Wigand to speak, laudably contains himself and emphasizes again that it must be Wigand who chooses. "Maybe," says Bergman, "things have changed." The banjo music that played when the FBI invaded Wigand's home earlier is cued up on the film's soundtrack, and he says, "A lot has changed," as he looks out to the border between water and land. Bergman replies: "You mean since this morning." "No," says Wigand, "I mean since whenever." Then, completely without warning, Wigand says, "Fuck it, let's go to court." There is something ultimately unfathomable about the man, some elusive deepening human integrity that Mann insists must be at the heart of such moments of defiance. Scruggs announces Wigand's decision to every-

8. Reviewing the Dialogue

Searching for the right words near the edge of a void. Lowell Bergman (Al Pacino, left) awaits a decision from Jeffrey Wigand (Russell Crowe, right) in *The Insider*.

one, the security teams scrambles for their cars, and at the behest of one man's spoken word this war with the system is on.

As they drive to court, one still cannot help asking: *Why* is he doing this? He said it himself; there don't seem to be any logical criteria. But that is what Wigand is all about, perhaps what all of Mann's protagonists are about. Nothing about this man is predictable, nothing can reconcile the basic paradox of such a man, and this it probably why Mann is bringing him, and others like him, to our attention. He is the perfect protagonist for such circumstances. The descendants of Magua and Munro still seek control and hope to revive the deterministic paradigm, despite the fact that human beings like Wigand (not to mention Chingachgook and Nathaniel) exemplify how all of this runs counter to the sheer complexity of human beings who invariably resist absolute and dehumanizing types of control. And on a fundamental human level, while the particular reasons for Wigand doing this now aren't entirely clear, it does make perfectly good sense that he does this now. What, after all, is the alternative? His family will be in danger no matter what he does, as will his integrity. He faces the coercion of terror no matter what he does. If flight cannot bring security then why not fight? It is the one thing the control junkies never consider.

This particular fight is especially exciting because the legal team turns out to be every bit as honorable and determined as their rhetoric would indicate. Motley (Bruce McGill), the member of the team who will take Wigand's testimony, explains to him above board the game plan: speak your piece before another court, besides the one in his home state of Kentucky, can issue another restraining order. But, predictably, one of the lawyers from Big Tobacco is there and interrupts Wigand repeatedly with objections. Motley patiently replies that they've heard the objections, that the court recorder has already entered it in the record. But when Wigand proceeds again, the tobacco lawyer tries to cut him off and take control of the discourse, saying, "I'm instructing you not to answer that question. That means *you don't talk.*" And then, as if it is not enough for him to extend his zone of control over Wigand, the lawyer says, "Mr. Motley, we have rights here."

Motley, clearly annoyed by the outburst, nevertheless maintains his composure and deftly replies by shifting the question from this abstract conception of rights—which for the tobacco lawyer is clearly nothing more than a means to justify monological coercion—to the more pertinent issue of how Wigand's local, individual rights are what are really at stake here. He uses tropes of place here to parody and expose the extreme and dehumanizing political leanings of his globalizing totalitarian opponent: "You've got rights. And *lefts*. Ups and downs and middles. *So what?* You don't get to instruct *anybody* around here. This is not North Carolina, South Carolina, nor Kentucky. This is the sovereign state of Mississippi's proceeding."

Motley's move here is one away from disembodied abstraction and globalization to the local; it is the old argument that Southerners used to fight (under less laudable circumstances) the nationalist aggression of the North in the war between the states, ingeniously remodeled here to defend the right of the individual as having the same substantiality as the right of states to govern themselves, a right that federal and state courts still sanction locally and globally. The tobacco lawyer smiles in contempt of this maneuver, and Motley explodes in anger: "Wipe that *smirk* off your face! Dr. Wigand's deposition *will be part of this record.* I'm going to take my witness's testimony *whether the hell you like it or not!*" Everyone in the courtroom is shocked into silence. A thorough professional, even in his moment of moral outrage, Motley turns from his opponent, looks at Wigand and calmly says, "Answer the question, doctor."

It is a rhetorical tour de force, Motley using the sheer physical power of his voice when all else has failed, and he has lived up to his word. The team has scored a victory at the local level—Wigand speaks and reveals

8. Reviewing the Dialogue

the full terror of what impact boosting does: it allows nicotine to cross "the blood-brain barrier intact." Wigand is right, a lot has changed. What does it mean when the boundary between solid and liquid can be breached when it still exists even where water meets the shore? It means that even the mind is no longer a sanctuary, that everything is vulnerable to this new kind of assault. Oh yes, we've come a long way.

Spectacular as the victory is, it still offers dark portents of things to come. The only way to resist the force exerted against Wigand was through similarly coercive force, and it could succeed only in this limited space where, without a judge (representative of the global system) presiding, Motley could overpower his opponent through his presence. In the disembodied court of public opinion, itself a media creation, things become more difficult to manage. In short, everything at this point goes to hell. Mann must now show us that the media will destroy Wigand's message, and with it, any human sense of truth and justice.

The protagonists' lives and their efforts toward achieving justice disintegrate as they face the power of the global systems that resist them. Wigand's family is gone after he returns from the courtroom. Bergman, after editing a brilliant version of the interview, replete with images of the cigarettes being replicated as serial instruments of death, is told by CBS Corporate that if the piece airs, CBS could be sued with the result that Brown and Williamson could own CBS. Bergman is caught completely off guard—he has believed in the integrity of his business because it was based on the kind of truth spoken in the courtroom—but now he finds out that truth is no longer the distinguishing factor, the ally it once was, because information, truth itself, has been turned into a commodity. CBS Corporate lawyer Caparelli (Gina Gershon) tells him that the standards of the state of Mississippi for the truth are irrelevant in the world of CBS Corporate and federal law. Bergman retorts, "The standard I'll hang by is this guy telling the truth." But she presents the real logic that's in effect here: "The greater the truth, the greater the damage" to the tobacco companies. Bergman cannot believe his ears: "Come again?" Caparelli says, "They own the information he's disclosing. The truer it is, the greater the damage." Bergman's world is disintegrating before the hypermarket that consumes all things, the truth and meaning included. "Is this *Alice in Wonderland?*" he asks.

But it is he that initiated this trip to the other side of the looking glass, the cold indirect light of the simulacrum that reveals conflicts in him, just as it did for protagonists and antagonists alike in films like *Manhunter*. It is easy to lose oneself in there, easy to succumb to total isolation and delusion. Even though Bergman is able to demonstrate that, in truth, all of this is happening to secure the sale of CBS to Westinghouse, his allies desert him, including Mike Wallace. And Bergman too is vulnerable to the seductions of the system. When he learns that Wigand kept some truths about himself hidden, he becomes angry and hears himself making this amazing statement to Wigand on the phone: "It's not the fuckin' point whether you told the truth or not!" His own susceptibility to this smear campaign is clear here as the impact of the information is boosted, like the effects of nicotine, by the various spindoctors of the media. Mann underscores the power of this disinformation when Wigand rejects this man who is losing ground to the very forces they had fought together.

Things continue to deteriorate and both men spiral into isolation that denies them the shared territoriality that enables them initially to resist. Wigand checks into the hotel where he first met Bergman, and Bergman is forced to go on vacation, accompanied by his last remaining ally, his wife. After watching the Wigand segment, Bergman calls Jeffrey who has turned it off prematurely and seems to be losing touch with physical reality. Wigand sits before a huge mural that appears to date back to early nineteenth-century America, featuring spreading trees, winding country roads and, on one of them, near where Jeff is sitting, a cloaked figure on horseback madly galloping away from something unseen. The mural dissolves, and Wigand is sitting in his old back yard where he can see one of his little girls sitting on a tire swing. She moves laterally and joins the other daughter, the one he rescued earlier with the power of his voice. They stand beside the tomato plants we saw them planting in the yard in an earlier scene, a place denoting how they once shared time together, once made the past, present, and future come together, in free exchange with nature, with each other, because they shared what seemed to be a real private space. We see this past his head, we are inside and outside him, and it is like the effect of seeing the blindfold, this is something real and not real, filling our senses but not really a referent. Jeffrey has lost his territory and his subconscious is taking over as a substitute. We are watching him descend into psychosis induced by what Mann's visual style represents as the narcoticlike hallucinogenic power of the simulacrum Wigand and Bergman once fought together.

Surprisingly, Mann uses this moment to show that all is not lost, that some kind of resistance is still feasible. Bergman calls his hotel in a desperate attempt to work the magic of the voice, to make amends to Jeff, after telling Mike Wallace over the phone that the report was a disgrace. Wigand is so far gone that he cannot hear the phone. Bergman decides to use the modern equivalent of the trick that sometimes worked in *The*

8. Reviewing the Dialogue

Last of the Mohicans: translation. He persuades the hotel manager to help him save his friend. He makes the manager translate his words, even the tone, in a scene that shows Kittler (1999) may be right—audio technology does seem to reproduce reality differently from film and video (119), presence somehow is still there. Despite the reluctance of the manager to convey his anger, Bergman succeeds by making the manager equally angry by shouting into the phone exactly what he wants him to say to Jeff: "*Pick up the fucking phone!*" The translation works; the old angry Jeff is back, accusing Bergman of having "manipulated" him into this. Bergman works his last bit of sympathetic magic here, completely identifying with this man who is bruised by crossing so many boundaries, by violating some of his own principles, even as he tried to uphold them in the corporate world. They are both sick, they both need each other's help. Bergman, as no one else can, reminds Jeffrey of who he is: " I greased the rails for a guy who wanted to say yes.... You're not a robot Jeff. You got a mind of your own, don'tcha?" It is the one assumption that a man with a temper like Wigand's cannot desert—he did make choices freely. Bergman will not argue with Jeffrey in his depression, he will only give his honest assessment of a man whom he considers to be of inestimable value: "Jeffrey, where you goin' with this? You are *important*, Jeffrey. You think about that.... We're runnin' out of heroes, man. Guys like you are in short supply." Wigand is sobered by his words and returns the compliment as he returns to the exchange of language: "Guys like you are too." The bond of sympathy is secured when Wigand asks where Bergman is and he is told that he is on a forced vacation. They have both been deserted. His voice breaking, Wigand says, "You try to have a good time." Cut to a long shot of Bergman who has wandered far away from his beachside into the vast ocean, literally and figuratively out to sea as soon as the shared space and time created by the dialogue is over.

The magic has worked almost too well in some ways. Wigand is at least talking again, but now Bergman is tumbling into the abyss of depression. He too has been violated by the culture of impact boosting. In dialogue now with his wife, he questions his motives for being a newsman as Wigand once did:

> I'm Lowell Bergman from *60 Minutes*. You know, you take the *60 Minutes* out of that sentence and nobody returns your phone call. Maybe Wigand was right. Maybe I'm hooked. What am I hooked *on*? *60 Minutes*? What the hell *for*? Infotainment! Fucking useless.

Power, he is discovering, is addictive, no less than nicotine, especially when, like the carcinogenic drug, it is formulated as information.

It is itself a hallucinogen, not so different from what was being traded back in *The Jericho Mile*'s Folsom Prison. Mann brings the point home for Bergman and the audience. The illusion of control begets the illusion of security which cannot exist when control is exerted via these networks of information in such a way as to violate the sanctity of our humanity, our private space, our capacity to believe in (and therefore exercise) free choice. Whether you are a mule for Dr. D. or helping CBS boost its stocks, you are caught in the same absurd paradox that confronts the tobacco executives. The more you exert this kind of control, the less you have.

Bergman needs to see himself in this light in order to recognize where he has gone wrong, in order to disengage himself from the information enterprise cognitively in ways that help Mann explore alternatives. After renewed dialogue with his wife, he is able to get the "perspective" that she says he is lacking because he is not "listening" to her. Finally, though, she gets his attention by saying, "Really know what you're gonna do before you do it." She is right; he needs a game plan—but the distracted look on his face already seems to indicate that what he must do is something that will have unfortunate consequences.

He decides to betray this simulacrum of a profession by using its own methods against it, almost as if he were creating a parody of it. This is foreshadowed when he meets a couple during vacation at a mountain lodge and, after introducing himself as a producer at CBS, notes their disinterest in his revelation. At first this seems a sign of how low he and CBS have sunk in the court of public opinion, but that is not the case at all. He calls a friend, a federal investigator pursuing the Una Bomber, and informs him that he has just encountered two of his agents posing as geologists who do not have rough hands. Rather than risk having the operation ruined by Bergman, the friend promises to leak the information to Bergman regarding the bomber's location and arrest before the rest of the media can have it. Bergman agrees.

Mann accomplishes two things with this scene. First, he reiterates the comparison between the media and terrorists as mutually engaged in a symbiosis of destructive informatics. Second, he is able to show how Bergman is adopting a new stance for dealing with all of this. His identification of the agents shows his awareness of simulacra and the necessity of dealing with it in a different way. He once mingled coercion with rhetoric. Now he allows the system to coerce itself. He never said he would reveal information about the agents. He lets his colleague jump to that conclusion and give him what he wanted. But, of course, this is merely a more effective form of coercion, because it simply observes

8. Reviewing the Dialogue

what is true about the coercive community of informatics: it cannot conceal. What it is concealing is what Baudrillard (1997) said that Watergate concealed—namely, that there is nothing to conceal because there is no longer a difference between illusion and reality (14–15). There is no reality. There is only perception that comes from the manipulation of information. What is left is hyperreality, something that is more real than real. But that is a little like the slogan of the android designers in *Blade Runner*, later picked up by the rock group White Zombie: "More human than human." What is more human than human? Something that is not human. And what is more real than reality? Something that is not real at all.

Placed in such a world, Bergman implements a similar tactic with his friends in the newspaper business. He lets them draw all the conclusions, which they can do accurately because nothing about this can be concealed; the cat, as Bergman later says, is already *way* out of the bag. Precession rules here. Bergman merely answers with a no if they get something wrong. We never hear him say no.

It is simply a matter of getting out of the way and letting the whole perverted mess consume itself. Neither his bosses nor Mike Wallace ever fully understand all of this. Wallace gives a long speech on the value of posterity, of history, of time—and it is clear what is at stake here for him—that disembodied bit of information valued so much in the news business, image. He makes the right decision but he is clearly hooked on the videoscope as Bergman once was. The camera is a mirror—instant feedback on how wonderful we all are, and it will last forever. When Wallace sides with Bergman against the bosses, he is chided by his boss for worrying about something that will have a fifteen-minute shelf life. Seizing upon the Andy Warhol trope, Wallace says, "No, that's fame. Infamy lasts a little longer." But does it? Without this film to remind us of what happened here, we might not remember it at all. Time in the videoscope is not like the time shared in the physical space created by the presence of speakers. It is itself hyperreal, making us focus on the present moment because nothing else is left as the videoscope consumes space and physicality. Will anything be remembered in a world where the present consumes everything in the empty synchronous time of our posthuman imagined communities? Of course not, forgetting the past is what unites us all in this hallucinogenic state. The alternative, of course, is to live in the kind of time shared by Bergman and his wife, or Bergman and Wigand, where chance meetings can produce shared values. But how long can they last in the vacuum created by power? Fifteen minutes? Sixty?

Eventually the segment is aired, and Bergman's always trusting wife says to him, "You won." They are in their bedroom, trees outside visible beyond the network of windowpanes, and he replies, "Yeah. What'd I win?" The next day, CBS scoops everyone on the Una Bomber and a colleague congratulates him saying, "You know, we beat everybody." Bergman—who has showed no signs of happiness throughout the end of the film, not even when Wallace supported him, seems untouched by this. He seems to know what all of this adds up to now. He signals to Wallace that he needs to share a moment with him, and after they leave the newsroom he says, "What got broken here doesn't go back together." He must resign; he can't say to his next source, "Hang in, you'll be fine—maybe." Wallace is visibly saddened and can say nothing. What, after all is there to say? Bergman is right. You cannot repair a community based on trust, on selfless commitment, on symbolic exchange when it has been violated by something like this. Once the basis of such exchanges is violated—the concept of and belief in free choice—then there is no reversing the damage. He is right: to introduce an analogy that does not occur to him, it would be like apologizing for rape. Robbing the victim of free choice destroys the grounds for offering and accepting apology. Where there is no speech community, there is no society. There is only the hollow simulacrum of all that and its pandemic terrorism and implosive violence.

Bergman leaves Wallace, whose face is framed by multiple video monitors, serial reflections of the videoscopic industry. Wallace turns as he leaves and punches the security code that allows him to return to the inside of the newsroom, that translucent world that creates him as it uncreates him and everyone else. Mann seems to ask: Where else is there to go?

As if in answer, Bergman walks out the same kind of revolving door that we saw Wigand approaching in the film's beginning. He walks away from the camera; everyone in the street traverses the screen laterally. Fit image of a man who not only has no place but who, unlike all the others out there who are likewise directionless in the simulacrum, painfully knows it. And that is the paradox of all Mann's protagonists, the same one that bedevils Baudrillard and others who are aware of the posthuman condition. Is it better to know? Perhaps. But what does it accomplish? Via Bergman, Mann suggests one form of action—parody the parody. But that does not return to us a sense of dignity or integrity—or the capacity to trust. In a world of windup dolls, we alone know that we are not real. And here is the worst part of the paradox: knowing this makes us want to act, even though we must realize that any resistance

8. Reviewing the Dialogue

will fail ultimately to change the global aspect of the problem even if we do sometimes resist forcefully, effectively, on the local level. We cannot give up this idea that we live in a world of shared value; if it were not there, we could not perceive the absurdity and the evil of the simulacrum and the misguided evolution of the control revolution. What is one to do?

For Mann, in his next film, it is time to look again to the past.

9

A Blast from the Past: Being the People's Champion in *Ali* (2001)

Champ, the more real you get, the more unreal it's gonna get.
Ali quotes John Lennon to his fiancée
Sonji Roy on the topic of fame.

The more things change, the more they stay the same: we end as we began. Of all Mann's twentieth-century human protagonists, only two never study themselves from their reflected image in a window or a mirror: *The Jericho Mile*'s Rain Murphy and Muhammad Ali. Few artists would be so daring as Mann in suggesting that these two men have anything in common, but *Ali* clearly indicates that this is the case. It seems an incredible assertion: Ali was a media creation, was he not, a man who played the camera as deftly as he played opponents in the ring, someone who promoted, quite selfconsciously, a hyperreal image of himself— he was nothing like the self-sacrificing Murphy. But Mann's film shows that even in such a context as media-hyped professional boxing, one can still make sacrifices, still engage in meaningful symbolic exchanges. One can share time with others in that exchange and, even if it lasts only for a moment, one can indeed be, in the truest sense of the phrase, the People's Champion. However fleeting, such a moment of identification offers a deeper sense of selfhood and accomplishment than anything the media infected world of acquisitiveness and information control could ever offer.

Ali's long opening sequence sets up the film's thematic conflicts concerning information by presenting the basic conflicts in Ali's life, conflicts having to do with information and art, conflicts that we see influence him as a child growing up and as a grown man training in February 1964. The Columbia Pictures logo is on the screen and we hear voices, the crowd; cut to a black screen and a voice announces: "We'd like to introduce the star of our show, the young man you have all been waiting for." We might anticipate that it will be Ali, but then we hear, "How 'bout it for *Sam Cook?*" We cannot see him yet, but we can sense that he is interacting directly with the crowd as he asks them, "How are you doing out there?" Cut to Ali (Will Smith), jogging in 1964, a white sweatsuit hood covering his head, masking him, as he runs by walls covered with iconography, scales of justice, all perfectly balanced, all on a white background. Now back to Cook, brilliantly lit before an audience of adoring fans, who respond with roars of approbation as he asks more emphatically, "How are you *doing?*" The crowd repeats what he says: "Oh yeah!" Cut to Ali encountering policemen in a cruiser who zap him with the siren and ask him, "What are you running from son?" Cook continues singing and now he is saying, "Don't fight it" as we cut to Ali hitting the speed bag. Don't fight what, all that "good" feeling out there? Clearly Ali is preparing to fight someone, and we see who in the next flashback cut—Sonny Liston, who, after pummeling an opponent, turns to Ali and says, "Beat you ass like I was you daddy."

The opening montage isn't even close to finished, and already we have seen so many contrasts and conflicts in the informatics of Ali's world. Sam Cook engages via dialogue with an audience that responds as a massive group soul, a tribute to his music's origins in African-American churches where such responsorial dialogism is the norm for choirs and audiences, just as it is for preachers and laypeople. This is contrasted with the coercive monological question of the police who represent a purely coercive type of informatics. The thematic implications grow with these images—the scales of justice beg the question—where is justice in such a white world? Even a black man running with his identity concealed cannot hide from the racist authorities. Perhaps going it alone isn't the right thing—perhaps the group identity of the chorus is where he belongs. And yet, another black man, Sonny Liston, coerces him, using language like the white officers, condescending, treating Ali as if he were less than a man, challenging his right to any kind of selfhood. Oppressive language and iconography are everywhere you turn in Ali's world.

The next few shots further complicate this cultural scene. We see Ali as a child watching an artist (whom we later learn is his father) laying down white paint on a wall, overpowering the green and black ele-

9. A Blast from the Past

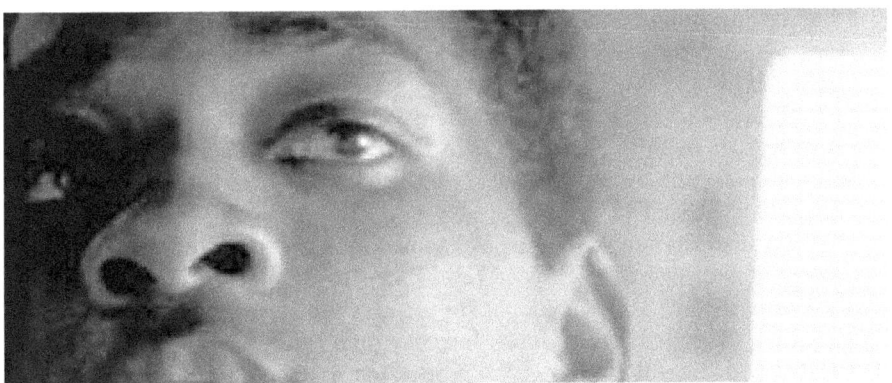

As the culture bombards him with conflicting and conflicted images of identity and community, Muhammad Ali (Will Smith) responds by pounding the speed bag to prepare for the Liston fight in the opening montage sequence of *Ali*.

ments we can just see in the background of the picture. Cut, and a long shot reveals that this is a picture of a blue-eyed, blond haired Jesus about to go beneath the water with his equally Caucasian associate John the Baptist. The child looks skeptically at the artist and at the scene from the side of his eyes. Cut back to Cook and his crew, where an immaculately coiffed African-American woman is standing up in front of an audience in a dazzlingly white gown. Cook sings, "Don't fight," and the image perhaps implies a connection as it implies a question—could these seemingly disparate types of discourse and iconography merely be different manifestations of a whitewash, both dialogue and image focusing on good times to the exclusion of other serious considerations? Could they be as oppressive, potentially, as the language of the white officers? The conflicting elements of the scene are being used to draw us into the world of the film; Mann is setting up a rhythm here that invokes a dialogical relationship between spectator and film. Conflicting images provide the opportunity for the audience to question the conflicted nature of Ali's world, his early postmodern culture.

The camera now follows the child Ali onto a segregated bus where white letters on a black background announce "Colored Only." As shots of the adult Ali pounding the bag interrupt, we see the youngster transfixed by a newspaper held by an old man on their side of the color line. The headlines shout: "Nation Shocked At Lynching of Chicago Youth." Closeup of the bandaged head of the victim; it is the shocking image of Emmett Till's face. The old man sees the child studying the frightening image and thrusts it toward his face, making him recoil in fear. Closeup now on Ali's adult eye, seemingly emotionless, as he pounds the speed bag. How can there be any good feelings in a world like this, where they can rob you of your identity in so many ways, where control is based on an informatics of terror that dehumanizes and desensitizes almost everyone on both sides of the color line, where it is everyone for himself or herself?

As if in answer, we cut now to Malcolm X (Mario Van Peebles) who offers an alternative—organized resistance—to a vocally responsive crowd of sympathizers. He casts doubt on the idea that good times will get better, that "We Shall Overcome," because "the times will never get better unless you *make* them better." There is the first hint here that Malcolm is proposing something even more radical than the other leaders of the Nation of Islam offer. He acknowledges Elijah Muhammad's belief in the law, but he adds "if anyone puts his hand on you, you see to it that they don't put their hand on anybody else." Ali listens intently; then cut to another apparently spiritual influence in his life, Drew "Bundini" Brown (Jamie Foxx), who became Ali's corner man, and who offers him what he gave Sugar Ray, "my Power, my Voodoo, my Magic." Here are the alternatives, seemingly, to the whitewash—resistance, empowerment through the spirit, through magic, identification with what will provide an alternative identity to the white man's version of what a black man should be. But as is so often the case in the world of Mann's protagonists, these alternatives are not as different as they seem. They hurtle toward each other with implosive force in ways that complicate Ali's attempts to find justice for himself and other African Americans, to establish an identity that will allow him to be the People's Champion. Resisting the simulacrum turns out to be as difficult for Ali as it is for all of Mann's protagonists. But there are alternatives to the system that Mann can present to us in all of their rhetorical force with the example of Ali's life as the plot unfurls.

The difficulties Ali will encounter in achieving the status he desires surface in his fight with Liston. The Cook song score continues, now changing to the words "Bring it on!" and Ali already seems to be engaging in a kind of superficial even hyperreal showmanship that belies the serious nature of the human being we see in various stages of his life in the opening. Entering the arena, he shouts, "Sonny Liston, you ain't no champ!" Where is the quiet determination of the Ali we see in the mosque, in training? Is this how you get respect, doing anything to get the crowd's attention? He is asked invasive questions about his religion and with his trainer Angelo Dundee's help, avoids direct answers. It makes

9. A Blast from the Past

sense, of course—who would not recognize the risk involved in revealing his character in this public arena? But who can make claims to being more of a real champion, much less the people's champion, when he is engaging in such chicanery, such evasion, such simulation? Liston, a bigger and stronger fighter, senses the falseness of all this bravado and cuts it off with a brutally honest comment: "Keep talking. I'm gonna fuck you up." It is the familiar arena for Mann's protagonists and antagonists, a place where one's real worth will be determined by one's capacity to live up to one's word, the word that constitutes face, presence, courage—the only tools for resisting the simulacrum on the local level. The time shared inside the ring with an opponent will determine Ali's worth as a real human being, not the theatrics outside the ring.

In the process of rising to this challenge, Ali seems to discover things about himself that neither he nor we could have known previously. In the ring, when time is passing, the crowd roaring, pretense briefly vanishes. Ali uses evasion when he can, but Liston keeps coming even after the bell rings. Ali mugs for the cameras on the break, but in the ring he is all business with an opponent who fills the field of view at times; the lights above the ring with their contrived geometry of diagonals seem to be on a separate plane of (un)reality from the two boxers who, in this heartfelt battle, become the only reality for boxer and spectator alike. The determination of Liston and his people seems without limits; at ringside Howard Cosell (Jon Voight) will "not prognosticate anything but his [Ali's] survival." Cosell's caution is vindicated; in the ensuing round Liston's people apparently put something on Liston's gloves (ammonia?) that temporarily blinds Ali. He survives the round purely by a combination of determination, timing, and intuition. There can be no real strategy or psych game in these moments—he either has the human courage to stay in that ring with such an automaton of destruction or he does not. He does; his eyes clear in the sixth round where he gives Liston such a pounding that Liston eventually spits out his mouthpiece in surrender. Here, in the ring, Ali seems to show that he is sometimes more than an entertainer and a poseur—here in this world that seems so real and so physical, surely the truth about oneself emerges. But the cameras have been clicking the whole time, and as Sam Cook joins him, Elijah Muhammad watches on television, already planning to exert his control over Ali's life with his powerful network of information and coercion.

Mann has intensified the thematic conflict even as he has shown Ali's victory by implying that, as in the case of so many Mann protagonists, the first round of battle leaves much to be done before one can offer any real resistance to the system. Ali's conflicted world is reflected in a conflicted identity that simultaneously makes him capable of resisting the system and susceptible to being destroyed by it. Who will win the battle for Ali's soul, Mann seems to ask; the hyperreal showman or the warrior?

Ensuing scenes reemphasize the importance of identity for Ali, the importance of asserting himself in such a way that he will not betray himself yet still allow him to be the "People's Champ" as he calls himself. Interviewed on the street while being followed by throngs of admirers, Ali is asked if he wants to be like Joe Lewis, and he says, "not exactly." Under the watchful eyes of some Muslims, he indicates, "I no longer want to be called by that slave name," Clay; he is Cassius X. Ali will be "the kind of champ I want to be," not the kind the media wants him to be. In another scene he makes fun of a show on TV about a mummy stalking victims—he sees himself as someone who can detect the unreal nature of media simulacra. He is above all that—he thinks.

Nevertheless, the next scene when he is visited by Malcolm X shows how difficult it is to be oneself whenever one seeks identity through identification with ideological systems, in this case the one professed by the Nation of Islam. In the intimacy of the moment, Ali pulls himself away from the TV as Malcolm initiates the dialogue by asking him, "You ever think you'd lose it? Really lose it?" Ali confesses that the lynching of Emmett Till in his childhood had that effect on him. Malcolm clearly needs someone he can open his heart to, someone before whom he does not need to censor his words, someone who can accept him for himself. He makes his angry confession:

> When I first heard about those little girls that got bombed in that Birmingham church, the prohibition of the Honorable Elijah Muhammad prevented me from speaking my thoughts and actions. Because Birmingham was part of the civil rights struggle, you know, begging for a place at the white man's table. But dead children are dead children. So the anger I felt I had to contain. I locked it up so tight my muscles seized. I lost control over the right side of my body. My leg gave out. Right arm gave out. "I'm having a stroke," I thought. But I had to hold it in because all I wanted, brother, all I wanted to do was find something and *break* it, break any part of the system because you are so provoked in your heart and your spirit as a human being at dead children. And I can do—nothing. Everyone knows, I can't do nothing anymore. So Elijah Muhammad has suspended me as a minister in the Nation of Islam.

This is perhaps the longest speech anyone delivers in a Mann film and it reveals much about this man's struggles. He has been prohibited

9. A Blast from the Past

from acting and speaking as his conscience bids him by someone with whom he thought he shared a common value system. He seeks desperately to find someone who does share those values—notice the switch from the pronoun "I" to "you" toward the end to the speech. Notice also his initial focus on himself and his struggle with Elijah and how he then switches his focus to how he is being seen in the eyes of his fellow Muslims. His crisis is not so much over who he is or what he believes but rather why it is that no one shares his values and how this denies him his sense of identity in his chosen community. How can he function like this? His utter rejection of the white man's system seems to speak to something more radical and more immediately human in him than he can articulate with the ideologies and types of discourses he has at his disposal. What is he to do? Without a community of believers who share in his values, he is paralyzed—for all intents and purposes he no longer exists, he is a phantasm. Even a man as genuine as Malcolm, Mann implies, can be swallowed up by the simulacrum when its codes are reiterated in the only seemingly radical rhetoric of the other Muslims. It is the terrible fact that Ali, like many other people in his time, does not want to face.

Not surprisingly, Ali cannot really enter the dialogue here and has no real advice, other than telling Malcolm to try to fix things when he returns from his trip to Africa. Ali is as naïve about his partnership with the Nation as Malcolm was previously, something later events will show when Ali is also excommunicated. Sadly, this initial naiveté will lead him into conflict with Malcolm and his own family as he becomes more deeply involved with an ideology that only *seems* to confirm and support his unfolding sense of an identity unlike that bestowed by the dominant social and cultural system. Elijah confers upon him a new name, Muhammad Ali, because he is "special." Ali's father is angry because he feels that it is the family that made Ali. Ali responds angrily, saying, "*I* made me," and defending Elijah as a better role model than his father: "He ain't drinkin', goin' back on his wife or prayin' to no blue-eyed blond-haired Jesus." The father protests that he (presumably the father, not Jesus) put "food on the table, clothes on your back." Ali is like Frank in *Thief;* he is desperate for masculine role models (that he cannot see have already been co-opted by the system he fights) and naïve about how significant an impact economics have on one's convictions and one's ability to act on them. But his conflict is made more complex by the fact that unlike Frank, unlike any of Mann's protagonists except for Rain Murphy, and Nathaniel with his Mohican brethren, he seeks to establish a sense of self that not only disallows the power of money but also seeks a kind of mythic social reality beyond the bonds of individual friendships. This will take him on an arduous path, but one with much greater potential for the rewards he is seeking. He wants social bonds based on shared values that point to an overarching symbolic spiritual bond, not just blood ties or the disembodied ties supplied by the iconography of the system.

But he shows himself to be woefully far from achieving that goal when he sees Malcolm in Africa, where Mann's visual style demonstrates how difficult it is to achieve what Ali and Malcolm really seek. Malcolm is entering that later stage of enlightenment in his spiritual life where he begins to see Islam as a unifying force that could transcend political, geographical, and racial boundaries. He is wearing African dress, associating with Maya Angelou, speaking excitedly of the pilgrimage to Mecca, of seeing "blue-eyed, blond-haired Muslims" there. Ali seems suddenly distracted, looks strangely at Malcolm, and the camera tilts up past his shoulder to reveal an open window in the hotel behind him. A surveillance team of some kind is watching them, composed of both black and white agents whom we see in close-ups and medium shots. Cut back to the conversation and a now glassy-eyed Ali hears a voice in his head, his own, disembodied, speaking these words: "You shouldn't have quarreled with the Honorable Elijah Muhammad." He then speaks these very words aloud to Malcolm who reacts with shock as Ali leaves him.

It is one of those moments when we as viewers know more and understand more than Ali because Mann's style allows us to see and hear more. Malcolm has been under surveillance ever since arriving in Africa; even his conversations with his wife by telephone are being recorded. But this is the first time that we have seen a black agent involved. This is preparing us for what we learn later; agents representing both the United States and the Nation of Islam are working together to watch the movements of a man who is threatening them. Eventually their mutual interest in corralling him will lead to the assassination of Malcolm. Ali cannot anticipate this, and to see him reacting to the voice in his head implies that, without realizing it, he is complicit in the attempts to control Malcolm's thoughts and actions. Ali is allying himself with a coercive force that is not much different from the white culture that he seeks to rebel against. He does not realize yet that money is what links all of these powers together—but he will. He has not found a larger family and social unit in the Nation as it was operating in his and Malcolm's life. He has instead found the same type of simulacrum, an imitation of social and familial ties, that the British and French white fathers used to lead Magua and Munro astray in *The Last of the Mohicans*.

9. A Blast from the Past

While Ali is establishing himself with the sensual and (as it later turns out) too secular Sonji Roy (Jada Pinkett), the plot against Malcolm is progressing. A white agent talks to one of Ali's Muslim associates about taking Malcolm out and the man asks, "Will I be reimbursed for my expenses?" The agent replies that he will reimburse him for "the dry cleaning" and implies that something similar needs to be done about Ali as well. Ali is being betrayed by the only organization that at this point in the movie seems to transcend political and racial bounds, the Kingdom of Money, the world of coercive informatics and its code that, as Baudrillard (and Benedict Anderson in his critique of nationalism cited in chapter 6) warned us, sustains the racist and political bounds that it seemingly violates. As Baudrillard (1997) says in *Simulacra*, "Conjunction of the system and of its extreme alternative" (18). Or, to put it more directly, in the current culture, "Everything is metamorphosed into its opposite" (19). The agents out to destroy Malcolm seem to understand the necessity of such metamorphoses to sustain their power.

When Malcolm is killed, the still innocent Ali cries but remains unshaken in his conviction that the Nation is the way to go. After defeating Liston a second time, he breaks up with Sonji simply because she will not dress like a good Muslim wife. He clearly still cares for her, holding one of her red dresses close just after she goes—but in the Nation he sees something more important than even their love. Bundini displays his magic as a kind of one-man chorus here, parodying Ali's extraordinary loyalty to a transcendental code that costs him his beautiful and loyal wife: "I'm the only normal person left around here. I'm a black Jew, I can't read, and I'm half drunk." But he still knows better than to let someone like Sonji walk out of his life. Nevertheless, for Ali her appearance is the reality, because, as he says, "*How* I am says something." His focus on the ideology cheats him of his ability to appreciate the very real sacrifices that she does make for him from time to time. Mann is saying that Bundini is right: something is so wrong here that even a drunken man can see it.

But a new fight is on the horizon that will help educate Ali about himself in a new way—one brought on by his convictions about Vietnam, convictions that will drive a wedge between him and his fairweather friends, the Nation of Islam and the institution that provided the isomorphic foundation of its power structures, the United States Government. Ali, after his good-natured assault on Howard Cosell's toupée in the public eye of the cameras, has a more serious conversation with the sportscaster in private. Like Ali, Cosell is a more serious individual away from the videoscopic eye, and he warns the boxer, "They're coming after you because they're scared of black militancy in the inner cities." Ali again exposes his naiveté by saying that he is not like H. Rap Brown and Stokely Carmichael. Cosell explains it as best as one could back then: "All they are is political. You're the heavyweight champion of the world." In short, Ali has become an icon through the medium and he cannot be dismissed like the other rebels—if he does not conform to his role as a symbol in the empire of signs, in the simulacrum, he must be destroyed. The words of John Lennon he had quoted to Sonji have come back to haunt him (as they would Lennon): his attempts to make himself real, to create himself as a public subject, have made his life something not real, and therefore no longer secure because it is no longer his own. Information is a commodity, as are those who are part of the system of informatics.

Thinking that his seeming allies in the public arena will stand by him, Ali speaks without reservation and indicts the American war effort as racist oppression. He seems to sense intuitively that this oppression is part of the not real system that is trying to deprive him of his own presence as an individual subject. In a telephone interview he says, "Yeah, I know where Vietnam is. It's on television. Southeast Asia? What, you mean it's there too?" This attempt at parody does not deter his opponent, and he rises to the bait, taking the system head on: "Man, I don't got no quarrel with them Viet Cong. Ain't no Viet Cong ever called me nigger." His friends try to warn him that he could make enemies this way and he says, " So what? So what? I ain't got to be what no one else want me to be." He continues on this course, even as his handlers tell him that they cannot promote any fights for him, even when he must answer a formal inquisitor in a public hearing who asks him if he is still "acting like the people's champ." His unhesitating reply: "Yes, sir." Outside, he steps up the attack on the racist culture he detests and says to reporters, "I ain't goin' no 10,000 miles to help murder and kill other poor people." Attacking the representatives with even greater vigor he further indicts them and the culture they represent: "You *my* enemy.... You my oppressor when I want justice." In fact, he adds "You won't even stand up for me right here at home."

He has at least begun to sense that there is a conspiracy, but he still does not realize how vast it is, this collusion between informatics and the racist hierarchy. In his fight with Terrell, he asks his opponent repeatedly, "What's my name?" as he beats him in a rage provoked by this assault on his freedom and his identity. But when it is all over and he turns to the crowd, some chant his name and others boo.

9. A Blast from the Past

Thus begins the downward spiral that constitutes the middle section of the film. Ali is sentenced the maximum penalty for draft evasion, five years in prison and $10,000. After seeing Ali on television with Cosell still claiming he is the champ, the Honorable Elijah Muhammad does something to dishonor his connection with Ali—he suspends him "from the practice of Islam" on the grounds that Ali loves the sporting world too much. He is forbidden to have "conversation with any Muslim whatsoever." In short, Mann is indicating that both the system Ali opposes and the one he thought supported his battle against racism deny him his voice, his presence, his capacity to assert himself as a subject. He is where Malcolm was, a victim of the economics of coercion. Even his old friend Bundini, he is told, has sold the championship belt to support his drug habit. He faces the isolation all of Mann's protagonists encounter when they divorce themselves cognitively from the social simulacrum based on acquisition and oppression.

His second wife, who says she "never stopped" loving him, like all of the kids in the old neighborhood, begins to point out the weakness of his strategies in the past. If he should ever get a fight again, she says, he should have all new management. She rightly sums up the problem with his non-self-sacrificing allies: "They all over you when you got it, then they just drop off of you when you don't." Through her, Mann emphasizes the need to adopt alternative strategies that allow protagonists like Rain Murphy and Lowell Bergman to minimize their complicity with the system. Ali does not comment, but after this significant oral exchange he nevertheless begins to work on other strategies to try to save the situation.

He turns to Howard Cosell who is willing to help but can offer little hope since his "bosses only give a damn about Nielsen ratings." In private, Ali says, "I guarantee it will be a historical and momentous night" if he fights Joe Frazier. When he appears on television with Cosell, we are expecting more mugging or more naïve protests. What we see instead is an Ali using a kind of reverse psychology on both the networks and the mass audiences that, as Baudrillard would say, both create and are paradoxically created by each other. Ali surprisingly says, "I'm through fighting." He then goes on to depict what the fight would have been like in rhyme but sadly announces that this momentous occasion will never take place even though he will take on his next opponent, "the U.S. Government."

People in the control booth watching him and Cosell succumb to laughter while the telephones start ringing off the hooks. It is one of those strange moments when the goal of a tactic is so obvious that it works, partly because of its strange simultaneous confirmation and negation of the simulation and artifice of the medium. Ali is creating interest in the fight and an appetite, much as the networks do, but in a different way. He has adapted his mugging style, his tendency toward self-parody, to achieve his ends differently. It is somewhat like Lowell Bergman's parody of the parody where he allows the transparent system of the media culture to betray itself. Here Ali lets the medium's coerciveness betray itself. Both strategies remind one of what Baudrillard (1997) once said: perhaps one of the more effective examples of resistance is that of a young child. Knowing that it cannot resist the overwhelming coercive power of adults it adopts a strategy of truculence—if it is asked to behave like an object, it acts like a subject, and if it is asked to behave like a subject it acts like an object (83–85). In short, in a purely perverse fashion, one does the opposite of whatever one is asked to do. The illusion of power seems to evaporate at such moments, as any high school teacher can attest. Ali has topped his faceless opponents through a bizarre gesture of reflexivity, a disingenuousness that oddly attests to the sincerity of his desire for an honest fight.

But outside the videoscopic arena, Ali still relies on an anachronistic sense of honor and obligation to get back in the ring. Picked up by Joe Frazier as he is cruising the streets in his sedan, the observant Ali quips, "You look like the heavyweight champion of pimps." Frazier does seem to be succumbing to the seductions of acquisitiveness; when Ali challenges him to fight, Frazier's reply reflects the fact that he is thinking more like a businessman than a warrior: "I ain't got nothin' to win, but I got everything to lose." Ali, using the intimate oral exchange to full advantage, replies with the verbal equivalent of a body shot: "You ain't the real champ yet." What can Frazier say? He's right—until he fights Ali, the title means nothing because it is, for both of these men, about something more than money; it is about self-respect. Frazier agrees to fight him if Ali can beat Jerry Quarry. The conversation ends on a note that shows that Frazier, much like Ali, is a man living in two worlds, one of honorable competitive exchange and one of materialism. "By the way," says Frazier, "you need money?" Ali lies, saying, "I'm fine."

Ali can play a parodic game but still wants something more, as is made clear in the earlier scene where he rejects Bundini for selling his championship belt. Bundini is no longer the man of magic and faith that he claimed to be. He is living in a very empty place where he feels God has forgotten him and given him a terrifying freedom, one that Mann indicates sadly attests to the emptiness and alienation of the human condition when we give in to the hallucinogenic lure of power and money. On the train Ali takes when he leaves Bundini, someone calls Ali champ

9. A Blast from the Past

and he turns away; he is less than he was because of this scene with Bundini. His bonds of sympathy with Bundini are still strong—he needed this flawed yet insightful and sensitive man who seemed to offer a real kind of healing magic, the exchange of humanity that expresses itself as friendship. It was like the dialogical dance between Bergman and Wigand in *The Insider*: only men who share the same weaknesses can work the magic of saving each other from the diseases of the soul. Without such friendship and love (exemplified also by Molly's relationship with Graham in *Manhunter*), Mann suggests, one is lost in the world of the simulacrum. Without it one returns to the world of *Heat*—there is no hope for symbolic exchange.

Ali's need for Bundini becomes all the more clear when, after Ali's conversation with Frazier, Bundini makes his comeback, clean and sober, claiming it is "God's act." He and Ali complete a rhyme together: "Your hands can't hit / What your eyes can't see / Float like a butterfly / And sting like a bee." Ali accepts him—the bond of sympathy working here because Ali to is about to make his comeback and strangely, Bundini is working a sympathetic magic of exchange with Ali. If Bundini can beat the lure of the hallucinogens, the drugs and the booze, money and power, then Ali perhaps can stand up to the not real forces that threaten to destroy him too. These men share in a human ritualistic magic based on identification, based on words they share in time to the beat of the rhyme. It is, after all, the only strategy that is making sense at this point, the totemistic identification with animals in a ritual symbolic exchange that makes you both bee and butterfly. The symbolic exchange outlines the strategy for life inside and outside the ring, perhaps inside and outside oneself as well, when battling the demons the system places inside of you and in your way. You are *not* where your enemies expect you to be when they strike; you *are* there, with stunning energy and presence, when you return the compliment and engage.

As Ali begins to rise again, his wife's predictions come true and his fair-weather friends return, allowing the system to renew its assault on Ali and his attempts to construct an identity for himself. He takes out Quarry, the crowd chants "Ali," and Herbert Wallace and other representatives of the Nation rally around him after the fight. His wife says, "you don't need their management," but they have come to offer Ali $5 million for the fight with Frazier. Moreover, they will restore his public identity as a Muslim: "The Messenger has lifted your suspension," says Herbert. But he and the others don't realize that they are dealing with a more sophisticated Ali than before. Ali replies, "So you're saying I can be a Muslim again." When they affirm it, he says, " I ain't never stopped, just like I ain't never stopped being the Champ." They emphasize the money and he says, "I love the Nation, but it don't own me." Nevertheless, after a few moments of consideration, he tells them to "Go on out there and you make the Frazier deal." A close-up on his wife shows her extreme disappointment, then cuts to Bundini praising Ali for accepting him despite the religious differences and confessing his addictions to pork and white women. Ali's sympathetic bonds cut in many ways. He has reached a point where, like Malcolm, he realizes that he can devote himself to a faith without the support of the visible religious institution. But like Bundini (and like Frank in *Thief* and Lowell Bergman in his low point in *The Insider*) he is still hooked on the various aspects of the system that appears to give power and license. The cost of equality and justice seems to come very high, since, as the saying goes, freedom isn't free.

Ali and Bundini nevertheless show an increasing awareness of this, and this enables Mann to show that their exchange has not been completely compromised by what has happened. Howard Cosell calls during Ali's celebratory dinner to tell him that he has won a TKO over the United States Government. Ali informs his wife: "The Supreme Court just set me free." Bundini in his never completely sober mental state gives the only reliable reading of this unexpected verdict one can make, a reading that implicitly could be applied to the Nation's change of heart as well. He says, "They want to be on your side now because the Truth has showed itself to the Power, so the Power is coming to the Truth, and that's what it is, and the Truth tastes good when it's a belly full of lies." Ali responds with "What?" and they both laugh as Bundini says, "It don't matter." Indeed it doesn't. They grasp as well as anyone could at this time what Baudrillard has always said about the media and the simulacrum—they actively consume the truth as they pursue nonexistent and purely hallucinatory modes of empowerment.

This leaves Ali at something of an impasse—he is back in the game but at the same cost that Frank pays in *Thief*, for he is making a deal with the very forces that threaten to rob him of his integrity as an individual. But as is so often the case with Mann heroes, the world turns out to be an unexpectedly complex place. Ali will absorb two blows he did not anticipate. First, he loses his fight to Joe Frazier. Second, he watches in horror as Frazier loses the title to a larger and more dangerous opponent, George Foreman.

This puts him at the mercy of two equally formidable foes—Foreman and fight promoter Don King. King stands for everything Ali's wife will later decry when she points out that money is all that Ali's friends have ever really cared about. King declares that the fight in Zaire between

9. A Blast from the Past

Foreman and Ali will be "The Rumble in the Jungle. That is the name I have given it." His commercial interests are evident in his hyperreal promotion of the event: "I dream of overcoming ... racial depression" in hopes of seeing a "new day of liberation—financial and otherwise." He goes on to make ridiculously bad rhymes about the event, until Ali feels compelled to cut him off and end the spectacle: "Man, Don, you crazy."

Ali finds himself in the midst of a King inspired media frenzy that Foreman seems to contribute to when he threatens to back out due to a mishap in the ring, something that immediately makes Ali's trainer Angelo Dundee suspicious. Mann seems to be asking us, as he did in the film's opening montage, just what *is* real here? At this moment, the answer seems even less apparent than it did an hour earlier in the film. Nevertheless, this return to Africa turns out to be a pivotal moment for Ali and for the film. Ali suddenly and unexpectedly comes in contact with something genuine; he is caught by surprise just as his friend Malcolm was in Mecca when, one day, Ali quite literally leaves the beaten path and encounters an Africa he has not known. Like other Mann protagonists, he is about to learn the art of translating between the culture of materialism and the world of symbolic exchange.

It is already beginning when he gets off the plane and the crowds are cheering "Bumaye Ali!" He asks a guide to translate, and the man tells him it means, "Ali, kill him." An interesting way to put it. Why not say, "Ali kill Foreman"? It is as if the other man's name does not matter. Who and what are being killed exactly?

Until later in the film, when he takes a detour, Ali hasn't a clue. At the first meeting with Foreman, we see the usual media parlor tricks— Ali beating native drums and shouting, "The champ is here!" But, as it turns out, that's not where he is. That space is not real, no more than what he shares with Cosell when they're on camera. Reality space and the real champion are to be found somewhere else, a place Mann transports us to through his visual style.

Cut to an overhead traveling bird's-eye shot; all we see is the red earth of Africa. Then Ali enters the frame, and gradually others, children pacing him and calling his name. Cut to other shots as they run and we see a landscape not unlike that of the opening Middle East sequence in *The Insider*: signs in various languages and then one with a photograph of President Mobutu's face, an icon of control. Ali does the unexpected here, turning down a narrow dirt path that is bordered by green hedges, moving away from this icon of coercive informatics. It is like a trip through time; sign systems are getting simpler and in this place they are hand made—he runs past a door with the words "BABILONYA

HOUSE" painted on it above a painting of a man's face. No photographic representations here. Cut back to a white reporter asking at the juncture where did Ali go? No one can say. You have to experience this place in an earlier ritual time if you are to know it. Neither we, nor Ali, find it by following street signs.

He is moving into a place where everything he does is imitated by the throngs of youngsters that follow him, and this is Mann's initial representation of how this man will become a champion of the people just as Rain Murphy did. Ali passes a hand painted image of himself on a wall with the words *BUMAYE ALI* written beside it. Away from the cameras and the media, he is experiencing a different kind of identification and communion, a human society unlike that in the simulacrum. He finds himself in a large market, where nothing but fresh produce can be seen, near a wall where images of Africans painted in modern dress stand beside the words *Bar du Marche*. It is a place between two worlds, where the European influence is there, but is being translated into something that does not feel European at all. Each home, each market stall, is its own place; boundaries are felt presences here as they were in the burial ground scene in *The Last of the Mohicans*. A man stops and boxes playfully with Ali, something few of his admirers would do back in the States. It is as if they have always known him, as if they were expecting him— no surprise, only joy and instant recognition, as if somehow he were returning to his true home. He runs past another wall with an all black painting of the continent of Africa. Then past an image of himself on a blue wall with arms raised in victory. Each image is distinct, unique; each has its own aura, to borrow a phrase from Walter Benjamin (1999), and represents the inner aura, the felt life, of the man, the leader with whom they identify, not as a flat image serially replicated or as some reflection of an archetype from the "subconscious" mind but as a living presence. This is art produced by a people collectively for no profit—it is pure representation, it is the art of a people who understand the value of symbolic exchange.

Ali stops before the largest and most impressive of these images. On the left, a house with a cross on it, some sort of sanctuary. On the right, himself, with the bees of the rhyme he shared with Bundini floating like butterflies nearby. Someone is behind him playing a large green boom box, while the song from the soundtrack *Tomorrow* plays, a song that starts in an African language but ends in English. A translation process is taking place while Ali stands before his portrait transfixed by its aura, his own aura, a new identity represented by the only kind of art that can effect such a transformation in a human being. So many people are there

9. A Blast from the Past

Ali (Will Smith) is arrested in his journey by an image of himself produced by the collective symbolic exchange of the Africans who have captured his aura and begun his transformation into a true champion of the people before his fight with Foreman in *Ali*.

that we can barely see these giant images—but Ali can see it all in this moment that he shares with them, in this ritual moment where they present him with this sacrifice, this gift, a gift which cannot be repaid in money but only with similar selfless sacrifice. He is *there*, entering the image, not absently absorbing it, but contemplating it. As Benjamin would say, a painting affects us differently from serially produced photographs and films. Without editing and other cinematic tricks to distract the mind, "the spectator can abandon himself to his associations" and meditate (748). And what does Ali see—a giant who kills tanks with his fists, who stands undaunted before fighter jets and modern soldiers. He is as powerful as a nation state but he is something more than that—the future People's Champion, a leader whose identity emerges in this moment of exchange. The wall says, *ALI BUMAYE*. He belongs to them, and finally, at long last, he belongs to himself. No more subject and object, those reflections of human relationships in the immateriality of materialism. Something much more than that—the very thing Rain Murphy became. He is the people who sacrifice for him and for whom he must now sacrifice. He is ready to become the People's Champion, a true warrior.

He jogs on, now moving into the more urban neighborhoods, people living in the urban squalor of broken down homes, serial copies of one another in the high rises that look ready to fall down—products of the system that sees all things, even human beings, as serial replicas in the simulacrum of society. But the experience at the wall is still with Ali; we can see it in his face. It is all the same now. He is deeply shaken by this. Men on a truck drive by and signal him with the raised fist. Closeup on his face, still deeply moved, he belongs to these people, it is not about himself, it is about them, and that is where he is finding himself, his aura, his living presence and soul in *them*. Rain Murphy understood this too and the need to do something to repay these people. In Mann's world this is the only way to make a difference, to resist the system.

Ali still must struggle, though. Unlike Murphy he is still part of that nonmaterial material world. He and his wife fight about this. She says that Don King and Mobutu do not care about Africa, they care about themselves. Ali counters, King promoted the first black fighter, but his wife argues, "He thinks green." Ali cannot really deny this but tries to explain that it is the only way to get the job done. And what, she asks, "if you get killed?" He is stung: "Is that what you think?" She cannot understand why her Muslim husband is letting himself "get strung up on a cross." This is not the moment for these words. If these people whom he has never met can have such faith in him, why can't his wife? He needs her faith just as much as he needs theirs. It is the beginning of the end of their relationship. He has a kind of faith that she does not have, one based on symbolic exchange that has a place not only in that village environment but in marriage too. Love is important for Ali as it is for all of Mann's heroes; it is the last place where such selfless exchanges can exist. She leaves as Veronica Porsche enters his life—he cannot fight without a woman by his side, a woman who can understand the kind of man he is becoming. His wife's cynical political stance is not enough for him now.

Meanwhile a breach opens between himself and Don King as the date of the fight approaches and it is a breach that Mann focuses on to show that he is becoming contemptuous of King, that Ali is rejecting the other man's culture, even if his motives are different from those of Ali's wife. Using his parodic style to make Foreman fight—Foreman whom he claims has "knocked hisself out"—Ali notices that King is putting down Angelo Dundee behind his back. Without warning, Ali loses his temper with King and says, "You ain't callin' the shots around here, you ain't callin'nothin'!" He shifts from parody to an angry sincerity, saying that everyone "miscalculated; they got it wrong" when they said the myth of Ali was gone. It all sounds like the usual Ali bluster, but the shocked and silenced crowd (even King is subdued) seem to sense something is different. The experience of running with the local people has changed his outlook. Despite his breakup with his wife he appears to be understanding now that King really can't be an ally. But Ali also seems to be seeing more than she does as he discovers a different kind of faith.

As the minutes and hours wind down to the fight, Mann demonstrates that the world of the simulacrum is conspiratorial on a vast scale. The eerily depraved looking President Mobutu meets with a white American banker who compliments him for bringing the fight to Zaire. "Zaire," says the banker, "is the center of the world" now. Cut to a shot of Herbert, the Nation of Islam's representative, shaking hands with Don King. Mann uses these moments to create a backdrop for the fight. Once again Mann emphasizes that the global battle turns against men like Ali, even if they do score local victories. What Nathaniel called the sickness of greed in *Last of the Mohicans* is universal, no matter what this fight means to Ali—or to the spectators, both on screen and off.

But for all that, the moments in time that Ali has shared with the impoverished Africans, and the moments he is about to share with them are important—for they help him to accomplish the impossible and they allow Mann to emphasize that one should never completely dismiss the human potential for resistance. The arena is huge, and as Foreman moves beneath the huge iconographic emblems of Mobutu, Foreman seems like a pawn of an enormously powerful and inhuman system. Ali had earlier compared Foremen in a news conference to a mummy, and, like the one Ali saw on television and derided in an earlier scene, he has a kind of hyperreal, not quite human quality about him, he is an automaton of destruction. The early rounds reveal how remote Ali's chances for victory are against such a man—Ali is taking a terrific pounding from a man much larger and more powerful than Liston. Caught with a solid blow, Ali is on the verge of unconsciousness, holding onto the larger man. But he looks into the crowd and sees a man with a green boom box exactly like the one that a man was carrying earlier in the village. He gathers his strength to shake it off, says to himself, "Been there before. Hello dream room. Open that door.... Got to get *out!*" He can move out of the disembodied dream space, once he sees the reminder of the different space of symbolic exchange he shared in the marketplace. Mann is showing that the symbol can indeed overpower the simulacrum when the power of the people is there.

Ironically, Bundini and Dundee seem to lose faith in Ali at that moment, shouting at him. But Ali is getting in touch here with an even greater magic than those men wield. He turns to the crowd, the source of his power, and they chant the litany, "Bumaye Ali!" Ali in a clinch whispers to Foreman, "Runnin' out of gas big fella," as if to announce his strategy openly, now that is too late for Foreman to recover. It is the same as the fight with Liston—wear him down and humiliate him—but this time the stakes are higher and Ali is in touch with a part of himself that he has not known before. Nothing is more important than beating this man. This is what it means to be a People's Champion. Total self-sacrifice; repaying the gift that the people gave him. That is who he is. He is the man that nothing and no one can stop because defeat before these people is utterly unthinkable. Ali says it to himself and to Foreman simultaneously as he pointedly challenges everything that can keep them both from being these people's champion: "Can't let you get that second wind that you don't even know is out there for you. You want the title; want the round? Nose broke, jaw broke, face busted in, are you ready for that; is that *you*? This is a man that will die before he let you win."

The next round will make all the difference. The African girl carrying the round card winks at him and he winks back. He is still *here*, in this ring, in the shared space right now. The bell sounds and soon Ali is back on the ropes where Foreman is pounding him, exhausting himself, beating himself even as he takes it to Ali. The song *Tomorrow* that played as Ali ran with the local people, the song that initiated this translation process, begins to play and Ali, finding that second wind he was waiting for, now takes the fight to his fatigued opponent. Ali lands a solid blow and Foreman goes down, the icon of Mobutu apparent over his head until the camera tilts with Foreman's descent and the image vanishes. Both Ali's wife and Veronica Porsche look relieved. As Foreman tries to struggle to his feet, we cut to a low angle shot of Ali waiting and watching. Above him, far in the distance a white dove flies upward to the spotlights above the arena as if to signify that something of a miraculous nature is about to happen. It does. Foreman can't get up and Cosell sums it up accurately: "It is *over!* It is *over!* Muhammad Ali has done the impossible. He has taken the crown that was taken unfairly from him in 1967! What a moment of history in this arena!"

It is that rarest of rarities in Mann's world, a moment of justice. Sacrifice has given a man what he rightly deserves. He has won more than a title. After raising his arms above his head as in the African paintings of himself, Ali collapses. He has answered the gift of sacrifice from the people and beaten the system that denied him a truly meaningful identity by surrendering to the ritual of exchange. He has survived the ritual, but it has been almost too much for him.

Ali's powers return to him as the people chant for him. Then, Don

9. A Blast from the Past

King approaches, offering perhaps congratulations, but Ali, at least at this moment, will have nothing to do with him. He shouts something at King that we cannot make out in the roar of the crowd, and it is as if Ali is speaking for everyone there. Whatever may happen later in their professional lives, this is *not* Don King's moment. It belongs to Ali and the people who made this impossible victory happen by giving him the kind of respect and faith that he could have found nowhere else in the modern world. They are the community of shared values that Ali had always searched for in his fight against oppression and racism. They have given him a special sense of identity in this moment. It belongs to them, not the bankers. King looks astonished.

A thunderclap sounds and rain pours down on everyone. At first the scene seems dominated by those icons of nationalism, the flags of Zaire and the United States. Then Ali pushes past all of the photographers and raises his arms before the screaming crowd, again looking like the portrait in the paintings. He stands up on the ropes as the rain falls and we see behind him a huge clock that records the moment where he and the people share time, share this place, share the meaning of sacrifice. Time is luck. Freeze frame. We look for the image of Mobutu, for the flags. They are nowhere to be seen.

The English section of *Tomorrow*, the film's anthem of shared time and translated symbolic meaning in time, has begun, and the voices are saying "See you tomorrow," as we now look at a rain soaked cityscape—perhaps Chicago—through the windshield of a car. Beside the car, youngsters are running like the children who ghosted Ali's run in Africa. It appears to be raining all over the world, a world at least temporarily united and cleansed by Ali's victory.

Ali and Rain Murphy achieve the impossible through a kind of sympathetic magic that is very rare in Mann's posthuman world. Such moments of sharing where we seem to experience something divine yet human are extraordinary, but they are real, Mann seems to insist. If they were not, why would we feel such exhilaration when hearts beat in unison? Mann's stories, his plots, his characters show that this is not idealism. What happens for Rain Murphy and Muhammad Ali exists in a world where the forces that make the huge machinery of our world run, often drown out the better part of our natures. And Mann's portraits of the modern world since the 1980s, where the videoscopic revolution for Mann seems to become more pervasive and more sinister than ever before, make clear that part of the effectiveness of Ali and Murphy is linked to the time and place in which they lived. This is true even for the protagonists of *The Last of the Mohicans* where the world of symbolic exchange is just beginning to be compromised on a global scale. Still, with *Ali*, Mann teases us into thought. If this kind of exchange could give Ali the capacity to defeat such a powerful opponent, could it be that we are counting it out too soon? What else might be done with such extraordinary strength? What potential for change might exist if enough people decide to make a different kind of choice? As in the final image of *Thief*, Mann will not commit himself to complete pessimism in a world as complex as this. He leaves the door open so that dialogue can be renewed and human potential can develop and be examined in the future.

Thus Mann will give us no easy answers. For now, it is more important to ask the questions. If we want to know more, we must wait. The answers will come in time.

10

Summation and Conclusion

> *The exchange gift, to be exact, operates not according to the evaluation or equivalence of exchanged goods but according to the antagonistic reciprocity of persons.*
> Jean Baudrillard, 1975,
> The Mirror of Production

In this final chapter I would like to do two things: sum up the general rhetorical thrust of the Mann films I have discussed here and then move on to discuss some differences between terminology used in the study and that used by Baudrillard in his criticism by way of offering a clarification and synthesis of what Mann's work implies about information and symbolic exchange in modern times.

Mann's works and the philosophy expressed therein bring to mind, in at least one way, what is sometimes said of the efforts of early modern writers like Alexander Pope and Samuel Johnson. While there is a persistent and detailed examination of themes in such artists' work that promotes the evolution of a kind of epistemology and philosophy, the thinking and art of these people is surprisingly consistent in its outlook on human life and culture. Mann, in short, seems never to alter the basic premises he outlines in his earliest films. The films that follow add depth and detail to his understanding of culture, information, and the way informatics impact the individual. But the fundamental elements of the original vision emerging from *The Jericho Mile* and from *Thief* remain unchanged.

The Jericho Mile introduces the concept of symbolic exchange in its purest form possible in modern times, compared to what we see in his later films (except for *The Last of the Mohicans* and *Ali*). It is almost as if Mann had anticipated where the rest of his cinematic career was headed—this film is indeed a prologue to all of the rest. It defines the nature and significance of symbolic exchange so that we have a norm whereby we can consider the progress and effectiveness of other protagonists who likewise attempt to defy the coercive aspects of modern informatics. It establishes the basic narrative and stylistic form for the other films with its opening montage of conflicting images paralleling the conflicting elements of the culture that in turn set up the thematic conflicts in Mann's films (always involving variations on how human symbolic exchange opposes disembodied coercive informatics). This presentation of the culture's conflicts via this representation of the culture in a microcosm leads in turn to the unwinding of a plot where characters find themselves in conflict with the simulacrum that can be resisted only through symbolic exchange. The plot dramatizes how the protagonist(s) gradually learn to implement the atavistic exchange of symbol that is effective only on the local level. *Jericho Mile* is perfect for the purpose of this prologue (or proem); it gives us a protagonist whose relative isolation from the mainstream economics of the simulacrum can enable him to establish himself briefly as a tribal chieftain who finds a stable identity through the exchange without succumbing to the role of subject or object in the simulacrum, roles that lead humans to be deconstructed along with space, time, and context in the simulacrum. *Jericho Mile* thus allows Mann to establish his basic critique of postmodern culture and it shows how and why this empty posthuman parody of a human society can be battled only locally in spaces that have not been completely overtaken by the coercive informatics of the simulacrum.

From here Mann can go on to show what is the major culprit in this culture's crime against humanity—the urbanization of culture as it constitutes itself as an oppressive imagined community that promotes globally the spread of nationalism, imperialism, and totalitarianism. This Mann begins to make clear in *Thief* as he shows an individual with essentially the same strengths and capabilities as Rain Murphy—the ex-convict and professional thief Frank—who cannot successfully establish symbolic exchanges like Murphy because every form of exchange in his life is contaminated by the politics of greed that have created a simulacrum destroying his gestures toward friendship and familial relations. Hence, he cannot achieve symbolic exchange with nature or humanity because the disembodied informatics that invades the urban technologized environment like a cancer makes this impossible.

In *The Keep*, Mann explains how this posthuman situation came to be by exposing the abuses of information manifested by the Nazis' totalitarian approach to controlling human society. The Nazis' misguided

10. Summation and Conclusion

prometheanism is nothing less than an attempt to assert absolute control over the human population by creating a terrorist culture where human beings are reduced to abstract information. Their interest in controlling the subconscious mind and in blurring the distinction between technology and biology points to the Nazis as the founders of a uniquely modern form of evil. Their strange attraction to the Golem represents their obsession with technologizing every aspect of human life by reducing it to abstract information (genetics). Their desire for control manifests itself as a human catastrophe wherein human territoriality is destroyed in an implosive social simulacrum where the serial replication of Nazi war machines institutes serial production of death and murder. The physical manifestation of the Golem as a doppelganger also points to the potential to make living things into serially produced creations, something that ultimately divests them of their uniqueness, their living presence, and, ironically, their physical materiality as they are subsumed by the serially produced phantasm of society, the simulacrum created by the Nazis.

The Nazis of *The Keep* thus might seem to represent the ultimate in irresponsible exploitation of informatics in late modern times—until Mann introduces us to an even more dangerous vehicle of destruction—the videoscopic culture he decries in *Manhunter*. Here Mann explicates the worst effects of the control revolution. The Nazis, themselves fearful of losing control, contribute to the culture's obsession with control; *Manhunter* shows how absolute control and any kind of security are impossible in the deconstructed spaces created by the videoscope's invasive eye. When ecological and geographical spaces are obliterated by instant relaying of visual information, a threat is created that is far worse than the Nazis' attempts to use archetypal icons to destroy the shared territory of symbolic exchange and thus control the subconscious mind of the human subject. For now, within the context of the posthuman, the videoscope can be conceptualized, as Sconce and Virilio imply, as a kind of consciousness in itself devouring the event commutated by the videoscope that transforms space and physical reality into light energy. The result ultimately is a monstrosity like Hannibal Lecktor, the serial murderer who inherits the mantel of serialized destruction from the Nazis in a videoscopic simulacrum. Serially reproduced doppelgangers on film and video become Mann's metaphor for the death of human symbolic exchange in the disembodied hyperreality of our posthumanity.

It is this examination of the ultimate abuse of technology, the videoscope, that lends an even darker and often more tragic tone to Mann's works immediately following *Manhunter*. For all its epic grandeur and high romantic passion, *The Last of the Mohicans* is still a tragic reminder of how humanity almost seemed destined to create the terrifying informatics manifested in *The Keep* and *Manhunter*. Its depiction of the destruction of the Native American tribal cultures after the invasion of the imagined communities produced by European urbanized civilizations clearly shows that the antecedents of this can be traced back for two hundred years or more. The world of *Heat* also shows the continuing effects of this culture in late twentieth-century times, as does *The Insider*, which describes the overt legalization of information as commodity—the making of truth into a form of legal liability—as the death knell for our capacity to resist the damaging effects of a misguided informatics that threatens individuals, families, and the security of an entire global culture that has now become dominated by many manifestations of terrorism.

Nevertheless, *Ali* reminds us that throughout all of this Mann has continued to emphasize the value of love and friendship, whereby time can be shared meaningfully by individuals in various attempts to resist the coercive aspects of this culture. *Ali* takes us to a time where perhaps information has not yet become quite as invasive as it is by the time of *Manhunter*, although it is still depicting a time close to the videscopic revolution, at its very inception. Ali's astonishing victory shows that even postmodern human beings can implement symbolic exchange. The theme of translation, introduced primarily in *The Last of the Mohicans*, and resurfacing in *The Insider* and *Ali*, maintains the hope that the fundamental elements of humanity, our capacity to share oral language in symbolic exchanges that discharge meaning and obligation instantly, cannot be completely annihilated by modern culture. Its capacity to change us for the better may be limited to the local scene, as it was in *The Jericho Mile*, but it is still there. And Mann's deliberately open ended renderings of these issues points to the necessity to maintain an open mind when considering our potential for improving the human condition. The value of the exchange cannot be completely compromised. Changing the global system today may be beyond our grasp—but perhaps this is only a temporary state of affairs. Mann seems to argue for patience. His visual style itself, plus his effective use of plot and character to translate, takes us back to the shared time and reality of the exchange, thereby attesting to its continuing value for human beings.

Now, in the course of this study and in the course of my summation above, I have sometimes spoken of the values shared by Mann protagonists who share time together and make symbolic exchanges usually in oral discourses (though there are other means of instantiating exchanges

10. Summation and Conclusion

as in Muhammad Ali's encounter with street art and the use of graffiti in *The Jericho Mile*). What I mean here by "value" is the value of the exchange itself, where the process of sacrifice and giving points to an alternative to the larger socioeconomic system of informatics (what Baudrillard calls "the Code") that typically coerces people to conform with a system using fear and violence to secure its ends. It is a system based on the turning of signs into commodities that can be owned by the acquisitive power brokers in the culture who ironically lose power as they try to assert control over human beings. The value of the exchange is that which is diametrically opposed to such a system.

I should point out, however, that Baudrillard used the term *value* somewhat differently from me, and in ways that may help further elucidate the elusive concept of symbolic exchange and how it is important for understanding Mann's films. For Baudrillard, value is not something associated with symbolic exchange; value is something one has only as a result of a surplus of meaning that occurs when the signifier is made into a commodity in the monopolistic system of informatics. Value, in this sense, is therefore something always imbued with the values of the system of disembodied information with its emphasis on exchange value, abstraction, and the concomitant dehumanizing qualities of the politics of greed in the simulacrum. Poetry, at least for Baudrillard, represented just the opposite of all this for he believed that it is a true form of symbolic exchange. In *Symbolic Exchange and Death* (1993) he said, "The model of exchange also exists within the field of language, something like the core of political anti-economy, a site of extermination of value and the law: poetic language" (195). In poetry signifiers seem no longer to be guided by the linear code that dominates in the culture (197). The words have no surplus value when they are used by the reader and poetic speaker, and the words answer the mutual needs of both in the discourse. For in the poem, "nothing remains" afterward, and thus it cannot be interpreted by a linguistic approach to analyzing signification (198). Hence poetry does not speak the values of the ruling system and represents something outside the field of values created by an oppressive culture.

Given all that has been written about the politics and epistemologies of poetry in the past three decades, it would be easy to take issue with Baudrillard's claims here about poetry, but the greater significance of what he said in this passage is in how it illuminates the distinctive quality of symbolic exchanges. For Baudrillard, our abstract, disembodied conceptions of value, codes of conduct and law are the antithesis of what symbolic exchange is all about. As he said in his discussion of law in *The*

Mirror of Production (1975), the laws and codes governing postmodern society represent a "rupture of exchange and the loss of the symbolic" (61). Thus this abstract doctrine destroys symbolic exchange "in favor of the law of castration and value" (63). Put more simply, abstract systems of value like the code and its legalism are substitutes for a more genuine form of exchange between human beings. A culture based on sacrifice and loss, instead of selfish acquisition, has no need for these systems. Behavior is regulated by exchanges that benefit all of the participants. In such a system, values and laws in the abstract logo-centric sense are unneeded. Behavior is guided, and order is maintained by the ritual that invokes exchange between people and the natural environment. Restraint in a more abstract sense is not necessary, and for the participants in a purely primal system, probably not even conceivable.

Hence, as Baudrillard said in *Symbolic Exchange and Death*, poetry represents a special kind of *jouissance* that destroys "the repressive *logos*" (230). Poets and shamans work this magic in the same way, by focusing on limited fields of signification that allow exhaustion of signification in ritual: "The shaman and the prophet ... act on ... limited phonemes or formulae, exhausting them in a maximal configuration of meaning." Likewise, poetic expression works on "the *restricted* corpus of the signifier." Thus, "The signifier, ... follows the same movement as the gift and the counter-gift...; it is a reciprocity where the use-value and the exchange-value of an object cancel each other out," thus yielding the emptiness of value and the delight associated with genuine social relations and poetic expression (204).

At this earlier more optimistic stage of his career, Baudrillard saw this as a revolutionary gesture that could be repeated at the global and the local level. "What the poetic accomplishes with the phoneme-value at the microscopic level, every social revolution accomplishes over the entire flanks of code of value" (204). However, as we saw in chapter 1, this attitude did not prevail in Baudrillard's later career, and it has never been evident in Mann's films. Mann sees the value of the exchange as a rejection of the prevailing value code, but he never sees in it any potential for changing the entire system. Instead, for Mann, the informatic codes and their instrumentalities generally deny the kind of physical presence and intimate connection required for symbolic exchange. Globalization always ends with a recapitulation of the coercive codes that create and sustain the system, ideologically and technologically.

Nevertheless, Mann does all he can to allow the audience to experience the limited fields of discourse in which sacrifice and exchange can take place. A case in point: a scene toward the end of *The Last of the*

10. Summation and Conclusion

Mohicans. After Colonel Munro is killed by Magua on the battlefield, Nathaniel, Chingachgook, Uncas, Cora, her sister, and Duncan flee the scene and hide beneath a waterfall, hoping to lose Magua's pursuing war party. Inside the hideaway, Nathaniel and his Mohican fellows discover their powder is too wet and they cannot make a fight of it. They speak first in English then switch to the Mohican language as they try to come to a difficult decision. Suddenly, speaking above the roar of the waterfall, Cora says, "Yes, *go!*" She has intuited what they are discussing—and most likely the audience has too—namely that Nathaniel, his brother, and his father must leave Cora and the others if there is to be any chance of the group surviving.

How does she know this? How do *we*? We might be able to guess from context based on their observations about the wet powder—but what creates that context? Symbolic exchange and the culture of sacrifice are the context for this scene. We are not translating linguistically, any more than Cora is; we are reading symbolic gestures that are not dependent on a specific kind of linguistic competence. We know Nathaniel and the Mohican way; this is just like the scene where the Camerons were left behind unburied. If we judge by an abstract decontextualized and disembodied code of value here at the waterfall or at the Cameron place, as Duncan does, we misjudge. Cora has learned not to do this. She has accepted the ritual play of signifiers on a symbolic level where their meaning is exhausted in the limited field of activity identified and contextualized by actions that, quite literally, speak louder than words alone. Nathaniel, a shamanistic warrior like his Mohican father, has brought her to a new place. The audience is there too.

One can debate whether symbolic exchange exists in poetry today as Baudrillard argued at a more optimistic stage in his life; but one would be hard pressed to deny that Mann brings such exchanges to life in cinema. He also dramatizes their death on the global level even as humanity struggles to keep them alive in specific local circumstances. The sacrifice between Bergman and Wigand in *The Insider* is fully realized in the moment where Bergman brings him out of his psychotic reverie at the hotel. Nevertheless, Bergman is clearly right when he says something was lost in the long run when CBS Corporate and the Big Tobacco companies were brought into the mix. Similarly, Molly, Will Graham, and their son have moments of exchange—but the film *Manhunter* rightly asks, who can escape the videoscopic eye that invades and destroys the kinds of intimate spaces and limited discursive fields that are required for true exchanges? No one can escape it, if *Heat* is any evidence of how this game is going in modern times. The oppressive code persists.

But if Baudrillard's career is one of a gradual descent into darkness and pessimism, the same cannot be said for Mann. Yes, he argues that things are getting worse as information systems and the system associated with them become more oppressive. But even in his most recent films he had insisted that sacrifices go on, that people can have moments in which they give up much for others in their lives. We can find ourselves in others without being limited to the grotesque video doppelgangers of *Manhunter* and *The Keep*. Mann maintains faith in the doubling that occurs in the symbolic exchange as described by Baudrillard in *Symbolic Exchange and Death*:

> Between the primitive and its double, there is neither a mirror relation nor one of abstraction, as there is between a subject and its ... consciousness.... The double is no longer a fantastic ectoplasm, an archaic resurgence issuing from guilt and the depths of the unconscious.... The double ... is a *partner* with whom the primitive has a personal and concrete relationship [141].

Agencies that oppose such relationships are everywhere in Mann's world, but they cannot completely deny the capacity of the individual to share time in exchanges that do not signify value in Baudrillard's sense of the word, though clearly Mann does value them for what they are. Identities are confirmed in gestures that deny the usual system of signification that insists we must be either a passive object or an active subject (when in the moment of exchange we can realize the ends of both roles simultaneously), for these gestures deny the ideology through their genuine lack of selfishness in moments of intense identification between speakers who are not alienated from themselves through each other. Such moments of total selfless identification between partners take place, and they do not require relationships that are perfect or without conflict, as Baudrillard implies in the chapter epigraph. All that is required is a moment in which an exigency is met by self-sacrifice, without selfish calculation. It can happen in the most unexpected places, as Mann has shown—a prison yard, a courtroom, or a boxing ring. These can become places of exchange and they can establish an embodied place where the oppressive abstract informatics of logos are banished for being the phantasmal yet destructive enemies of humanity that they are.

And the exchanges can happen to anyone, regardless of race, gender, or social position because those categories cease to have significance in the exchange. Molly in *Manhunter* is the initiator of the exchange in her world where only marginalized people seem to fully appreciate and embrace the exchange outside the mainstream videoscopic culture that

10. Summation and Conclusion

has clearly dominated the men who reign at the top of the system. But in *The Last of the Mohicans,* it is Nathaniel who initiates Cora because she has fallen under the influence of the European culture that denies exchange. Both men and women can be initiators and recipients in exchange—what makes the difference is not gender or race but one's relationship to the ruling culture and the degree to which one can operate without being completely dependent upon its economics and the coercive information systems associated with them. In the end, one either chooses to embrace symbolic exchange or one doesn't. Duncan's sacrifice at the end of *The Last of the Mohicans* proves that even social position and class are not determinants here. Instead, what mainly determines one's participation is willingness to try and experiment. In the end, it comes down to a matter of *choice*. Mann insists on the necessity of choice for the exchange; he insists that it still exists, despite all of the attempts that have been made to take it away from us.

With each film, Mann's assessment of the situation has grown more complex. He observes the growing complexity of the information culture his characters are immersed in and he translates this to his films with extremely complex visual style and narrative form. He reflects the "growing awareness" described by Hayles in *Chaos Bound* (1990) evident between the 1960s and the 1980s "that the world itself had become (or already was) a complex system economically, technologically, environmentally" (5). Hayles indicated that this conception of a world linked by vast complex (chaotic) dynamic systems of information could seem "oppressive" but might also "offer the liberating possibility that one may escape the information net by slipping along its interstices" (5–6). Mann recognizes this possibility, but his films show that as information systems grow increasingly complex, the chances for resisting the more oppressive influences of informatics on any level will most probably decrease. Nothing, in all likelihood, can destroy symbolic exchange completely, but any potential it could have for changing the system clearly is not increasing. Indeed, Mann's films seem to show succeeding generations of protagonists struggling harder to establish effective symbolic exchanges as the influence of information technologies has expanded since the eighteenth century.

Where does this leave the (post) human condition for Mann? The future holds little hope. In each film the concept that is essential to human freedom, justice, and decency is, again, that of *choice*—and that is the one thing the system seems to compromise more severely with time. *The Insider* surely demonstrates this—if the truth becomes a commodity and we sometimes cannot establish our right to expression, then we are losing our capacity to participate as equals, as human beings who respect the right of others to have integrity, dignity, a sense of self. The system is indeed implosive, a vortex. But Mann will insist that even the smallest victory is nevertheless important. His focus as a filmmaker is unlike Baudrillard's as a theoretician. Baudrillard focuses on the masses—while Mann studies the individual. Mann insists that, as individuals, we cannot deny the deeper significance of the exchange. No system can completely extinguish—so far—our capacity for sacrifice. By the same token, a means for asserting symbolic exchange at the global level is by no means apparent. But the symbolic exchange can no more die than Stiles did in *The Jericho Mile*. Baudrillard said in *Symbolic Exchange* that in archaic societies the living have exchange with the dead (141). Mann suggests that the same thing is true today in a way. Sacrifice is always significant. It is beyond what the code can destroy or fully explain. It is the one thing that makes humanity indestructible in a symbolically collective sense, even if we no longer appreciate its ritual significance as a global culture.

Beyond this, Mann's films do not offer many answers to questions we might have about the future, about our society. However, his films do create awareness on our part regarding the kind of society we live in. They help us understand why the culture we live in offers terrific challenges to human freedom and why meeting those challenges is more difficult than appearances might suggest. A complete victory over this enemy is not at present within our grasp. But the deeper significance of the symbolic gesture does not depend on victory in such a narrow sense. The only real defeat is in the failure to recognize the significance of sacrifice. All of Mann's films speak to this, and, at least for the time being, how we will respond as individuals is still our choice.

Bibliography

Anderson, Benedict. *Imagined Communities: Reflections on the Origins and Spread of Nationalism.* New York: Verso, 1991.
Bataille, Georges. *The Accursed Share: An Essay on General Economy.* Vol. 1. Trans. Robert Harley. New York: Zone Books, 1988.
Baudrillard, Jean. *The Mirror of Production.* Trans. Mark Poster. St. Louis, MO: Telos Press, 1975.
―――. "Requiem for the Media." *For a Critique of the Political Economy of the Sign.* Trans. Charles Levin St. Louis, MO: Telos Press, 1981. 164–165.
―――. *Simulacra and Simulation.* Trans. Sheila Faria Glaser. Ann Arbor: the University of Michigan Press, 1997.
―――. *Symbolic Exchange and Death.* Trans. Iain Hamilton Grant. Thousand Oaks, CA: Sage, 1993.
Benjamin, Walter. "The Work of Art in the Age of Mechanical Reproduction." *Film Theory and Criticism: Introductory Readings.* 5th ed., Ed. Leo Braudy and Marshall Cohen, New York: Oxford University Press, 1999. 731–751.
Brewer, John. *The Sinews of Power: War, Money and the English State: 1688–1783.* Cambridge, MA: Harvard University Press, 1990.
Callado Rodriguez, Francisco. "Fear of the Flesh, Fear of the Borg: Narratives of Bodily Transgression in Contemporary U.S. Culture." In *Beyond the Borders: Re Defining Generic and Ontological Boundaries,* Edited by Ramon Plo-Alastrue. Heidelberg, Germany: Carl Winter, 2002. 67–69.
Cawelti, John G. *The Six Gun Mystique.* Madison: Popular Press, University of Wisconsin Press, 1984.
Connor, Steven. *Postmodernist Culture: An Introduction to Theories of the Contemporary.* Oxford: Basil Blackwell, 1989.
The Directors: Michael Mann. Dir. Robert J. Emery. Videocassette. Fox Lorber/Center Stage, 2000.
Dzenis, Anna. "Impressionist Extraordinaire: Michael Mann's *Ali.*" July 14, 2003. http://www.sensesofcinema.com/contents/01/19/ali.html
Fuller, Graham. "Making Some Light: An Interview with Michael Mann." *Projections* 1 1992), July 14, 2003. http://www.geocities.com/Hollywood/Theater/5784/heat/3interview.html
Haraway, Donna. "A Cyborg Manifesto: Science, Technology and Socialist Fem-

inism in the Late Twentieth Century." In *The Cyberculture's Reader*, Ed. David Bell. New York: Routledge, 2000. 291–324.
Hayles, N. Katherine. *Chaos Bound: Orderly Disorder in Contemporary Literature and Science*. Ithaca, NY: Cornell University Press, 1990.
———. *How We Became Post Human: Virtual Bodies in Cybernetics, Literature, and Informatics*. Chicago: University of Chicago Press, 1999.
Hill, Carloyn Erickson. *Writing From the Margins: Power and Pedagogy for Teachers of Composition*. New York: Oxford University Press, 1990.
Jackson, Rosemary. *Fantasy: the Literature of Subversion*. New York: Methuen, 1981.
James, Nick. *Heat* London: British Film Institute, 2002.
Jung, Carl G. *The Archetypes and the Collective Unconscious*. 2nd ed. Trans. R. F. C. Hull. Bollingen Series, Vol. 20. Princeton, NJ: Princeton University Press, 1959.
Kittler, Friedrich A. *Gramophone, Film, Typewriter*. Trans. Geoffrey Withrop-Young and Michael Wutz. Stanford, CA: Stanford University Press, 1999.
———. "The City is a Medium." *New Literary History: A Journal of Theory and Interpretation* 22 (1996), 717–729.
Mann, Michael, dir. *Ali*. Perf. Will Smith and Jon Voight. 2001. Videocassette. Columbia Tristar Home Entertainment, 2002.
———. *Heat*. Perf. Al Pacino, Robert DeNiro, Jon Voight, and Val Kilmer. 1995. Videocassette. Regency/Warner Home Video, 1998.
———. *The Insider*. Perf. Al Pacino and Russell Crowe. 1999. Videocassette. Touchstone Home Video, 2000.
———. *The Jericho Mile*. Perf. Peter Strauss. 1979. Videocassette. ABC Video, 1988.
———. *The Keep*. Perf. Scott Glenn and Jurgen Prochnow. 1983. Videocassette. Paramount, 1989.
———. *The Last of the Mohicans*. Perf. Daniel Day-Lewis, Madeline Stowe, Russell Means, and Wes Studi. 1992.Videocassette.Fox Video, 1993.
———. *Manhunter*. Wide Screen Director's Cut. Perf. William Petersen, Dennis Farina, and Brian Cox. 1986. Videocassette. Anchor Bay Entertainment, 2001.
———. *Thief*. Perf. James Caan and Tuesday Weld. 1981. Videocassette. MGM/UA, 1996.
Markley, Robert. *Fallen Languages: Crises of Representation in Newtonian England 1660–1740*. Ithaca, NY: Cornell University Press, 1993.
Mauss, Marcel. *The Gift: Forms and Functions of Exchange in Archaic Societies*. Trans. Ian Cunnison. New York: W.W. Norton, 1967.
Mauss, Marcel and Henri Hubert. *Sacrifice: Its Nature and Function*.Trans. W. D. Halls. Chicago: University of Chicago Press, 1964.
Mead, G. R. S. *Thrice Greatest Hermes: Studies in Hellenistic Theosophy and Gnosis*. Vol. 1. London: John M. Watkins, 1964.
Ong, Walter J. *Orality and Literacy: The Technologizing of the Word*. London: Methuen, 1982.
Porter, Roy. *English Society in the Eighteenth Century*. New York: Penguin Books, 1990.
Pratt, Annis. *Dancing With Goddesses: Archetypes, Poetry and Empowerment*. Indianapolis: Indiana University Press, 1994.

Rose, Cynthia. "Michael Mann: Using Style to Shatter the Status Quo." *British Vogue*. (1992); July 14, 2003 http://www.muchacreative.com/Journalism/Mann.html

St. Armand, Barton Levi. "The Mysteries of Edgar Poe: The Quest for a Monomyth in Gothic Literature." *The Gothic Imagination: Essays in Dark Romanticism*. Ed. G. R. Thompson. Pullman: Washington State University Press, 1974. 65–93.

Sconce, Jeffrey. *Haunted Media: Electronic Presence from Telegraphy to Television*. Durham: Duke University Press, 2000.

Sragow, Michael. "All the Corporation's Men." July 14, 2003 http://www.salon.com/ent/col/srag/1999/11/04/mann/.

Steensland, Mark. *Michael Mann*. Harpenden, U.K.: Pocket Essentials, 2002.

Sterling, Bruce. "The Virtual City." *Paradoxa* 2.1 (1996), 46–60.

Thoret, Jean Baptiste. "The Aquarium Syndrome: On the Films of Michael Mann." *Simulacres* 1.3 (2000): July 14, 2003 http://www.sensesofcinema.com/contents/01/19/mann.html.

Virilio, Paul and Patrick Camiller. "Indirect Light: Extracted from *Polar Inertia*." *Theory, Culture and Society* 16.5 (1990): 57–70.

Index

Page numbers in italics refer to illustrations.

Allen, Joan 105
Anderson, Benedict 117–119, 121, 181
Archetypes 77, 83, 85, 88, 89, 90, 91, 96, 105, 107, 112

Bataille, Georges 19, 24–25, 26, 121, 130
Belushi, Jim 57
Benjamin, Walter 78, 96, 188, 189
Beowulf 59
Baudrillard, Jean 6, 7, 8, 10, 11, 15, 17–22, 25–29, 30, 31, 38, 49, 95, 144, 157, 170, 183, 186, 199, 204; *The Mirror of Production* 26, 28, 195, 199–200; "Requiem for the Media" 21; *Simulacra and Simulation* 21, 28, 29, 58, 66, 78, 79, 84, 121, 151, 169, 181, 184; *Symbolic Exchange and Death* 27, 28, 67, 106, 107, 199, 200, 202, 204
Blade Runner 56
Brewer, John 117

Caan, James 55, *64*
The Cabinet of Dr. Caligare 53
Camiller, Patrick 93
Cawleti, John 66
City as information system 62n.
Clones and cloning 79, 106
Collado Rodriguez, Francisco 81n.
Connor, Steven 20, 21, 25
Control Revolution 115–116, 127, 151, 163, 171, 197
Cox, Brian 96

Crowe, Russell 5, 151, *163*
Cyborg 16, 106

Day-Lewis, Daniel 4, 7, 20, 33
Dennehy, Brian 36
De Niro, Robert 136, 137
La Dolce Vita 53
Doubles and doppelgangers 32, 60, 63, 71, 76, 77, 78, 79, 84, 88, 90, 92, 97, 98, 104, 130, 131, 118, 125, 197
Dzenis, Anna 2

Easy Rider 21

Farina, Dennis 98, *100*
Feedback loop 19–20
Fellini, Federico 53
Foxx, Jamie 176
Fuller, Graham 3, 128n.

Glenn, Scott 85
Gothicism 17, 80–81, 87–88
Godard, Jean-Luc 10

Harraway, Donna 16
Hayles, N. Katherine 6, 7, 28, 38; *Chaos Bound* 17, 18, 19, 32, 103, 136, 203; *How We Became Post Human* 9, 16, 116
Hill, Carolyn Erikson 156
Hiroshima 84
Hitchcock, Alfred 66
Hubert, Henri 23, 42, 43, 88, 105, 130, 131

Index

Hyperreal 8, 17, 36, 74, 76, 77, 79, 81, 85, 95, 105, 135, 136, 146, 157, 159, 173, 178, 187, 191

Imagined Communities 117–119
Indirect Light 93–94, 101, 107, 108
Informatics 6–8, 9, 12, 16, 17, 18, 19, 30, 47, 52, 53, 55, 56, 57, 76, 77, 86, 95, 106, 115, 116, 118, 119, 128, 135, 154, 168, 174, 182, 183, 187, 195, 196, 197, 198, 200, 202

Jackson, Rosemary 80–81, 86
James, Nick 6
Jung, Carl 90

Kilmer, Val 136
Kittler, Friedrich 33, 93, 97, 167
Kurosawa, Akira 1

La Dolce Vita 53
Lecktor, Hannibal 6, 93, 96, 116, 197

Mann, Michael 1–8, 10, 11, 12, 29, 30, 32, 93n., 125n., 128n., 133n., 195–198, 201–204; *Ali* 11, 31, 33, 173–195, *175, 189,* 195, 198; *Band of the Hand* 31; *Crime Story* 31, 33; *Heat* 2, 4, 7, 11, 31, 135–150, *137, 157,* 153, 185, 198, 201; *The Insider* 2, 4, 5, 7, 11, 32, 33, 151–171, *153, 163,* 185, 186, 187, 197, 201, 203; *Insurrection* 3, 20; *The Jericho Mile* 11, 31, 33, 35–53, *38, 51,* 56, 58, 59, 160, 168, 195, 196, 198, 203; *The Keep* 3, 5, 11, 32, 77–92, *81, 90,* 116, 120, 132, 161, 196, 197, 198; *L.A. Takedown* 4, 31; *The Last of the Mohicans* 4, 7, 11, 32, 33, 115–133, *123, 129,* 138, 141, 146, 161, 167, 180, 188, 191, 193, 195, 198, 200–201, 202; *Manhunter* 3, 11, 32, 33, 56, 93–114, *100, 111,* 120, 122, 124, 131, 136, 138, 140, 141, 147, 165, 185, 197, 198, 201, 202; *Miami Vice* 3, 31, 33; *Robbery Homicide Division* 31, 33; *Thief* 5, 11, 55–76, *64, 74,* 79, 86, 120, 122, 140, 156, 179, 186, 194, 196
Markley, Robert 116
Mauss, Marcel 19, 23–24, 25, 26, 42, 43, 88, 105, 130, 131
McKellen, Ian 82

Mead, G.R.S. 87
Means, Russell 121

Nationalism 115, 117, 119, 122, 196
Nelson, Willie 59

Ong, Walter 22

Pacino, Al 7, 33, 135, *147,* 151, *163*
Paraxis 80–81, 83, 92
Peckinpah, Samuel 1
Petersen, William 96, *100*
Plummer, Christopher 159
Poe, Edgar Allan 87
Porter, Roy 117
Post human 6, 9, 12, 16, 17, 18, 28, 78, 79, 110, 138, 169, 170, 193, 196, 197, 203
Pratt, Annis 127
Prochnow, Jurgen 80, *81*
Prosky, Robert 62, *74, 82, 90*

Romanticism 87
Rose, Cynthia 3, 20, 120
Richie, Donald 1

St. Armand, Barton Levi 87–88
Sconce, Jeffrey 93, 197
Scott Ridley 56
Simulacrum 8, 17, 36, 37, 40, 46, 48, 49, 50, 56, 57, 59, 61, 67, 68, 70, 71, 72, 73, 75–76, 81, 85, 89, 91, 113, 120, 131, 136, 142, 144–145, 146, 147, 148, 149, 156, 157, 165, 166–177, *176, 177,* 179, 180, 182, 188, 190, 191, 196, 197, 199
Sizemore, Tom 136
Smith, Will 174, *175, 189*
Sragow, Michael 1, 2, 5
Steensland, Mark 2, 6–7, 10, 18, 29, 53
Sterling, Bruce 62n.
Stowe, Madeleine 7, 33, 123
Strauss, Peter 36, 39, *51*
Studi, Wes 124, 146
Symbolic Exchange 7, 8, 9, 10, 19, 22–28, 35, 37, 40, 41, 42, 44, 45, 46, 48, 51, 52, 55, 58, 59, 60, 61, 65, 76, 82, 83, 84, 91, 96, 101, 103, 115, 119, 124, 125, 127, 128, 130, 131, 132, 142, 143, 148, 158, 170, 185, 187, 189, 190, 192, 194, 195, 196, 199, 200, 201, 203, 204; and dialogue 7, 8, 10, 19, 21, 22,

25, 26, 27, 30, 31, 32, 33, 35, 37, 40, 41, 42, 45, 49, 52, 53, 58, 59, 66, 85, 96, *100,* 101, 103, 104, 105, 106, 108, 109–10, 111, 112, 113, 114, 125, 126, 127, 132, 135, 140, 142, 145, 146, 152, 154, 158, 160, 164, 167, 198; and film 8–10, 29, 33, 34, 52, 53; and poetry 8, 9, 10, 27, 199; and territoriality 33, 78, 105; and time 10–11, 32, 37, 39, 42, 43, 44, 45, 48, 50, 52, 53, 57, 61, 63, 68, 104–5, 107, 121, 141, 166, 173, 198, 202

Tangerine Dream 57
Tarantino, Quentin 10
Thoret, Jean Baptiste 6–8, 10, 17, 18, 146, 149
Trismegistus, Hermes 87

Unconscious mind 11, 28, 77, 78, 80–81, 83, 90, 91, 92, 105, 107, 144–5, 146, 166, 188, 197

Van Peebles, Mario 176
Vertigo 66
Videoscope 11, 93, 94, 95, 96, 98, 99, 100, 101, 103, 104, 105, 107, 108, 109, 120, 133n., 135, 138, 141, 142, 145, 169, 170, 193, 197
Virilio, Paul 7, 11, 33, 56, 93, 138, 197
Voight, John 139, 176

Weddle, David 1
Weld, Tuesday 60

www.ingramcontent.com/pod-product-compliance
Ingram Content Group UK Ltd.
Pitfield, Milton Keynes, MK11 3LW, UK
UKHW041956140426
5217IPUK00015B/823